T0319761

The Economics of Harmonizing European Law

NEW HORIZONS IN LAW AND ECONOMICS

General editors: Gerrit De Geest, *University of Ghent and University of Antwerp, Belgium and University of Utrecht. The Netherlands*; Roger Van den Bergh, *University of Rotterdam and University of Utrecht, The Netherlands*; and Paul Fenn, *University of Nottingham, UK.*

The application of economic ideas and theories to the law and the explanation of markets and public economics from a legal point of view is recognized as one of the most exciting developments in both economics and the law. This important series is designed to make a significant contribution to the development of law and economics.

The main emphasis is on the development and application of new ideas. The series provides a forum for original research in areas such as criminal law, civil law, labour law, corporate law, family law, regulation and privatization, tax, risk and insurance and competition law. International in its approach it includes some of the best theoretical and empirical work from both well-established researchers and the new generation of scholars.

Titles in the series include:

The Economics of Harmonizing European Law

Edited by

Alain Marciano

Professor, University of Corsica-Pascal Paoli, GREQAM-CNRS and IDEP, France

Jean-Michel Josselin

Professor, University of Rennes 1 and CREREG-CNRS, France

NEW HORIZONS IN LAW AND ECONOMICS

Edward Elgar
Cheltenham, UK • Northampton, MA, USA

Published by
Edward Elgar Publishing Limited
Glensanda House
Montpellier Parade
Cheltenham
Glos GL50 1UA
UK

Edward Elgar Publishing, Inc.
136 West Street
Suite 202
Northampton
Massachusetts 01060
USA

A catalogue record for this book
is available from the British Library

Library of Congress Cataloguing in Publication Data
The economics of harmonizing European law / edited by Alain Marciano, Jean-Michel Josselin.
    p. cm.—(New horizons in law and economics)
    Includes bibliographical references and index.
    1. Law—European Union countries—International unification—Congresses. 2. Law—Economic aspects—European Union countries—Congresses. I. Marciano, Alain. II. Josselin, Jean-Michel. III. Series.
KJE960.A8 E28 2002
341.242'2—dc21   2001033502

ISBN   1 84064 608 X

Typeset by Cambrian Typesetters, Frimley, Surrey
Printed and bound in Great Britain by MPG Books Ltd, Bodmin, Cornwall

Contents

Figures and tables

FIGURES

TABLES

Contributors

Jürgen G. Backhaus, University of Erfurt, Germany
Jean-Baptiste Calendini, University of Corsica, France
Michael G. Faure, University of Maastricht, The Netherlands
Bruno S. Frey, University of Zürich, Switzerland
Thierry Garcia, University of Corsica, France
Nuno Garoupa, University of Barcelona Pompeu Fabra, Spain
Sylvie Graziani, University of Corsica, France
Sophie Harnay, University of Reims, France
Jean-Michel Josselin, University of Rennes, France
Alain Marciano, University of Corsica, France
Alexander Neunzig, University of Saarland, Germany
Anthony Ogus, University of Manchester, UK, University of Maastricht, NL
Xavier Peraldi, University of Corsica, France
Michel Rombaldi, University of Corsica, France
Christophe Storaï, University of Corsica, France
Dieter Schmidtchen, University of Saarland, Germany
Hans-Jörg Schmidt-Trenz, University of Saarland, Germany
Jan M. Smits, University of Maastricht, The Netherlands
Roger Van den Bergh, Erasmus University Rotterdam, The Netherlands
Isabelle Vigouroux, University of Western Brittany, France

Preface

This book evolved out of a conference organized in May 2000 at the University of Corsica, under the auspices of the European Association of Law and Economics. Scholars invited to give papers were given carte blanche, but were asked to revise their contributions after the conference discussions. We present here a selection of them. They reflect the current research on the subject, unified by the same concern, namely understanding the law and economics dimension of European integration. They also show a diversity of opinions that we did not try to smooth. Underlying many contributions are strong preferences as to what the *jus commune* will be or should be in the future. This gives a wide-ranging approach to a most important subject.

We heartily thank Brigitte, our Corsican friends from the Restonica valley and our colleagues, the board of the EALE and all the participants in the conference, particularly Pierre Salmon and Christian Barrère who provided valuable comments and expertise. The publishing process has been both friendly and efficient. We are very grateful for that.

Introduction: The economics of the constitutional moment in Europe

Jean-Michel Josselin and
Alain Marciano

INTRODUCTION

Europe provides a fascinating and far-reaching field of investigation for economists. Agriculture, industrial policy, transport and so on, are many subjects that are thoroughly dealt with. But what about law? The provision and the use of law cannot avoid strategic behaviour by individuals or groups of interest. The creation and development of constitutional frameworks cannot be dissociated from rent-seeking. Judges are granted the right of *juris dictio* and as such they have a tremendous power that they can use to further their own private interest. At the same time, they must deal with possible strategic behaviour by the plaintiffs and must find rational criteria to provide sound decisions. Economics is particularly well suited for analysing such topics as private or public law. Public choice and constitutional political economy (Buchanan, 1990) are relevant approaches which consist of using economic tools to understand the choice of rules instead of simply studying individual or collective behaviour within an exogenously given set of rules. When this set becomes endogenous, the scope widens to comprehend constitution-making processes and the various ways of *juris dictio* by judges. Public choice, constitutional political economy and law and economics are close enough perspectives to all belong to the new political economy. Public choice mainly focuses on political mechanisms (Mercuro and Medema, 1997, p. 84). The emphasis can also fruitfully shift from the politician to the judge, from the vote to the court decision. A law and economics perspective has to focus on the mechanisms through which laws are passed and on the way their interpretation and efficiency evolve. In this matter, economics and the law are so intertwined that any attempt to provide compartmentalized analyses cannot but fail to reach its goal, if the latter is to explain things as they are or should be. Moreover, law and economics must build on both political economy and economic analysis.

1

It brings us back to the founding fathers of the discipline, Hume and Smith, but also rests on the more recent theoretical developments of the agency theory or the economics of information and collective decision making.

The chapters in this volume all belong to this tradition, which consists of analysing legal issues in a new political economy perspective. They show, through diverse and sometimes contrasting views, strong opinions or preferences as to what the *ius commune* will be or should be in the future. Contributors were asked to analyse the harmonization of law that results from the European integration process. The chapters then compare the respective vices and virtues of competition, a decentralized process of producing European common rules of law, and of harmonization, a centralized mechanism of creation of law. The book comprises three parts. First, the comparison between competition and harmonization is addressed from a general and theoretical perspective (Jan Smits, Roger Van den Bergh, Sophie Harnay and Isabelle Vigouroux, Anthony Ogus). Second, applied issues are investigated: criminal law (Nuno Garoupa), the European directives about product liability and product safety (Michael Faure), public utilities (Thierry Garcia and Xavier Peraldi), interregional co-operation (Sylvie Graziani and Michel Rombaldi), professional skills (Jean-Baptisite Calendini and Christophe Storaï). Rather than summarizing the previous debates, the third part builds on what we already know about Europe in order to shed some light on its future. As will be clear when reading the first two parts, the European institutions are still the object of the game, rather than merely its exogenous framework. The various players (individuals, regional or national jurisdictions, groups of interest) still have to define and stabilize the setting in which they will try to optimize the payoffs resulting from their interacting strategies. In this respect, harmonization is far from being the only way forward, as is advocated by Bruno Frey. Moreover, since the number of players is not yet fixed, the relevance and efficiency of enlargement must be at the heart of the agenda for future reforms (Dieter Schmidtchen, Alexander Neunzig and Hans-Jörg Schmidt-Trenz). At the same time, whenever collective decisions use institutions whose power goes beyond that of competitive protective agencies, the question must be raised of the control of the state. Constitutional safeguards must guarantee rational and efficient coercion (Jürgen Backhaus).

In the discussion that follows, we place these contributions in the perspective of the constitutional moment in Europe, an issue to which all the chapters in this volume are connected. The time is indeed clearly right for this constitutional moment. The European Union now has a past, a history of its own. Even if Europe is going to face some difficulties in going backwards because of a possible 'ratchet effect' (Vibert, 1995, p. 154), no institutional option is yet closed and new directions can still be taken. Mistakes and achievements are lessons for the future. But if a common past does have advantages, it also brings about drawbacks that further justify the constitutional moment. The sedimentation of institutions, the absence of constituent assemblies before the redaction of the different treaties and the democratic deficit all indicate the urgent need for reforms.

LETTING RULES SPONTANEOUSLY EVOLVE

There are many ways of creating or reaching a harmonized system of rules. In this respect, and to use broad categories, the evolutionist and contractual approaches still compete. Economists are of course not the only ones debating on this subject. Particularly when it comes to discussing the future of Europe, political scientists also find a split (European Journal of Public Policy, 1999). In fact, this is an old debate, dating back to arguments between Hobbes and common lawyers. While Hobbesian constructivism relies on rational calculus, common law jurists like Coke develop the evolutionist perspective of accumulated experience as the soundest possible basis for efficient judgements. Beyond that, and beyond the unbridgeable gap between the two underlying conceptions of human nature, the fundamental point is the way in which the publicity of the law is built. Coke and others were confident of a spontaneous process. On the other hand, Hobbes pleaded for contractual publicity. Much more recently, this argument has also been emphasized by lawyers like Kelsen and by philosophers like Rawls. In the field of economics, the concept of publicity of law relates to the different ways of building the common knowledge of the corresponding rules (Josselin and Marciano, 1995). Should we use accumulated experiences to build it? Is it realistic in the context of already existing nations? A great number of small and continuous interactions can indeed lead to this common knowledge. There remains to assess it with regard to the convocation of a constituent assembly whose purpose would be to explicitly build common knowledge instead of letting it emerge. In this section, we first analyse the theoretical background on which the evolutionist perspective rests. We then move on to the limits of this perspective, in general terms as well as in the field of harmonization.

Evolutionism, Spontaneous Order and Common Knowledge

Evolutionism as a theory of social and cultural evolution is mostly based, as Jan Smits (Chapter 2) and Anthony Ogus (Chapter 3) remind us, on the Hayekian argumentation in favour of spontaneous order. The instances of successful regimes of spontaneous law all have in common that they are systems of customary law. The English common law is usually considered as grounded on customs (see Hogue, 1966, pp. 190–200). It is then also and quite often considered as a unique example of how and how far a process of spontaneously selected rules can work.

In a constitutional political economy perspective where the framework for decisions is endogenous, this brings about a most important debate. Common law advocates do not of course rely on Hobbesian rational calculus to ground their position. The reference is rather that of the spontaneous order tradition, revived by the founding fathers of classical political economy during the Scottish Enlightenment. Repeated interactions between individuals lead to the spontaneous emergence of historical precedents; tacit norms or conventions then appear and next turn into more or less formalized rules. The latter do not result from the will and design of human beings but are rather the consequence of their actions: no one has explicitly decided to create them. However, everyone has decided to use them as guidelines and it is publicly known that everyone has done so. It then appears that these conventions are common knowledge rules. Therefore, no explicit agreement or communication about the sense of rules is needed. Coordination of actions, without reference to intentions, is a sufficient condition for successful communication (Josselin and Marciano, 1999b). In particular, it defines the legal culture of the group in which the interactions develop. From place to place, a phenomenon of imitation ensures the spreading or selection of the rules followed by successful groups. As noted by Hayek, 'this process of selection follows in many respects the same pattern as biological evolution . . . Cultural evolution, because it also rests on a sort of natural selection looks very much like biological evolution' (1988, p. 292). Hayek's enthusiasm as to the way common law evolved neglects the role that private interests have played in the evolution of law in England (Hogue, 1966). His argument, however, refers to organizational efficiency. Others have shared his enthusiasm concerning common law, arguing that economic efficiency is also at the rendezvous.

Theoretical insights provided by evolutionary biology have frequently been used and they are supposed to illuminate the debates about social and cultural evolution. In this perspective the selected rules are supposed to be the most efficient ones; in the words of biology only the fittest rules survive. A related issue is that normative questions are ruled out since efficiency is guaranteed by the process of natural selection. These points are elaborated in Jan Smits' analysis of European private law (Chapter 2). He thus considers that, beside the difficulties 'to predict to what extent the different areas of private law will evolve toward some uniform system', one can nonetheless argue that competition between different legal orders would promote efficiency in allowing the selection of the 'best available rules'. Smits also notes that it is 'inevitable' that 'not all the present social guarantees in the European legal systems (namely those that guarantee more than the European minimum standards) will be kept intact'. But '[w]orries about some mentality being strangled in this process are then not relevant anymore: that would be the irreversible consequence of an internal market coming about'.

Spontaneous Order and Evolutionary Background

One would not be surprised to find a reference to Darwin, as in Jan Smits' chapter, as a theoretical background for an evolutionary approach to the selection of rules. An explicit reference to Darwin would indeed help clarify the meaning of rightness and efficiency in this context. However, Darwin is not a frequent reference in theories of social evolution. In particular, his name rarely appears in Hayek's books and papers.

What is usually considered as the Darwinian theory of social evolution is due to Herbert Spencer rather than to Charles Darwin himself. For instance, the frequently used expression 'survival of the fittest' is proposed by Spencer and not by Darwin, who only used it in later editions of *The Origin of Species* and did not use it in *The Descent of Man*. Moreover, Darwin insists on the decisive role of moral sentiments or, more precisely, sympathy, which are concepts he explicitly borrows from Hume and Smith (Marciano and Pélissier, 2000).

The consequences for a theory of social evolution are twofold. First, because the process of natural selection in human societies rests on sympathy, the normative content of selected rules is assured (Josselin and Marciano, 2001). In other words, if we follow a Darwinian line of reasoning, rules could not be selected for their efficiency but for their capacity to generate a social order in which relationships are based on sympathy. This leads us to one of the limits of a spontaneous order process: we cannot be sure that evolution is just. Hayek even claims that 'evolution cannot be just' (1988, p. 20) which means that rightness must be found in the evolution process itself rather than in its outcome. Secondly, there is no certainty that evolution could select the most efficient rules. Among others, Brennan and Buchanan remark that

> social conventions that emerge historically and take on the status of 'unwritten rule' do not necessarily produce the best conceivable pattern of outcomes. Some modern social analysts (notably Hayek and his followers) display an apparent faith in the forces of social and cultural 'evolution' to generate efficient rules. There seems to be no reason to predict that these forces will always ensure the selection of the best rules. (1985, pp. 9–10)

Nozick gives a discerning illustration of this proposition in pointing out that chance can be a means of selecting a rule (1974, chap. 6). A convention might be institutionalized without any 'calculus of consent'. No one can be sure that chance has any bias towards efficiency.

The Spatial Limits of Evolutionary Harmonization:
Legal Culture and Induction

An evolutionist view on the European legal order rests on the possible hybridi-
sation of the different legal systems and thus assumes the possibility of 'legal
transplants' from one country to another. These transplants are made possible
when a rule is susceptible to being used, and then adapted, in different legal
regimes. A first problem consists in prohibitive costs of adaptation. A second
and more crucial point is made by Legrand in his radical criticism of legal
transplants. He argues that, because the specific 'legal culture', defined as
'those historically conditioned, deeply rooted attitudes of law and about the
proper structure and operation of a legal system that are at large in the society'
(1996, p. 52, quoted by Ogus in this volume), attached to existing legal
systems, transplants are impossible and then the convergence of the legal
regimes in precluded. His argumentation rests on the link between 'cultural
heterogeneity' and 'the situated, local properties of knowledge' (1997, p. 123,
ibid.). Legrand's argument is extreme. In a weaker form, it nonetheless
suggests the spatial limits of competition. The question concerns the possible
generalization of rules born in a specific context and dedicated to specific
recurrent problems. Are these rules likely to become applicable beyond the
initial boundaries within which they emerged, or to become relevant to
instances that were not concerned in the first place? Among the different
elements of a legal culture, labour legislation is one of the most important. In
this domain of law, as noted by Jean-Baptiste Calendini and Christophe Storaï
in Chapter 8, the probable tensions between the different national traditions
could be an obstacle to the spontaneous harmonization of law. The generalization, or transplantation, of rules has to solve a problem of induction. A
newcomer entering a game may face induction problems because of his inability to know positively the meaning another person gives to the rules or to infer
this meaning from the observation of her behaviour (Josselin and Marciano,
1995, 1999b). Therefore, evolutionism has to face problems of induction.

However, one should not too quickly conclude that transplants are impossible. The existence of a problem of induction 'only' stresses that a transplanted rule will never be the same again, both at home and where it is
transplanted. What is then important is the way in which the different rules are
made accessible. Therefore, the existence of a legal culture does not imply that
transplants are impossible. It affects the nature of the process through which
rules are likely to be transferred from one legal regime to another one. This
could be an argument in favour of a European social contract whereby the
common knowledge of rules would be explicitly constructed. One may
conceive that repeated interactions between individuals do lead to the spontaneous emergence of commonly accepted rules. One may even acknowledge

that such rules are efficient, at least in organizational terms. We should certainly be more cautious when it comes to making legal culture interact in order to breed a *commune ley*. The dynamics of legal systems remain a largely unknown territory, though Kelsen warned us quite a long time ago now that this is a major key for understanding law.

A purely evolutionist conception of harmonization has thus to deal with problems of induction which limit the efficiency of spontaneously selected rules. A covenant or a constitutional contract is a solution to the problem of induction. The underlying argument of this chapter is then that Europe cannot do without a social contract whose many possible forms must be discussed. For obvious reasons, the unitary mode of organization has never received great attention while federalism has been considered as a possible direction from early on. The choice between a competitive and a centralized federalism grounds the constitutional moment for Europe.

THE REGULATION OF COMPETITION BETWEEN LEGAL ORDERS

The Tiebout model is the soundest possible basis on which to ground federalism, even if the specificity of the European situation calls for some scepticism when it comes to applying theoretical principles of competition. Furthermore, the Tiebout perspective cannot comprehend all the aspects of the provision of public goods. In particular, the legal culture may display some characteristics of monopoly, which requires a careful design of the juridical institutions.

European Federalism and the Tiebout Model

Building on the American experience may not be as straightforward as it could seem at first glance. There are two reasons for that. First, caution is necessary because the USA has a very specific form of government; Australia or Canada could have also been designed as possible models. Furthermore, American scholars themselves do not recognize Europe as an illustration of their own federal structure. For instance, Buchanan writes: 'Europe, as observed does not correspond to the theorists' model for political federalism, and the course of history remains open as to whether or not any approximation to this model will ultimately be realised' (1996, p. 253). Buchanan's statement suggests a discussion about the capacity for the European Union to follow the path of the USA and, more generally, reveals scepticism as to the ability of governments to put good (at least Pareto-improving) ideas into practice. The gap between the institutional structures in America and in Europe stems from the differences in the respective situations of the US nation and of the European nations.

There is, thus, a second reason for being cautious: federating a nation is quite different from federating existing countries. The harmonization process in Europe is constrained by the necessity to take into consideration the diversity of ideas, cultures and policies that at the same time form the 'strength of Europe'; a variety without which Europe will 'lose its *raison d'être* and will lose its economic and political role' (Frey, this volume).

The Tiebout model provides a useful, even if partial, background for the European federalism. The use of the 'market metaphor' (Donahue, 1997) illuminates the workings of the legal markets. In this volume, Faure (Chapter 7), van den Bergh (Chapter 1) and Garoupa (Chapter 6) show that Europe could draw advantageous lessons from the economic theory of competition between jurisdictions. The argument is that federalism may be structured through competition between jurisdictions. The idea is to build a non-cooperative but at the same time non-conflicting game between local governments. The latter should be interpreted as the smallest functional units (Backhaus, 1997a) to which the provision of public goods is assigned.

Competition among local governments is expected to limit possible predation. It provides incentives to attract mobile factors and to reduce transaction costs on markets. The Schengen agreement has created an area of free circulation; it is thus an element in favour of a competitive model of federalism. However, beside this institutional prerequisite and from a practical perspective, free circulation requires for instance that the different degrees and qualification between nations be harmonized. This is a major contribution to the creation of a European harmonized labour market. These are two necessary conditions that need to be fulfilled in order to ensure the mobility of the labour factor. Jean-Baptiste Calendini and Christophe Storaï discuss this issue in Chapter 8. The respective historical backgrounds of the European labour markets provide many barriers to the creation of a unified market. Jean-Baptiste Calendini and Christophe Storaï insist on the link between the harmonization of qualifications and that of the labour market. They stress the difficulties that attempts at uniformity may face. The Commission did publish a white paper on *teaching and learning*, which presented the conditions required for a uniform norm for the recognition of 'skills'. But, the adoption of a common, consensual, definition of what 'qualification' means seems to be a strong requirement before going towards more flexibility on the labour market.

In counterpart, Nuno Garoupa in Chapter 6 shows that there is at least one type of skill that is general enough not to be bound by historical conditions and the features of national markets. These are the capacities individuals acquire and use on illegal markets. The only barriers that are likely to constrain the emergence of a European criminal market are the national frontiers. Once the limits are removed, the criminals face lower transaction costs and their activity is likely to increase. As these cases show, the framework of this competition must not let the players fall into a prisoners' dilemma. The government at the highest level must see to it. However, the process has some limits, which requires that the debate goes beyond the Tiebout model.

Going Beyond the Tiebout Model

As is vigorously stressed by Musgrave (1997) and Donahue (1997), Tiebout assignments cannot be so easily generalized since they largely build on a metaphor. Competition on the market for goods cannot be straightforwardly extended to jurisdictional competition. In particular, this competition may take place in a conflicting setting, just as in markets for goods the outcome may be that of a price war. Generalized strategic behaviour of local governments generates a race to the bottom. It can myopically be seen as beneficial by some jurisdictions, but others will soon be lured into grabbing short-term benefits. Non-optimal provision of public services will ensue. Moreover, voters themselves can display detrimental strategic behaviours. For instance, provision of law at lower levels of government may induce legal externalities. Corporate law is an example of how such externalities help citizens of a given jurisdiction catch the benefits of a law and transfer the cost onto the residents of other jurisdictions (Rose-Ackerman, 1992).

European rules should thus limit the scope for a race to the bottom. In other words, there are fields in which centralization and EC law could have positive effects. Corporate law, for instance, may be cited as one of these areas in which EC law has an important role to play. It is also at the core of Chapter 1 by Roger van den Bergh in this volume. Company laws in Europe are constructed to provide harmonization (Carney, 1997). To put it in other words, 'competition and harmonization may be complements, rather than substitutes' (van den Bergh, this volume). The Treaty of Rome, with articles 54 and 58, acknowledges that federating nations require the creation, not to say the construction, of a common market. During the process, rent-seeking may of course thrive. Competition on the market for corporate law would certainly weaken rent extraction, as is the case in the USA. However, the American common market spontaneously emerged along with the fledgling nation. This early and competitive creation produces fewer regulations and probably more efficiency.

The race-to-the-bottom argument should not be overemphasized since, as noted by Scott, 'there is almost no evidence that, under competition, the feared race to the bottom is more that theoretical' (2000, p. 204). Faure (Chapter 7) confirms that judgement by showing that this argument is not strong enough to justify a centralized provision of law in the case of product liability.

For all its insights, the Tiebout model cannot comprehend all the aspects of the provision of public services. First, Samuelsonian public goods cannot be dealt with by using exclusion mechanisms and preference revelation through mobility. If law is a pure public good then the market metaphor is quite useless. The American Federalists developed this argument when they advocated the shift from the Articles of Confederation to the 1789 constitution. Secondly, the Tiebout setting cannot comprehend spillovers. Indeed,

> the Tiebout argument of competition between local communities obviously works only if the problem to be regulated is indeed merely local. Once it is established that the problem to be regulated has a transboundary character, there may be an economics of scale argument to shift powers to a higher legal order that has competence to deal with the externality over a larger territory. (Faure, Chapter 7 this volume).

The centralized provision of law is required because of the transboundary effect of the regulated activities. Environment has repeatedly been presented as one of the type of activities in which centralization is required in order to avoid the cross-border effects of pollution. It is nonetheless important to remark that central authorities have many instruments at their disposal. The choice of the relevant legal tool must nonetheless be a cautious one. Can the same argument be replicated to different legal issues? In this volume, Michael Faure examines the case of product liability and product safety. His conclusion is: 'the mere fact that different states would hold different preferences with respect to product liability and product safety and that therefore different regimes would exist, can as such hardly be considered as an argument for centralisation as long as states are not capable of externalising harm to victims in third countries'.

Legal Culture: Natural Monopoly and Competition

One of the main assumptions of the Tiebout model is the perfect elasticity of the supply of jurisdictions. Among others, Donahue (1997) and Musgrave (1997) argue that this is not historically relevant, at least in the American case. In theoretical terms, rather than being anonymous and competitive suppliers, local governments display strategic behaviour in a non-cooperative game setting (Inman and Rubinfeld, 1996, 1997a and b).

Citizens themselves may not have uniform incentives to move from one jurisdiction to another. The level of the corresponding transaction costs may depend on their productivity or on their wealth. This may reinforce the negative aspects of the provision of public goods by local governments. Furthermore, when considering legal competition, the elasticity of location relative to the legal rules may be much closer to zero than for any other good. There is a 'portfolio effect' (Donahue, 1997) in this matter. As Michael Faure argues when considering this point, not only 'people may stay even if the (legal) regime does not suit their need optimally' (this volume) but also 'the legal regime may not be decisive [because] . . . job location and residence are that important in reality, there is often little left for people to choose' (Faure, ibid.; compare also Rose-Ackerman, 1992).

In Chapter 3 Anthony Ogus offers an original explanation of the link between legal culture and the impossible convergence of legal systems. He tells us that legal culture is a natural monopoly. He then writes that '[a] predictable consequence is that practising lawyers will exploit the situation, generating rents for themselves by, for example, promoting formalism and complexities and other features which enhance their income'. Such barriers to entry increase problems of induction, much to the advantage of lawyers who cannot but profit from the corresponding asymmetries of information. Industrial economics teaches us the need to regulate activities in situations characterized by natural monopolies in order to reach an optimal level of production. However, here lies a major problem, namely the existence of pressure groups likely to influence the regulation process. The rents created by regulation are then likely to be captured by the rent-seekers. This is typically what happens on the legal market.

Ogus notes that regulatory constraints are difficult to use and to implement 'because lawyers constitute a powerful pressure group, adept at influencing the law-making machinery'. This is the case as long as we consider competition within the field. To this first problem, a second one can be added, namely, as Tullock and Demsetz have argued, competition for the field itself. Their view of political competition as a franchise bidding for political monopoly can be usefully applied and further substantiated in order to highlight and discuss basic aspects of the European integration process. The provision of law is not organized as an ongoing market process. Instead of playing a competitive game among legal systems, suppliers of law may compete in order to reach monopoly power. Is it a matter of artificial barriers to entry, for instance through procedures that exacerbate problems of induction and hence asymmetries of information? Is it a matter of economics of scale in the provision of law?

The argument implies the possible competition between European and national judges. Roger van den Bergh, in Chapter 1, considers this situation and notes that 'the European legislator engages in competition with the national legislators rather than eliminate it by means of harmonization'. This is indeed competition for the field. In the same vein, Sophie Harney and Isabelle Vigouroux in Chapter 4 develop a model that describes European integration as the result of a process of competition between national and European judges. The model shows that competition does promote legal innovation. What could be considered as a positive effect also has the negative consequence of leading to judicial activism and the related judicial empowerment (to use the words of

Joseph Weiler). In this perspective, national judges have a vested interest in promoting the rules enacted by the European judges. Thus, competition increases centralization and harmonization. Sophie Harnay and Isabelle Vigouroux propose a conclusion that is similar to the one given by Anthony Ogus: we can expect an increase in the role of lawyers and judges. However, beside the virtues of the spontaneous evolution of law, Harnay and Vigouroux insist on the crucial importance of the institutional setting in which competition takes place or should take place. And some of these institutions may sometimes be distortional.

A POSITIVE ASSESSMENT OF EUROPEAN FEDERALISM

One cannot but deplore, as Roger Van den Bergh puts it, 'the lack of an appropriate European constitutional framework' (this volume). The agency theory provides an insightful means of analysing the strategic behaviours of the central institutions. A positive assessment of the present European constitution is then possible.

The Inappropriateness of the Institutional Framework

The inappropriateness of the European institutions clearly appears when one tries to list the impressive number of pressure groups influencing the provision of law and public decision making in Brussels. To say that Europe is a rent-seeking society is largely a euphemism. These strategic behaviours are made possible by a specific constitutional structure. There are of course many explanations for the existence of those pressure groups. One of them fits the micro-economic approach and the political economy perspective. European institutions are designed through, and evolve into, an agency framework whose incompleteness paves the way for inefficiency and rent-seeking. Constitutions can fruitfully be formalized as agency contracts (Anderson and Hill, 1986; Wagner, 1988, 1993). In this setting, economic models of agency help understand the nature of authority and power (Aghion and Tirole, 1997), administrative law or *Verwaltungsrecht* (Josselin and Marciano, 1997, 1999a). Usually, the focus is put on the efficiency of the agency contract, and the role of incentive or control mechanisms. We rather stress here the instability of the contract as a consequence of its incompleteness.

Incompleteness usually relates to the argument according to which the payoffs associated with the projects are unknown. What we emphasize here is the incompleteness of the set of projects itself. First, the number of projects may be unknown. Second, the contracting parties may not be able to clearly delineate what in a given project belongs to the field of competence of the principal. The agent then has some power to define his own domain of choice. He may then use this power strategically in order to displace his principal (Josselin and Marciano, 2000). When the agency contract is incomplete, conflicts inevitably arise between existing national laws and the emerging European law. Under article 164 EEC, the European Court of Justice settles these tensions and thereby completes the contract. The doctrines of *direct effect* (*Van Gend & Loos*, 1963) and *supremacy* (*Costa v. ENEL*, 1964) serve this purpose.

The European Court of Justice thus plays a major role in the evolution towards a constitutional status. In this respect, the decision made in the Van Gend and Loos case (*Van Gend & Loos v. Nederlandse Administratie der Berlastingen*, case 26/62, 1963, E.C.R. 1) is fundamental. It acknowledges the co-existence of two levels of principalship: the Community 'is a new legal order of international law ... the subjects of which comprise not only the Member States, but also their nationals'. The ensuing shift in principalship is only partial. The status of international organization no longer fits the situation since member states lose part of their prerogatives. They now share principal-ship with their nationals and the nationals of the other states. The European Court of Justice displays a judicial activism that leads to the constitutionaliza-tion of the treaties: The Treaty of Rome is defined as the 'basic constitutional charter' (*Parti écologiste 'Les Verts' v. European Parliament*, case 294/83, 1986, E.C.R. 1339). On the other hand, Europe does not for all that become a federation since two levels of principalship remain, thus partly preserving the states' rights that characterize a confederate organization; Holcombe (1991) shows in the American case how states can directly control their agent in a confederation. In the European case, the Court acts as a constituent power.

The Constitutional Status of Europe

Europe has no definite and precise constitutional status. Some scholars have stressed that Europe is 'unique in its structure' (Sbraggia, 1992); others have considered that the European constitution is 'hybrid' (Koslowsky, 1999). The reason is that Europe stands in the middle of the ford, between an international legal order and a constitutional order.

The first stages of the European integration process cannot be interpreted as directed, at least avowedly, by the aim of building a new state that would rest on a higher constitutional norm. Europe should rather be considered, at its origin, as an 'international legal order' (see for instance Schilling, 1996, or Weiler and Halpern, 1996). The regime builds upon a number of Treaties (ECSC, EEC, EURATOM) forming a compact that defines the European legal order. Since no constituent power intentionally designed it, this set of treaties cannot be considered as a constitution in itself. The process is that of intergovernmental conferences whose conclusions are ratified by national legislatures, the latter having no constituent power in this respect. The decision made in 1957 in the *Dineke Algera et al. v. Common Assembly of the European Coal and Steel Community* (joint cases 7/56 and 3–7/57, opinion of Mr Advocate General Lagrange, ECR, 69: 82) is a perfect instance of such a situation.

In an international legal order, member states are in the position of principals while the institutions of the European Community are their agents. Existing and constituted states do contract and they delegate precise and enumerated tasks to the central institutions. The agency contract thus defines the respective prerogatives of the two sides. On the one hand, the laws governing international treaties bound the actions of the EC institutions; there is no way for them to eradicate their subordination to the principals. On the other hand, the principals do intend to retain formal authority. Of course, the delegated prerogatives are in practice far from stated once and for all. But the tasks delegated to the agents are controlled by the principals who may change their extent according to the resolutions they manage to reach. Furthermore, following the decision processes of an international regime, changes in the prerogatives of the agents result from bargaining and negotiation between the principals who remain the ultimate enforcers. There is indeed no enforcement mechanism outside their own collective will. This obviously requires that a collective will exist, which is far from straightforward since the decision-making process is based on the rule of unanimity while each state keeps a veto power. A positive account of the difficulties to reach agreements in this setting is given by the failure of the first attempt in 1952 to finalize a treaty establishing a European Community of Defence.

Under this intergovernmental regime, there is no locus for a final authority external to the principals. The international or central institutions are not granted any compelling prerogatives. More specifically, there is no central judicial power. The European Court of Justice mainly verifies that the secondary law (legislation proposed by the Commission and enacted by the Council of Ministers and Parliament) fits the frame of the Treaty of Rome under the control of the member states. How far and how quickly will the Court gain more power? The case of the USA and the Supreme Court of Justice gives evidence of a trend towards centralized federalism. In the absence of a formal European constitution, the ECJ may have even more latitude to lead a movement towards a federal constitutional status. What will remain of the principalship of member states? Adding to that the fact that the Treaty of Rome allows majority voting with article 189, it happens that from the beginning Europe displays some attributes of a fledgling supranational state.

To move from an intergovernmental structure to a supranational regime requires a change in the agency relationship and a shift in principalship. The agency contract is now meant to take place between the citizens themselves, for instance through a constituent assembly, and the supranational level. Principalship thus moves from the states to the citizens. In theory, the people are now considered as the source of the power and decisions at the federal level should no longer result from bargaining processes between the member states. The federal level is a central and final level of authority, an agent supposedly controlled by the citizens–principals. In the wake of this shift in principalship, member states lose many of their previous prerogatives, among which their power of veto. The rule of unanimity is relaxed and replaced by majority rules of decision. Whereas under an intergovernmental regime negotiation is the way through which decisions are reached and prerogatives assigned to the central level, the power of the federal institutions is now explicitly stated in a constitution. This constitutional assignment is ultimately enforced by the guardian of guardians, namely the federal court of justice. The latter also checks the behaviour of the other parts of governments and contributes to the balance of powers.

A real shift towards a federation would have required that a constituent assembly defined the prerogatives of the central government. This is obviously not the case: with two levels of principalship, Europe is neither a confederate nor a federal structure. This unsettled situation may require a constitutional moment.

SUGGESTIONS FOR THE FUTURE CONSTITUTIONAL MOMENT

The preceding discussion has revealed the need for constitutional safeguards in order to control possible strategic behaviour as well as the necessity to go beyond the Tiebout model in order to define a framework for the European federation. Subsidiarity then appears as a key concept. However, one should not take the virtues of federalism for granted. Administrative law appears as a necessary and relevant way to control the state.

A Democratic and Competitive Federalism

It is not at all sure whether all the opportunities offered by the concept of subsidiarity have been explored in theory and in practice. It may require much more attention and application than is often given, with a few exceptions such as van den Bergh's paper (1994). The subsidiarity principle (Article 3B, Maastricht Treaty) can limit the set of activities of the EC institutions since it contradicts the doctrine of the supremacy of the European Community law.

Applied to environmental policies in Europe for instance (Backhaus, 1997b; van den Bergh, Faure and Lefevere, 1995), it appears to be a very effective instrument of analysis and reform. The economic interpretation provided by Backhaus (1997a, 1999), following the legacy of Wolff, gives a framework in which the various forms of federalism can be assessed. Constrained optimization of the choice of institutional structures requires that tasks should be delegated to the smallest functional units. Once this general principle is set, it can be implemented in three ways.

Lateral subsidiarity relates to institutions of the same rank cooperating in order to solve a given problem; confederations are mainly founded on this form of cooperation. That was the initial setting in which the early European Community worked. It still uses it when one follows the interpretation of the intergovernmental thesis. *Upwards* subsidiarity provides a means of finding solutions with institutions of higher level, as is the case with centralized federalism. This is in many respects the case with the USA, and Europe may tend towards this solution as well. However, the USA now seem to engage in a process of devolution (Tannenwald, 1998) that shows many characteristics of downwards subsidiarity, whereby communities of lower level are more likely to efficiently handle many problems. Europe may follow this path, both in spatial and functional terms.

A promising direction of research and practical implementation indeed relates to the spatial and *downwards* reorganization of governments. Since the devolution process in a unitary state like Great Britain, and since the formal acknowledgement of subsidiarity in the Maastricht treaty, one could claim that nations will never be the same again. Economic theory reaches a similar conclusion when it assesses the rationale for mergers and dissolution that constantly reshape countries. Wittman (1991) and Blum and Dudley (1991) have provided path-finding models that help understand why nations rationally form or break-up. Further models by Alesina and Spolaore (1997) or Bolton and Roland (1997) follow the same idea. This way of conducting an economic analysis of highly emotional subjects is fascinating since it reveals the rationality that grounds political decisions. This approach can of course be applied to possible reforms towards downwards subsidiarity in Europe. In this respect, decentralization provides strong incentives for governments to act efficiently (Salmon, 1987, 2000). Underlying this process is the idea of the constitutional liability of regions. Three arguments may provide a rationale for it. The first one rests on a classical political economy perspective. Hume shows how moral sentiments are scarce feelings usually restricted to areas of nearness. What we could label the 'topology of Humean sympathy' defines territories ruled by local norms (Josselin and Marciano, 1999b). The second argument takes the form of a dilemma. How to get both the efficiency of local public decisions in some matters and at the same time profit from the stabilizing coinsurance provide by national policies? An efficient status of regions in Europe rests on 'a trade-off between allocative efficiency, fostered by regional differentiation and financial responsibility, and risk-sharing efficiency, achieved through mutual insurance permitted by the adoption of uniform rules' (Drèze, 1993, p. 277). Of course, the increasing importance of regions comes from the decline of the nations. It is also possible to consider it as a consequence of the decline of the Welfare State, as is argued by Sylvie Graziani and Michel Rombaldi. In this respect, new forms of governance, based on interregional cooperation, could be required to correct possible disparities among the regions of Europe. Sylvie Graziani and Michel Rombaldi (Chapter 9) remind us that the Commission insisted on the need to consider interregional cooperation as a mean of harmonizing the European territory: 'the interregional cooperation programs have become indissociable from the European construction efforts'. The third argument rests on heterogeneous spatial clubs. The integration of regions showing quite specific preferences inside unitary states may be very costly. From an efficiency perspective, the constitutional enterprise is indeed spatially constrained (Josselin and Marciano, 1999c). This may provide a strong incentive towards federalism.

Another direction of research considers the functional dimension of feder-alism (Casella and Frey, 1992). Markets cannot instantly create geographical jurisdictions. Their supply is therefore relatively inelastic. This simple fact reinforces the necessity of organizing competition, in such a way as to provide the adequate institutional framework we referred to earlier. If we add to this the imperfect mobility of individuals, then jurisdictions may advantageously compete on a functional rather than territorial basis. They would geographi-cally overlap and provide a strong basis for a directly democratic and federal Europe. The corresponding concept of FOCJ (Frey and Eichenberger, 1996, 1997) emphasizes the efficiency attached to downwards subsidiarity. It also implies a variety of organizational forms, practices and institutions regulated by competition and direct democracy. And this brings us to the core of the argument presented by Bruno Frey: how to harmonize without losing the bene-fits associated with democratic and competitive governmental institutions (Chapter 10).

Competition and democracy may be the keywords that would guide any trend towards a larger Europe, that is, enlargement in scope and functions, but also in terms of the countries involved in the process. Competition in itself can lead to unjust outcomes, as we have seen before. Democracy is then the neces-sary complement to the spontaneous and competitive evolutionism described by Jan Smits. At the same time, the upper framework of the constitution is recognized as something much more important. This is the case in positive terms: the constitution is the necessary setting for organizing efficient compe-tition, as Roger Van den Bergh shows. This is also the case in a normative approach. Sylvie Graziani and Michel Rombaldi strongly advocate the regulation of competition.

The issue of enlargement thus crystallizes all the questions raised by the future of Europe: Which competition? Which democracy? Which constitution? The analysis by Dieter Schmidtchen, Alexander Neunzig and Hans-Jörg Schmidt-Trenz (Chapter 11) gives a clear view of the problem at stake. An augmentation in the number of the member states indeed increases the problems of harmonization between the different systems, the related issues of political distortions and that of the preservation of citizens rights. Schmidtchen, Neunzig and Schmidt-Trenz tell us that the Commission 'seems to take for granted that enlargement enhances the wealth of both the citizens of the EU and the citizens of the applicant countries'. Their chapter stresses the necessity not to jump so directly to optimistic conclusions. As they note, 'there is no free lunch. Increasing membership of a club may come along with congestion and decisionmaking costs'. The problem here is then to determine the optimum size of the European Union. Drawing on the theory of optimal legal areas, Schmidtchen, Neunzig and Schmidt-Trenz propose a model allowing evaluation of who the winners and the losers are from an enlargement of the European Union. Their message is that 'there is no guarantee that what is good for the Union, that is, maximizes Union welfare, is also good for the group as a whole'. To some extent, the impossibility of deriving a definite answer from the comparison between the benefits and the costs of enlargement provides another illustration of the difficulties to positively argue in favour of (spontaneous) harmonization or (conscious) regulation. Once again, decisions about enlargement are likely to remain political choices.

An Efficient Control of the Future European State

If the future Europe is to be a federation, then the choice of a specific form of federalism requires paying attention to the scope of the power delegated to the central institutions. In the absence of constitutional safeguards, the European federalism would have to be centralized, just as in the USA. In counterpoint, confederations are characterized by the delegation of few, limited and enumerated tasks – as is exemplified by the *Articles of Confederation* – under the control of the member states. Federalists emphasize the weakness of the central government as a major drawback of this kind of organization; for instance, Hamilton notes that under the Articles 'the government of the United States is destitute of energy' (Federalist Paper 15). A constitution must provide the upper level with prerogatives granting 'the means, and . . . methods, of executing the powers with which it is entrusted' (Federalist Paper 16). The need for a central judiciary power is then presented as a necessity in order 'to avoid the confusion which would unavoidably result from the contradictory decisions of a number of independent judicatories' (Hamilton, Federalist Paper 22). But, if confederations are sometimes paralysed by the trickiness of their decision processes, the reverse may be sometimes said of federations, which would be granted too many prerogatives. Admittedly, the veto power owned by each state is likely to prevent them from reaching an agreement; on the other hand, the federal court of justice possibly turns out to be a very powerful agent who may well get more power than initially planned by the framers of the constitution. Therefore, constitutional provisions are required to limit the authority of the central government. In the USA, the debates in and around the Convention of Philadelphia clearly revealed concerns shared – to a different extent of course – by both federalists and anti-federalists.

The problem is sharper in Europe since no constituent assembly presides over the making of the constitution: it happens to be the role of the Court itself. The constitutional safeguards required in a federation are still to be designed. First, the European parliament is initially conceived as a consultative structure. Its role has been increased through the introduction (Maastricht treaty) and extension (Treaty of Amsterdam) of the co-decision procedure. The parliament can now balance the power of the Court but its new competencies have mainly resulted from bargaining with the Court and have resulted in an increase of the power of the Court (Cooter and Drexl, 1994; Cooter and Ginsburg, 1999). Second, subsidiarity remains a vague principle. Section two of Article 3B of the Treaty of Maastricht expresses the stretch between the two levels of principalship – the member states on one hand, the citizens on the other – by putting emphasis on the relationship between the member states and the Community. It thus rests on the Court to balance powers by increasingly defending the rights of the other principal, the people of Europe.

Not so surprisingly, the subsidiarity principle protects citizens since it increases their possibilities to sue their own state. There exists another way to protect citizens' rights, namely the delineation of the scope of public utilities. In this perspective, the ECJ also plays a major role. The conventional view, especially in France, is that Europe threatens the French tradition of public utility. In Chapter 5 Thierry Garcia and Xavier Peraldi remind us of a statement of the French Council of State, arguing that 'Europe does not institute proceedings against public utility: it does worse; it unawares the concept of public utility and the existence of public utility'.

However, the problem is not as obvious as it could seem at first sight. Garcia and Peraldi argue in their chapter that, beside 'antagonisms which characterize the French and European approaches of public utility . . . , it is possible to detect a marked phenomenon of convergence'. It is indeed difficult to define a European conception of public utility, the reason being that the ECJ and the Commission do not systematically adopt the same point of view. The Commission uses a restrictive approach, based on the supply of a minimal service for a certain level of quality and an accessible price. The Court develops a wider conception, considering the necessity to take into account collective needs (political, social as well as economic). It is then interesting to note that the European Community links the definition of public utility to a principle of European citizenship. Not only does it reinforce the role of the people of Europe as a principal, but it also increases the level of protection of their rights. Thus, to focus on what citizens' rights should be, on the one hand, or to delineate the domain of public utilities, on the other hand, are the two available ways of controlling the State. These two perspectives also relate to the two major traditions that exist in administrative law, whose goal is to control the actions of the state, namely the continental and the British–American traditions. As noted in Chapter 12 Jürgen Backhaus, when presenting the different traditions in administrative law, there exists 'a deep divide separating administrative law'. It is thus said that 'the French approach emphasizes rules, procedures, and clearly circumscribed acts while the British inspired approach tries to structure the discretion of the civil servant by means of general principals that should guide this behaviour'. Furthermore, in the USA, 'the protection of the citizen is mainly contained in the Bill of Rights, administration as a much recent phenomenon has primarily taken on the form of regulation'. The question immediately arising relates to the possibility of creating a common administrative law in Europe. So an important gap between the French–German and the British–US traditions could prevent the emergence of a common administrative law in Europe. One can easily imagine what the practical issues that stand behind the theoretical debate are: Europe was born within the French tradition and evolved under the auspices of the Anglo-Saxon precepts. Once again, if Europe stands in the middle of the ford, the odds are great that the goal of administrative law will not be reached; the European State might remain uncontrolled. Jürgen Backhaus offers an integrative approach in his chapter. He works out the principles of administrative law that 'are in full agreement with economic reasoning, hence they can serve to facilitate the economic analysis of an issue in administrative law'. He then concludes that 'the principles of administrative law, as they embody economic reasoning, can usefully be introduced in arguments of the European Commission in particular and *in processes of European harmonization more generally*' (emphasis added).

CONCLUSION: TAKING EUROPEAN LAW AND ECONOMICS SERIOUSLY

This book intends to demonstrate that one cannot understand the making of Europe without taking into account its legal dimension. The debate between competition and harmonization will certainly shape the future constitutional moment. In this field, as in many others, law and economics matters.

REFERENCES

Aghion, Philippe and Jean Tirole (1997), 'Formal and real authority in organizations', *Journal of Political Economy*, **105**(1), 1–29.

Alesina, Alberto and Enrico Spolaore (1997), 'On the number and size of nations', *Quarterly Journal of Economics*, **112**(4), 1027–56.

Anderson, Terry L. and Peter J. Hill (1986), 'Constraining the transfer society: constitutional and moral dimensions', *Cato Journal*, **6**(1), 317–39.

Backhaus, Jürgen G. (1997a), 'Christian Wolff on subsidiarity, the division of labour and social welfare', *European Journal of Law and Economics*, **4**(2–3), 129–46.

Backhaus, Jürgen G. (1997b), 'Subsidiarity and ecologically based taxation: a European constitutional perspective', *Public Choice*, **90**(1–4), 281–310.

Backhaus, Jürgen G. (1999), Subsidiarity, in Jürgen G. Backhaus (ed.), *The Elgar Companion to Law and Economics*, Aldershot: Edward Elgar, 136–43.

Blum, Ulrich and Leonard Dudley (1991), 'A spatial model of the state', *Journal of Institutional and Theoretical Economics*, **147**(2), 312–36.

Bolton, Patrick and Gérard Roland (1997), 'The break-up of nations: a political economy analysis', *Quarterly Journal of Economics*, **112**(4), 1057–90.

Brennan, Geoffrey and James M. Buchanan (1995), *The Reason of Rules. An Essay in Constitutional Political Economy*, Cambridge: Cambridge University Press.

Buchanan, James M. (1990), 'The domain of constitutional economics', *Constitutional Political Economy*, **1**(1), 1–18.

Buchanan, James M. (1996), 'Europe as a social reality', *Constitutional Political Economy*, **7**(4), 253–6.

Carney, William J. (1997), 'The political economy of competition for corporate charters', *The Journal of Legal Studies*, **26**(1), 303–29.

Cooter, Robert and Josef Drexl (1994), 'The logic of power in the emerging European constitution: game theory and the division of powers', *International Review of Law and Economics*, **14**(XXX), 307–26.

Cooter, Robert and Tom Ginsburg (1999), 'Division of Powers in the European Constitution', in Peter Newman (ed.), *The New Palgrave Dictionary of Economics and the Law*.

Darwin, Charles (1859 [1988]), *The Origin of Species*, London: Encyclopedia Britannica.

Darwin, C. (1871 [1988]), *The Descent of Man and Selection in Relation to Sex*, London: Encyclopedia Britannica.

Donahue, John D. (1997), 'Tiebout? Or not Tiebout? The market metaphor and America's devolution debate', *Journal of Economic Perspectives*, **11**(4), 73–81.

Drèze, Jacques (1993), 'Regions of Europe: a feasible status, to be discussed', *Economic Policy*, **8**(17), 265–87.

European Journal of Public Policy (1999), Special issue: 'The social construction of Europe', **6**(4), 527–720.

Frey, Bruno S. and Reiner Eichenberger (1996), 'FOCJ: competitive governments for Europe', *International Review of Law and Economics*, **16**(3), 315–27.

Frey, Bruno S. and Reiner Eichenberger (1997), 'FOCJ: Creating a Single European

Market for Governments', in Dieter Schmidtchen and Roger Cooter (eds), *Constitutional Law and the European Union*, Aldershot: Edward Elgar.

Hayek, Friedrich August (1988), *The Fatal Conceit. The Errors of Socialism*, Chicago: University of Chicago Press.

Hogue, Arthur (1966), *The Origins of the Common Law*, Indianapolis: The Free Press.

Holcombe, Randall (1991), 'Constitutions as constraints: a case-study of three American constitutions', *Constitutional Political Economy*, **2**(3), 303–28.

Inman, Robert P. and Daniel L. Rubinfeld (1996), 'Designing tax policy in federalist economies', *Journal of Public Economics*, **60**(3), 307–34.

Inman, Robert P. and Daniel L. Rubinfeld (1997a), 'Rethinking federalism', *Journal of Economic Perspectives*, **11**(4), 43–64.

Inman, Robert P. and Daniel L. Rubinfeld (1997b), 'The Political Economy of Federalism', in Dennis C. Mueller (ed.), *Perspectives on Public Choice*, Cambridge: Cambridge University Press, pp. 73–105.

Josselin, Jean-Michel and Alain Marciano (1995), 'Constitutionalism and common knowledge: assessment and application to a future European constitution', *Public Choice*, **85**(1–2), 173–88.

Josselin, Jean-Michel and Alain Marciano (1997), 'The paradox of Leviathan: how to develop and contain the future European state', *European Journal of Law and Economics*, **4**(1), 5–21.

Josselin, Jean-Michel and Alain Marciano (1999a), 'Administrative Law and Economics', in Jürgen G. Backhaus (ed.), *The Elgar Companion to Law and Economics*, Aldershot: Edward Elgar, pp. 115–20.

Josselin, Jean-Michel and Alain Marciano (1996b), 'General Norms and Customs', in Jürgen G. Backhaus (ed.), *The Elgar Companion to Law and Economics*, Aldershot: Edward Elgar, pp. 233–9.

Josselin, Jean-Michel and Alain Marciano (1999c), 'Unitary states and peripheral regions: A model of heterogeneous spatial clubs', *International Review of Law and Economics*, **19**(4), 501–11.

Josselin, Jean-Michel and Alain Marciano (2000), 'Displacing your principal. Two historical case studies of some interest for the constitutional future of Europe', *European Journal of Law and Economics*, **10**(3), 217–33.

Josselin, Jean-Michel and Alain Marciano (2001), 'Public decisions in the Scottish Enlightenment tradition', *Journal of Economic Studies*, **27**(6), 5–13.

Koslowsky, Rey (1999), 'A constructivist approach to understanding the European Union as a federal polity', *Journal of European Public Policy*, **6**(4), 561–78.

Marciano, Alain and Maud Pélissier (2000), 'The influence of Scottish enlightenment on Darwin's theory of cultural evolution', *Journal of the History of Economic Thought*, **22**(2), 239–49.

Mercuro, Nicholas and Steve G. Medema (1997), *Economics and the Law. From Posner to Post-Modernism*, Princeton: Princeton University Press.

Musgrave, Richard A. (1997), 'Devolution, grants, and fiscal competition', *Journal of Economic Perspectives*, **11**(4), 65–72.

Nozick, Robert (1974), *Anarchy, State and Utopia*, New York: Basic Books.

Rose-Ackerman, Susan (1992), *Re-thinking the Progressive Agenda, the Reform of the American Regulatory State*, New York: The Free Press.

Salmon, Pierre (1987), 'Decentralisation as an incentive scheme', *Oxford Review of Economic Policy*, **3**(2), 24–43.

Salmon, Pierre (2000), 'Vertical Competition in a Unitary State', in G. Galeotti, P. Salmon and R. Wintrobe (eds), *Competition and Structure. The Political Economy of Collective Decisions: Essays in Honor of Albert Breton*, Cambridge: Cambridge University Press, pp. 239–56.

Sbraggia, A.M. (1992), 'Thinking about the European Future: The Uses of Comparison', in A.M. Sbraggia (ed.), *Euro-Politics. Institutions and Policy Making in the 'New' European Community*, Washington, DC: Brooking Institution.

Schilling, Theodor (1996), 'The autonomy of the community legal order: an analysis of possible foundations', *Harvard International Law Journal*, **37**.

Scott, Anthony (2000), 'Assigning Powers Over the Canadian Environment', in G. Galeotti, P. Salmon and R. Wintrobe (eds), *Competition and Structure. The Political Economy of Collective Decisions: Essays in Honor of Albert Breton*, Cambridge: Cambridge University Press, pp. 174–219.

Tannenwald, Robert (1998), 'Devolution: The new federalism – An overview', *Federal Reserve Bank of Boston – New England Economic Review*, May/June, 1–12.

Van den Bergh, Roger (1994), 'The subsidiarity principle in European Community law: some insights from law and economics', *Maastricht Journal of European and Comparative Law*, 337–66.

Van den Bergh, Roger, Michael Faure and Jürgen Lefevere (1995), 'The Subsidiarity Principle in European Environmental Law: An Economic Analysis', in E. Eide and R. van den Bergh (eds), *Law and Economics of the Environment*, Oslo: Juridisk Forlag: 121–66.

Vibert, Frank (1995), *Europe, A Constitution for the Millennium*, Aldershot: Dartmouth.

Wagner, Richard E. (1988), 'Agency, Economic Calculation and Constitutional Construction', in Charles K. Rowley, Robert D. Tollison and Gordon Tullock (eds), *The Political Economy of Rent-Seeking*, Boston: Kluwer, pp. 423–45.

Wagner, Richard E. (1993), *Parchment, Guns and the Maintenance of Constitutional Contract*, Shaftesbury Papers 3, Aldershot: Edward Elgar.

Weiler, Joseph H. and Ulrich R. Halpern (1996), 'The autonomy of the community legal order. Through the looking glass', Working Paper, Harvard Law School.

Wittman, Donald (1991), 'Nations and states: mergers and acquisitions, dissolution and divorce', *American Economic Review*, **81**(2), 126–9.

PART ONE

Competition and Harmonization

1. Regulatory competition or harmonization of laws? Guidelines for the European regulator

Roger Van den Bergh

INTRODUCTION

The academic debate on the merits of 'regulatory competition' versus 'harmonization of laws' offers useful guidance when decisions with respect to the appropriate level of government for particular legislative actions must be taken. Insights from this debate seem to have penetrated policy discussions to a greater extent in the United States than in the European Union. The regulatory competition-based argument for decentralized governance has been applied by its American proponents to diverse regulatory areas, such as corporate law (Winter, 1985), securities (Romano, 1998), antitrust (Easterbrook, 1983), and environmental law (Revesz, 1992). In Europe, regulatory competition theorists have argued that economic analysis may clarify the obscure principle of subsidiarity (Van den Bergh, 1994). If one takes the latter principle seriously, there should be a presumption in favour of decentralized regulation and powers should be granted to the institutions of the European Community, only when it has been established that they cannot be satisfactorily exercised by member states (Art. 5 EC Treaty).[1] The subsidiarity principle thus makes competition between legislators the rule and centralized governance (unification, harmonization) the exception.

Neoclassical welfare economics offers efficiency criteria supporting centralized law making: the need to internalize externalities across jurisdictions, the danger of a 'race to the bottom', the achievement of scale economies and the reduction of transaction costs. Economic distortions in the form of market imperfections on the European markets for legislation may thus justify (quasi-) federal rules. However, before jumping to the conclusion that centralization is needed to cure economic distortions, attention must be paid to the political distortions that may be caused by harmonization. Various pressure groups may benefit from centralization: private politics, not social welfare, may be the driving motive behind central government decisions. Politicians pursue their own goals, which may deviate from the preferences of the citizens. Whereas neoclassical public economists stress that market imperfections on markets for legislation do justify harmonization, political economists focus on political distortions and therefore largely reject harmonization (Frey and Eichenberger, 1996). Decisions about the optimal allocation of tasks to different levels of government must take account of both economic and political distortions. In addition, economic theory warns against a too simplistic 'either, or' view: harmonization of laws and competition between legal rules are not necessarily mutually exclusive but may be complementary devices. Optimal governance may require a flexible mix of competition and harmonization, bringing about the major benefits of regulatory competition whilst at the same time minimizing its costs.

This chapter argues that the academic discussion on regulatory competition has now evolved to a point where it is possible to draw an economic decision-framework, useful for policymakers. The challenge for European law is not to speed up harmonization of laws at any cost, but to guarantee a high level of regulatory quality both with respect to the level of decision making and the contents of the enacted rules. The task of European law could be redefined as creating an institutional framework allowing that regulatory decisions are taken at the most appropriate level of government. It should also be ensured that the responses of the European legislator are well targeted at the problems caused by regulatory competition and that the risk of political distortions is minimized.

The structure of this chapter is as follows. After this introduction, it is explained how rules of European law may guarantee that benefits of regulatory competition are achieved in those areas of law where such benefits may be considered to be important (Section 1.1). Thereafter, it is shown how European law may cope with economic distortions on markets for legislation: the risk of a 'race to the bottom' and the need to internalize interstate externalities. Attention is also paid to other reasons for centralization: scale economies and transaction cost savings (Section 1.2). In Section 1.3, the problem of political distortions is addressed. Section 1.4, then, continues with two illustrations taken from different European policy fields: environmental law and competition law. In the conclusions, the main arguments are summarized and questions that should be part of an economic decision framework are formulated. In 1995 the OECD published a checklist for regulatory decision making (OECD, 1995), which included as a fifth question the problem of the most appropriate level (or levels) of government for the envisaged legislative action. In the OECD's wording, 'regulators should choose the most appropriate level of government to take action, or, if multiple levels are involved, should design effective systems of co-ordination between levels of government'. This vaguely formulated guideline may be substantially improved upon. The appendix to this chapter presents its main conclusions in the form of an integrated, stepwise Law and Economics checklist.

1.1 GUARANTEEING BENEFITS FROM COMPETITION

1.1.1 Economic theory

Competition between legislators generates several benefits: different laws can satisfy more preferences and allow for different experiences. Enterprises and citizens may have heterogeneous preferences as to their preferred set of laws: the more legislators compete, the more preferences may be satisfied. Firms and individuals may 'vote by feet' (Tiebout, 1956) and choose the jurisdiction which in their view offers the best set of laws. Competition between legislators also generates the benefits of a learning process. Differences in rules allow for different experiences and may improve the understanding of the effects of alternative legal solutions to similar problems.

The advantages flowing from satisfying heterogeneous preferences and learning processes will vary across different fields of law. The more homogeneous preferences are, the weaker the argument in favour of competing rules will be. In contrast, with heterogeneous preferences regulatory competition will generate important benefits. One may safely assume that most people want a minimum level of safety, but may have divergent preferences with respect to the food they wish to consume. Hence, centralized rules on the safety of nuclear installations or safety devices for cars seem to interfere less with citizens' diverging preferences than the regulation of the composition of foodstuffs. The achievement of the advantages of regulatory competition presupposes a sufficient number of rule-makers, information about the alternatives that are available and mobility of citizens or production factors.

Another major advantage of competition between legal orders is that different rules allow for different experiences. Competition, seen from a dynamic perspective, is a process of 'trial and error'. Learning processes are particularly important in fields of law characterized by information problems on the part of the legislator. Diversity in laws makes it possible for states to experiment in their search for efficient and workable rules of law. On this point it should be stressed that competition between legislators and legal uniformity are not mutually exclusive. Competition between legislators does not necessarily imply that rules will greatly differ. States may decide to amend their codes in response to legal solutions adopted in other states. If legal rules can be envisaged as a homogeneous product, convergences between jurisdictions are likely spontaneously to occur (Ogus, 1999). Whereas unification and harmonization by means of central rules (Regulations, Directives) implies forced coordination of legislative provisions, dynamic competitive processes may produce voluntary harmonization. If states do not amend their codes in response to another state's innovation, they run the risk that firms will move to the state which is most responsive to firms' and consumers' demands for legislation. The scope of a voluntary harmonization through dynamic competitive processes may be larger than the degree of uniformity brought about by centralized decision making. Directives often contain escape clauses or grant the member states a number of options to choose between that impede full harmonization. If states voluntarily choose to adapt their legislation to superior rules of competing states, a greater degree of uniformity may be reached. If one is willing to take competition between legal systems seriously, the answer to the question whether harmonization is needed must be left to the competitive process itself.

1.1.2 Lessons for European Law

European law does not fully profit from the lessons from economic theory. Even though some parts of EC law may be understood as devices to enable efficiency-enhancing regulatory competition, other parts hinder the efficient outcomes of competition between legal orders. If the European regulator took competitive processes seriously, he would in the first place 'organize' competition between the member states' laws and would only enact rules of substantive law if and where such competition cannot lead to efficient outcomes. Competition among rules of law is related to the sovereignty of the member states. Therefore, the creation of a legal framework for competition between legal orders is a matter of constitutional design. At present there is no European constitution, which creates sufficient scope for diverging legal rules and spells out rules of conduct for the competing legislators. At best, the current text of the Treaties may be qualified as a quasi-constitutional framework, which contains the first building blocks of a European Constitution. It should be improved upon to become a general legal framework ('*Ordnungsrahmen*') safeguarding the beneficial effects of competition between legal systems, whilst at the same time coping with economic distortions on markets for legislation.

The formulation of basic principles of European law does not completely coincide with what could be termed efficient law. It will be indicated below that the principles of attribution of powers and subsidiarity can be given an economic meaning; they can be further elaborated upon to create a framework for competition between member states' laws. Competition between 'sellers' of laws requires that 'buyers' are informed about contents and effects of alternative rules, and can freely choose the set of laws best adapted to their preferences. On both points European law can play an important role: by guaranteeing 'mobility' through enabling free choice of law, and by improving information on the markets for legislation, in particular by laying down measures of standardization. Finally, competition requires a sufficient number of legislators to make sure that varying preferences can be satisfied. From this perspective, it must equally be noted that the European legislator can further stimulate competition by offering European rules as a sixteenth choice (as a complement to the fifteen legal systems of the member states) for firms and citizens. Offering additional choices, rather than harmonizing immediately certain rules of substantive law, will also preserve the benefits of competition as a dynamic process.

Attribution of powers and subsidiarity
Even though the European Treaties have evolved slowly from statutes of economic cooperation to constitutional documents (containing goals of political integration alongside an ever-increasing economic integration), the lack of an appropriate European constitutional framework to guarantee regulatory competition must be deplored. The current quasi-constitutional framework of the EC provides scope for competition between legislators, but it does so only to a limited extent. Some scope for competing legal rules is safeguarded by the principle of attribution of powers (Art. 5 (1) EC Treaty). The Community institutions have only the powers given to them expressly or impliedly by the Treaties and may thus not pre-empt member state action totally. However, in practice the scope for Community action tends to increase at the expense of member states' regulatory competences. In contrast with the US and German constitutions, the European Treaties do not provide any detailed assignment of competences. The absence of competence catalogues creates scope for broadly described functional Community competences (for example, environmental policy, consumer policy, social policy and so on). Article 94 EC Treaty empowers the Community to take measures 'which have as their object the establishment and functioning of the internal market'; this broad formulation can be abused by the Commission to pre-empt member state action totally. The interpretation of the functional Community competences ultimately lies with the European Court of Justice, which as a Community institution, may take a clear pro-integrationist attitude rather than emphasizing the protection of member states' competences. In the past, the process of negative integration[2] has created scope for competition between the home state and the host state's legal rules concerning production and distribution of goods. With respect to the regulation of sales methods, the Court has, however, changed direction in 1993.[3] Marketing techniques which are lawful in the exporting country may not be used in the importing member state if they violate the latter's rules. In contrast with the competition on the market for rules governing production of goods, the resulting decentralization – as

far as the regulation of sales methods is concerned – leaves no scope for competition between legal orders.

As a mechanism to limit overcentralization, the subsidiarity principle (Art. 5 (2) EC Treaty) was included by the Maastricht Treaty on the European Union. However, this principle does not cover the full scope of EC policy fields but only the domains of mixed competences. The subsidiarity principle does not apply to areas falling into the Community's exclusive competence: for instance, external commercial policy, agricultural policy and some parts of competition policy.[4] Consequently, economic criteria cannot be used for reviewing the whole political and administrative structure of the Community. If a power has already been assigned exclusively to the supranational level, it should remain there forever. There is no legal instrument to 'repatriate' policy responsibilities back to the national level (Kirchner, 1997). This defence of the *status quo* may exclude competition in areas where it may be desirable. It is also important to add that decentralization, which is favoured by the subsidiarity principle, is no synonym for competition between legal rules. If member state laws apply exclusively to the transactions and business involved, subsidiarity is met but competition will not work if mobility between states is hampered.

Mobility
Competition between legal orders implies that enterprises and citizens are free to move to the jurisdiction that offers laws best adapted to their preferences. Mobility should not be understood solely as physical mobility, relating to free movement of persons *à la* Tiebout. As an alternative to physical migration, firms and consumers should be able to select the jurisdiction whose principles are to apply to their transactions. Physical mobility is largely guaranteed through the provisions in the EC Treaty regarding free movement of goods, persons, services and capital. It should be added, however, that some restrictions to these freedoms have been accepted in the case law of the European Court of Justice. As a consequence, the legal system of a host member state may attract business from abroad but at the same time limit competition with (some of the) legal rules of the member state of origin. For example, 'mandatory requirements of general interest' may preclude the application of foreign law and oblige professionals to obey national rules of conduct when performing services in a host member state (Van den Bergh, 1999). In cases where no physical migration is involved, another important limitation to competition between legal orders may be caused by rules of international private law of the host member state that do not allow free choice of the legal rules governing transactions or business. To increase competition, the European legislator should enact provisions directly concerning conflicts of law. However, Directives on harmonization of rules of substantive law do not ordinarily

contain such stipulations. In this respect, an interesting novelty is Article 65 EC (inserted by the Amsterdam Treaty) concerning cooperation in trans-boundary civil law cases, including measures to enhance the compatibility of member states' laws on collision and conflicts of jurisdiction. It is to be seen in how far this new provision will be used to increase competition by allowing for a greater freedom to choose the legal rule that will apply to the parties' transactions.

Information measures

Competition, obviously, also requires information on the precise meaning of alternative legal rules. If the European legislator took competitive processes seriously, European law would take a dramatically different form: instead of programmes of harmonization, one would rather see measures to improve information flows, such as standardization. Currently there is no common terminology in the laws of the member states; the common law uses a language that is not easily understandable to civil lawyers (for example, notions such as 'privity of contract' or 'estoppel'). Comparison of the strengths and weaknesses of different legal solutions concerning issues such as the formation and validity of contracts and remedies for non-performance is difficult because of information deficiencies caused by a non-uniform termi-nology. Standardization would be extremely helpful to make competition on the market for legislation work. Lowering information costs on alternative legal rules is needed to create a framework for competition on these matters. Standardization will enable the distinguishing of real from superficial differ-ences. In some cases divergent legal formulations lead to similar outcomes. In other cases, the application of diverging principles entails real differences and thus justifies the use of divergent legal formulations.

Adding a sixteenth choice

An equally important method to stimulate competition between legislators is the enactment of European rules which are a complement to, but not a substi-tute for, state laws. In the latter case the European legislator engages in compe-tition with the national legislators rather than eliminating it by means of harmonization. Some European rules do indeed have a supplementary charac-ter. The Product Liability Directive does not affect any rights which an injured person may have according to the rules of contractual or non-contractual liability in the member states.[5] The same is true for specific liability systems, which existed at the moment when the Directive was notified. Consequently, victims of product accidents may choose between different liability rules to claim damages. For example, in Germany they may base lawsuits on four different grounds: contractual liability, tort liability, specific rules (in cases of defective medicines) and the liability for product defects as contained in the

EC Directive. Such a competition between legislators allows individuals to choose the legal rule that most efficiently regulates their problem and implies the lowest costs to solve the conflict. In its Green Paper, the Commission invites comments on whether the Directive should be revised to become the common and sole system of liability for defective products (European Commission, 1999). A dynamic view of competition between legal rules is at odds with such a suggestion. As argued in another paper, also a static view focussing on the optimality of the outcomes of competition on the market for product liability laws does not provide much support for full harmonization, and the current Directive does not adequately cope with the relevant economic distortions (Van den Bergh, 1998).

1.2   CURING ECONOMIC DISTORTIONS

1.2.1   Economic Theory

As is the case with markets for ordinary goods, markets for legislation are not perfect. Market failures may take different forms. The most relevant problems caused by decentralized decision making in markets for legislation are negative externalities across states and the danger of a 'race to the bottom'. There is also the problem of increased transaction costs and the risk that scale economies are lost when competition between legislators is preferred to harmonization. These arguments are not always equally relevant. Also here one should distinguish across different fields of law. For example, in the field of environmental law the need to internalize across the border externalities (air pollution) is more powerful than in the area of private law, where externalities of a similar magnitude are absent. Similarly, the danger of a race to the bottom is more plausible in the field of tax law than in areas such as environmental law or competition law. Finally, competition may not be the best institutional arrangement if important scale economies get lost or if transaction costs increase to such an extent that they outweigh the benefits of diversity. The strength of the latter argument will also vary across different fields of law. Scale economies may be relevant when product safety standards must be set but are less so when it comes to harmonization of tort law.

The first two arguments in favour of centralized governance need some further clarification. To justify unification or harmonization, the European Commission often argues that diverging legal rules create unequal conditions of competition within the EC and that such differences should be minimized in order to create a 'level playing field' for industry. In the United States, a related argument is made: interjurisdictional competition may lead to a lowering of standards to the detriment of citizens in need of protection against abuses (workers, consumers) or degrade important quality standards (environmental conditions, protection of health). This fear of destructive competition, which is extensively discussed as the danger of a 'race to the bottom', may be exaggerated. Game theory has shown that, depending on the assumptions made, either a 'race to the bottom' or a 'race to the top' will result when states engage in legislative competition (Markusen, Morey and Olewiler, 1993 and 1995). Given the uncertainties resulting from theoretical studies, the question whether a race to the bottom is feasible is ultimately an empirical issue. The evidence available does not seem to warrant far-reaching centralization (Van den Bergh, Faure and Lefevere, 1996).

Most commentators will agree that the problem of interstate externalities is a more powerful argument to justify centralized governance than the risk of a race to the bottom. However, the former argument should also be limited to its right proportions. The seriousness of the problem depends on the magnitude of the cross-border effects. A too broad interpretation of the requirement that interstate trade must be affected will unnecessarily limit the scope for state law. It must also be emphasized that only in specific circumstances are national laws unable to internalize the negative external effects caused by the private law of another state. For example, generally a tortfeasor will not be insulated against liability for harm he causes outside his home state. Hence, the argument in favour of centralized governance is valid only in cases where forms of damage are difficult for state law mechanisms to redress.

Centralized governance may cure economic distortions in different ways. A full comparative institutional approach cannot be limited to a comparison of costs and benefits of alternative legal remedies at the (quasi-)federal level; it must also include the effects of 'doing nothing' (leaving the issue totally to lower levels of government) and the feasibility of contractual agreements between states. The most appropriate remedies to cure economic distortions will vary depending on the characteristics of the particular economic distortion. If an externality affects only a limited number of countries and the risk of strategic behaviour may be mitigated, negotiations between states on the basis of previously assigned property rights may lead to efficient outcomes (Coase theorem). The central rule-maker could then limit itself to organizing these negotiations and seeing to it that the agreements made are respected. If further-reaching intervention is appropriate, particular emphasis should be put on the need to devise solutions that are well targeted at the problem at hand. Centralized rules that are ineffective as mechanisms to internalize across-the-border externalities (or curing other economic distortions on markets for legislation) only reduce the benefits of regulatory competition, without bringing any compensating advantages.

1.2.2   Lessons for European Law

Again, it must be emphasized that appropriate constitutional rules are needed to make Community action possible in cases of economic distortions. The presumption should remain that states are able to achieve the relevant policy goals, but corrective measures may be needed when interjurisdictional competition leads to suboptimal outcomes. A system of concurrent powers perfectly meets this need. In such a system states retain the right to enact legislation as long as the Community institutions do not make use of their power to achieve Community objectives. The next step, then, is to make sure that the response of the European regulator is adequately targeted at the problem at hand and does not go further than necessary to reach the goals of the Treaty.

From this perspective, the *proportionality principle* enshrined in Article 5(3) [old 3 B] EC Treaty may be seen as an important element of the quasi-constitutional framework safeguarding competition between legislators. The proportionality principle requires that Community acts must be appropriate to the aim to be achieved and may not go beyond what is necessary for that purpose. It is a central notion of EC law that has received much attention in the Court's judgements on free movement of goods; it seems possible to deduce from that case law guidelines for division of competences between the EC and its member states. Different methods of harmonization may be used: total harmonization, optional harmonization, partial harmonization, minimum harmonization and alternative harmonization (Slot, 1996). The best framework for competition between legislators is provided by a system of mutual recognition, which is not a harmonization method in the strict sense of the word but a technique to eliminate trade barriers. Since legal rules regulating production and distribution in one member state are regarded as equivalent to rules in other states, enterprises and citizens remain free to choose the law that best conforms to their preferences. Obviously, mutual recognition is no viable alternative in cases of significant interstate externalities or when a race to the bottom is likely. Some degree of harmonization will then be needed. Minimum harmonization still allows competition between legislators, but only above the floor of rights set by European law. If harmonization is restricted to the imposition of minimum standards, competition remains possible as far as member states wish to enact rules stricter than those of the minimum standard do. Optional harmonization provides enterprises with an option to follow either the harmonized rules or the national rules. Goods that are traded across the borders of member states will have to meet the harmonized standards or the standards of the import country. While permitting the member states to enact stricter rules for products manufactured on the national territory, optional harmonization forbids them to oppose the marketing of imported goods if they respect the provisions of the directives. Hence, competition between the European legislator and the rule-maker of a particular member state remains possible to a limited extent. In cases of total harmonization such competition is ruled out entirely. It will be difficult to reconcile this far-reaching intervention by the European legislator with the proportionality principle.

If one takes the proportionality principle seriously, costs and benefits of alternative solutions, ranking from legislative action representing a low degree of interference to highly interventionist measures, must be compared. A full comparative institutional approach necessitates comparing the strengths and weaknesses of (1) leaving the issue to the member states ('doing nothing'), (2) agreements between member states, and (3) regulation at the community level, including a comparative analysis of varying methods of harmonization. The second option for Europe would be to stimulate Coasian bargains by assigning property rights to member states and providing for an obligation to hold consultations in the event of across the border externalities. Uniformity brought about by total harmonization is not necessarily the best response; neither with respect to the problem of interstate externalities, nor regarding the risk of a race to the bottom. In the latter case, minimum harmonization may suffice as a response. Such a Community intervention sets a floor of rights which member states may not derogate from, but upon which they may improve by setting superior standards.

1.3   COPING WITH POLITICAL DISTORTIONS

The private interest theory of regulation stresses that, besides market failures, regulatory failure is also possible. Agencies imposing regulation are under the influence of regulated industry and may become 'captured'. Politicians acting out of self-interest may provide interest groups with economic rents in exchange for votes and other support. Also bureaucrats serve their self-interest by maximizing their budget or increasing their status and improving the quality of work (for an overview, see Ogus, 1994). And finally, even judges' behaviour may be explained by their desire to gain prestige or to lower the pressure of work.[6] These insights are not only relevant to explain the contents of substantive law, but also to clarify the actual allocation of competences between a central authority and legislators at lower levels of government. A division of competences that does not coincide with economic welfare criteria may very well be explained by the private interest theory.

The choice between regulatory competition and harmonization may be distorted by different interest groups if the law reform affects their rent-seeking potential. Firms established in jurisdictions with more costly legal structures, which have already invested resources in complying with such regimes, will wish to keep their competitive advantage over newcomers and thus oppose cost-reducing reforms. Lawyers are often seen as an influential pressure group in relation to law reform, but heterogeneity of interests may prevent them from successful rent seeking. On the one hand, specialized lawyers may profit from competition between legal systems, since this will increase the demand for their services from firms wishing to choose the rules best adapted to their preferences. On the other hand, lawyers with a vast experience in the law of the jurisdiction of establishment will benefit from constraints on competition. As a consequence, harmonization may be retarded. Sub-groups, such as comparative lawyers pursuing an academic career, may have more homogeneous preferences and may thus constitute an effective lobby in favour of harmonization, which guarantees a demand for their services and brings them increased prestige. In sum, the central lesson from Public Choice that the most powerful interest groups are small, single-issue oriented and well-organized is equally relevant to explain why the actual allocation of competences deviates from optimality.

European bureaucracy may equally be a source of political distortions. The functional competences, enabling the harmonization of all sorts of policy areas, may be used by the European bureaucrats to increase their power and prestige by expanding the budget, personnel and functions of the central government (Vaubel, 1992, p. 13). The members of the Commission are appointed by the national governments but they must, in the performance of their duties, 'neither seek nor take instructions from any government or from any other body' (Article 213, al. 2 EC Treaty). Consequently, Commissioners should act in what they perceive to be 'European interests', which may remarkably parallel their own interests. EU bureaucrats typically argue that harmonization of laws is required for the functioning of the European internal market. In their opinion, the achievement of market integration should be regarded as an exclusive competence of the European Community. This view severely limits the scope of the subsidiarity principle and may expand the scope for European law outside areas where the economic distortions require centralized governance.

Given the inefficiencies that ensue from political distortions, devices are needed to reduce the risks of rent-seeking and regulatory capture. A future European Constitution should offer remedies which adequately cope with these problems. In this respect three axioms are crucial: independence, transparency and accountability (compare, with respect to competition policy: Neven, Nuttall and Seabright, 1993, pp. 153–213). Political independence should guarantee that the voting public at large, rather than interest groups, has an important impact on law making. More efforts are needed to cure the often deplored democratic deficit of the European Union. The European Parliament's position has been improved, but it must be seriously questioned whether the voting public's participation in political decision making can be achieved by strengthening the powers of a large group of professional politicians. In this respect, an increased use of referenda may be much more effective. In addition, the role of many non-elected bodies in the decision-making process is a continuing reason for concern. As put by Frey and Eichenberger (1996, p. 341): 'Paraphrasing Adam Smith, one may state that people rarely meet in Commissions to stimulate competition, but rather to suppress it by harmonizing tax policy, and government policy more generally'.

Transparency should reduce information problems and aid the European legislator to commit himself to a welfare increasing policy. At present, the Commission is active in many policy fields and often argues that in designing a particular policy account must be taken of the impact of a certain decision on other EC policies. In this view, no single policy is autonomous and decisions are always the result of a trade-off between different policy goals. For example, competition policy may be perverted by considerations of industrial policy (protecting firms from competition by non-European competitors), environmental policy (allowing environmentally friendly cartels) or social policy (exempting collective labour agreements from the ban on cartels; see Van den Bergh and Camesasca, 2000). A change of decision structures making it clearer which motive was overriding, and thus bringing about more transparency, may reduce the scope for political distortions.

Together with independence and transparency, increased accountability will reduce the risk of the political distortions discussed in this chapter. Mobility is one of the best guarantors of accountability. Exit constitutes an important mechanism to force legislators to respect citizens' preferences. Member states feeling that they are no longer able to enact legal rules, which do not cause economic distortions across European jurisdictions, must be able to exit. Hence, the right to secede should be explicitly provided for in a future European constitution (Buchanan, 1991). Considering the fact that the advantages and the disadvantages of centralization differ across various areas of law, taking competition seriously also implies that member states should be able to opt out with respect to a particular policy. Frey and Eichenberger's concept of FOCJ (functional, overlapping and competing jurisdictions) can be seen as a model of selective exit, which is based on interjurisdictional competition (Frey and Eichenberger, 1997). This concept also powerfully illustrates that a real democracy presupposes a bottom-up approach, rather than a top-down decision process by a central government.

1.4   TWO ILLUSTRATIONS FROM EC POLICY FIELDS

Two fields are chosen to illustrate the economic strengths and weaknesses of the functional definition of competences in the European Union. First, environmental law is discussed. Pollution may cause significant interstate externalities.

However, EC law also intervenes when no such externalities exist; further-more, it neither creates sufficient scope for a complete 'comparative institutional analysis', nor always uses responses that are well targeted at the problems at hand. Second, examples from competition law will be used to illustrate the importance of regulatory competition as a learning process. Also in this policy field, EC rules affect transactions not having a significant impact on interstate trade. It is also indicated how EC law may limit the scope for a race to the bottom in the field of competition law.

1.4.1 Environmental Policy

The goal of internalization of pollution externalities cannot explain substantial parts of European environmental law. Many Directives deal with relatively localized pollution. There are a number of pollutants for which local control may well represent the appropriate level for environmental management. Examples include noise and municipal waste. If, by contrast, the spillovers across boundaries are likely to be large, decentralized decision making will not produce satisfactory outcomes. Some pollutants travel over substantial distances (acid rain) and some environmental problems require worldwide action (depletion of the ozone layer, greenhouse effect resulting from CO_2 emissions). Between both extremes, the magnitude of the interstate externalities varies. For example, there seems to be more scope for state-specific standards relating to water quality than for decentralized decision making to combat air pollution. Given these differences in the extent of transboundary effects, it is remarkable that EC environmental law covers both local and community-wide pollution, without always making the relevant distinctions between local, regional and interstate pollution. Directives have been enacted with respect to noise levels,[7] municipal waste[8] and the quality of drinking water.[9] In these cases, the interstate externalities seem either absent, or at least less severe, than in other fields, such as air pollution.

Internalizing interstate externalities is a prominent rationale for vesting regulatory responsibilities with a central authority. Environmental policy is a most expedient example to illustrate the different ways in which centralized governance may cope with interstate externalities. If a country's pollution affects another country, the first attempt to solve the problem should be to properly specify property rights. If property rights are well specified, information is perfect and transactions costs negligible, an efficient solution will result without any further intervention by a federal authority. Even if there are many member states, and the costs of negotiation and enforcement must not be neglected, there may, in some instances, be opportunities for Coasian-type bargains among jurisdictions. A comparison between standard setting at the central level and agreements between the member states involved is needed to make a case for managing the joint environmental resources directly from the central level. The European regulator could assign property rights and organize negotiations between countries and see to it that the agreements reached are respected.

Many externalities will not affect all fifteen member states, but only a limited number of them. This may then create scope for Coasian bargaining. An example of agreements between member states aiming at solving transboundary pollution is the Rhine Action Plan, which was agreed upon by France, Germany, Luxembourg, the Netherlands, Switzerland and the EC, after the fire in a chemical warehouse owned by the firm Sandoz in Basel, Switzerland. The Rhine Action Plan has substantially decreased pollution from industrial sources, but was less successful in reducing pollution from agriculture and towns. In spite of the progress made, the Rhine Action Plan may be criticized for not relying on precise cost–benefit analyses and for not having paid sufficient attention to pollution from agriculture and towns (Centre for Economic Policy Research, 1993). There are, however, reasons to doubt that action at the EC level would have been more successful. European farmers, who have succeeded in capturing a major part of the European budget, are a powerful pressure group in Brussels. Moreover, in public opinion, industries, not households, are usually seen as the polluters who should pay.

If regulatory solutions are superior to negotiated agreements, another important question remains: what form should the federal rules take in order to adequately cure the economic problem at issue? Revesz (1992) has expressed serious doubts with respect to the adequacy of the American federal legislation on air pollution as an instrument to internalize interstate externalities. These criticisms are also relevant in the European context. Community legislation on air pollution establishes minimum air quality standards and maximum emission standards for certain harmful substances; it also aims at reducing the emission from pollutants from cars and other motor vehicles. The central feature of the air quality Directives[10] is an obligation to observe certain air quality limit values, which are defined as concentrations of pollution that must not be exceeded throughout the territory of the member states. Measures limiting emissions from industrial plants can be found in Directives on large combustion plants,[11] municipal waste incineration plants[12] and hazardous waste incineration plants.[13] At the heart of the large combustion plants Directive are emission limit values for sulphur dioxide, oxides of nitrogen and dust. To prevent air pollution caused by vehicles, member states must see to it that emissions meet the standards laid down in the Directive.[14] Given these rules, the same criticisms as those relating to American environmental law apply. The emission standards do not regulate the number of sources within any given state or the location of the source and, therefore, are not a good means to combat the problem of interstate externalities. The air quality standards are overinclusive

because they require a state to restrict pollution that has only in-state consequences and underinclusive because they do not prevent states from exporting
pollution to downwind states by locating sources near the interstate border.
Overcoming the current inefficiencies may be more difficult in Europe than in
America. A major obstacle to adopting efficient rules is one of the fundamental principles of European environment policy.[15] According to the 'source
principle', environmental damage should preferably be prevented at source.
This principle implies a preference for emission standards rather than environmental quality standards. Solving the problem of interstate externalities by
using marketable permits in units of environmental degradation in the downwind state rather than in units of emissions may be incompatible with the
source principle. Politically sensitive principles of environmental law may
thus cause substantial inefficiencies.[16]

1.4.2   Competition Law

Competition law offers prominent examples to illustrate the argument that
regulatory competition brings all the benefits of a learning process.
Competition law is a very difficult field: without a proper understanding of the
underlying economics no sound rules may be developed. It is also important
to profit from different experiences and to improve competition law on that
basis. A learning process may bring about spontaneous harmonization
confined to the 'best' rules. In contrast, if states are put under pressure to copy
each other's rules (or rules enacted at the central level), it can not be avoided
that they will also copy each other's mistakes. A dramatic example is the treatment of vertical restraints in European competition law, which has also been
introduced in the competition laws of the member states. The European rules
prohibit absolute territorial protection and the fixing of minimum retail prices,
because these practices interfere with the goal of market integration.[17] This
strict rule is imposed for political reasons in spite of the ensuing inefficiencies.
At the member states' level, however, market integration is not an issue. As a
consequence only the efficiency losses flowing from the absolute ban on territorial protection and minimum resale price maintenance remain.

Even though competition lawyers tend to like competition, they often
disfavour competition between competition laws. More scope for competition
on the latter market should be created in the first place by downsizing the criterion of 'impact on interstate trade' in European competition law. The very
broad interpretation by the European Court of Justice brings many agreements
of an apparently domestic nature within the reach of the prohibition. It has
enabled the Commission to exercise jurisdiction in a number of areas, where
the degree of effect on trade between member states appears to be minor. A
few examples may illustrate this point. According to the case law of the

European Court of Justice, the Commission has jurisdiction over nationwide distribution systems reducing the attractiveness of market entry for importers,[18] aggregate rebate systems discouraging the imports of foreign products[19] and refusals to supply local retailers without objective justification.[20] The latter case is the most dramatic example of the use of EC competition rules to combat restrictive practices without any international spillovers. The market affected was clearly national (even local) with at most minor effects on imports or exports. Also with respect to the other cases the argument may be advanced that the costs of market power were borne by the consumers of the country to which exports were discouraged. Therefore, it seems more natural to have the foreclosure effects controlled by the antitrust agencies of the import country. A narrow interpretation of the requirement that interstate trade is affected would not only be consistent with the role of centralized rules in coping with significant externalities across states (see below), but at the same time contribute to quality improvement through enabling learning processes in the market for competition laws.

The second section of this chapter has shown that a typical task for a central regulator is to minimize the risk of destructive competition between states leading to 'bad' law. European rules should thus limit the scope for a race to the bottom. Competition law may serve as an illustration of how this goal can be achieved. EC law indeed restricts the scope for member states to engage in a race to the bottom. Easterbrook suggests the following wish list for firms in search of monopoly profits. First on the list would be a monopoly protected by the state but not regulated in any other way. Second on the list would be a cartel enforced by the state. Third on the list would be a law lifting the antitrust laws (Easterbrook, 1983). Current EC law limits the scope for member states to grant firms any of these wishes. Existing state-protected monopolies have been deregulated, also in markets which were long considered natural monopolies.[21] Cartels protected and enforced by state regulation may be combated on the basis of a combined use of the articles 3(g), 10 (old art. 5) and 81 (old art. 85) EC-Treaty.[22] Member states may not adopt or maintain in force any measure, which could deprive the competition rules of their effectiveness. Following this principle, the European Court of Justice struck down several national regulations restricting competition, such as the Belgian rule requiring travel agents to observe the prices laid down by tour operators and prohibiting the grant of rebates to consumers.[23]

CONCLUSIONS

The question whether harmonization of laws is needed requires careful analysis and can be answered only with respect to the particular rule of law under investigation. Nevertheless three general lessons may be derived from the economic analysis of regulatory competition.

First, diversity in legal rules may generate important benefits. The more legislators compete, the more preferences can be satisfied. Competition is also a learning process generating important information about the efficiency of alternative rules. Given these advantages, European law should in the first place create an institutional framework that makes competition between legislators possible in those areas where such benefits may be deemed to be important. The quasi-constitutional framework, under which the European Community currently operates, already creates scope for competition between legislators. This framework should, however, be improved upon to fully profit from economic insights. To make competition on the market for legal rules work, this chapter has suggested an economic interpretation of the principles of attribution of powers and subsidiarity, measures of standardization to facilitate comparison of contents and effects of legal rules, harmonization of rules on conflicts of laws, and the enactment of European rules as a sixteenth choice.

Second, when competition between legislators does not function properly because of market imperfections on the market for legislation, corrective measures coping with such economic distortions should be taken. Here lies a second task for European law: the institutional framework should minimize the risk of a 'race to the bottom' and provide remedies to cope with negative externalities across jurisdictions. It should also make sure that scale economies are achieved in areas of law where these are important. The institutional framework should also guarantee that informed decisions which are well targeted at the issue at stake are taken. Given heterogeneous preferences, full harmonization should remain an *ultimum remedium*, confined to areas of law where competition between legal rules causes substantial costs without any compensating benefits.

Third, the risk of political distortions must also be mitigated. Increased political independence, transparency and accountability should reduce the impact of pressure groups. Also European bureaucrats may profit from excessive centralization; the latter problem seems difficult to cure from within the existing European institutions. Whereas the Treaty in its current form does already provide a quasi-constitutional framework to cure economic distortions, it remains far from what would be needed to avoid political distortions. To cure the latter problem, democratic forces from below should gain momentum and appropriate new constitutional rules should be fixed.

Economic analysis of regulatory competition has evolved to a point where it is possible to create integrated, step-by-step guidelines for decision making, allowing a sensible evaluation of costs and benefits of competition between legal systems. The current OECD Guidelines can be improved upon by an integrated

Law and Economics Checklist of the type suggested in the Appendix to this chapter. Starting from the insight that competition between legal systems may generate important benefits, the first set of questions inquires whether such advantages are indeed important with respect to the envisaged legislative action and can be achieved within the existing institutional framework. In areas where the argument of heterogeneous preferences is strong, but competition does not function properly, rules of European law that guarantee mobility or cure information deficiencies may contribute to an efficient market for legislation. Market failures (interstate externalities or a 'race to the bottom') and scale economies provide arguments for centralized decision making but, given the benefits of competition in a context of heterogeneous preferences, legislative measures leaving the largest possible scope for competition between legal rules should be preferred. If a race to the bottom is realistic, it will suffice to set minimum standards, to be seen as a floor of rights from which member states may not deviate. By contrast, if preferences are largely homogeneous, competition may lead to a spontaneous harmonization of laws. Centralization may then still be justified to 'speed up' this process in case of important scale economies and/or transaction cost savings. Finally, when harmonization seems appropriate, attention must be paid to the risk of political distortions at the level of the central government. The enactment of inefficient rules, benefiting interest groups (or bureaucrats) to the detriment of society at large, must be avoided. The checklist below includes an assessment of the main factors. (Additional sub-questions may be needed to give well-informed answers to the checklist; the latter are not further developed in this chapter.) Even though checklists do not guarantee first-best outcomes – in particular when answers to the relevant questions may force the regulator to restrict its powers and no adequate judicial control is provided for – such decision procedures will improve the quality and increase the legitimacy of the regulations issued. At present, given the current lack of democracy in the European Union, answering the last question of the checklist may have the effect of rejecting harmonization measures altogether. This conclusion forcefully stresses the need to improve the democratic legitimacy of the European institutions, to guarantee that economic distortions caused by failures of inter-jurisdictional competition are not replaced by political distortions.

NOTES

This chapter is based on an earlier publication in *Kyklos*; see R. Van den Bergh (2000), Towards an Institutional Legal Framework for Regulatory Competition in Europe, 53(4) *Kyklos*, 435–466.

1. Except for matters falling within the exclusive competence of the European Community Institutions.

2. The Court may consider existing legislative measures of the member states contrary to the fundamental freedoms of the EC Treaty (free movement of goods, persons, services and capital). This is called 'negative integration', in contrast with the approximation of laws brought about by Regulations and Directives that is called 'positive integration'.
3. Cases 26–268/91 *Keck and Mithouard* [1993] ECR I-6097.
4. Concentrations having a 'community dimension' (depending on thresholds concerning the turnover achieved by the post-merger firm) are controlled exclusively by the European Commission. See Reg. 4064/89 as amended by Reg. 1301/97.
5. Art. 13 Council Directive 85/374/EEC of 25 July 1985 on the approximation of the laws, regulations and administrative provisions of the Member States concerning liability for defective products, OJ L 210 of 7 August 1985, 29–33.
6. The latter explanation seems most powerful in the *Keck and Mithouard* judgement (cited above, note 3), in which the Court itself took notice of the increasing tendency to invoke (old) Article 30 of the EC Treaty and therefore considered it necessary to re-examine and clarify its case-law (paragraph 14).
7. Examples include: Directive 70/157, Motor vehicle exhaust systems, OJ 1970, L 42/16; Directive 78/1015, Motorcycles, OJ 1978 L 349/21; Directive 84/533, Compressors, OJ 1984 L 300/123.
8. Directive 91/271, Urban waste water, OJ 1991 L 135/50.
9. Directive 80/778, Water for human consumption, OJ 1980 L 229/11.
10. Directive 80/779, Sulphur dioxide and suspended particulates, OJ 1980, L 229/30; Directive 82/884, Lead, OJ 1982, L 378/15; Directive 85/203, Nitrogen Dioxide, OJ 1985, L 87/1.
11. Directive 88/609, OJ 1988, L 336/1.
12. Directives 89/369, OJ 1989, L 136/32 and 89/429, OJ 1989, L 203/50.
13. Directive 94/67, OJ 1994, L 365/34.
14. Directive 70/220, OJ 1970, L 76/1 lastly amended by Directive 94/12, OJ 1994, L 100.
15. According to article 174 [old art. 130R (2)] EC Treaty these principles are: the high level of protection principle, the precautionary principle, the prevention principle, the source principle, the polluter pays principle, the integration principle and the safeguard clause. For a discussion of these principles, see Jans (1994, pp. 19–32).
16. Inefficiencies may also be the consequence of the application of the 'high level of protection' principle if the diversity of situations in the various regions of the Community is not sufficiently taken into account and may equally follow from the 'precautionary principle' which requires environmental regulation even before scientific evidence has been made available which incontrovertibly shows the causal connection between a certain activity and the harm.
17. Commission Regulation (EC) Nr. 2790/1999, *O.J.*, 1999, L 336/21.
18. *Centraal Bureau voor de Rijwielhandel (Dutch bicycles)* [1978] OJ, L 20/18.
19. Case 73/74, *Groupement des Fabricants de Papiers Peints de Belgique v. Commission* [1975] ECR 1491.
20. Case 126/80, *Salonia v. Poidomani and Baglieri* [1981] ECR 1563; [1982] 1 CMLR 64.
21. The deregulation of the telecommunications sector may serve as an example.
22. Case 13/77, *Inno v. ATAB* [1977] ECR 2115; [1978] 1CMLR 283.
23. Case 311/85, *Vereniging van Vlaamse Reisbureaus v. Sociale Dienst (Flemish Travel Agents)* [1987] ECR 3801; [1989] 4 CMLR 213.

APPENDIX

Integrated Law and Economics Checklist for the Allocation of Competences in the European Union

1. Are preferences of firms and citizens with respect to the envisaged legislative action heterogeneous?
   - if yes: presumption in favour of decentralized governance, unless positive answer(s) to questions 3, 4 and/or 5.
   - if no: go to question 6.
2. Given heterogeneous preferences, is there a sufficiently large range of legal rules to choose between, is information on alternative legal rules easily available and is there a sufficient degree of mobility, so that firms and citizens can move to the jurisdiction offering them their preferred set of laws?
   - if yes: strengthen the competitive process by applying the rule of mutual recognition.
   - if no: consider EC rules to enhance competition, such as adding a sixteenth option, measures of standardization and harmonization of rules on conflict of laws.
3. Given heterogeneous preferences, does decentralized governance imply significant interstate externalities?
   - if yes: (1) consider Coasian solutions in the form of agreements between the states involved; (2) in cases of high transaction costs or opportunistic behaviour, consider harmonization measures reflecting the degree of preference's diversity; (3) make sure that the solution chosen is well targeted at the problem at hand; (4) go to question 7.
   - if no: harmonization measures are not needed, unless positive answers to questions 4 and/or 5.
4. Given heterogeneous preferences, does competition between member states' laws entail the risk of a 'race to the bottom'?
   - if yes: (1) take measures of minimum harmonization to guarantee a floor of rights; (2) go to question 7.
   - if no: harmonization measures are not needed unless positive answer to question 5.
5. Given heterogeneous preferences, are there important economies of scale or significant savings on transaction costs when the competence is assigned to the European Union?
   - if yes: (1) take harmonization measures allowing the maximum degree of diversity; (2) go to question 7.
   - if no: no harmonization measures required.

6.   Given homogeneous preferences, are there important scale economies or transaction cost savings to be achieved by centralized governance?
     – if yes: (1) full harmonization may be appropriate; (2) go to question 7.
     – if no: no harmonization.
7.   If the answers to the above questions provide support for harmonization measures, is the risk of political distortions (impact of pressure groups on policy making) minimized? Does the decision-making process satisfy the requirements of independence, transparency and accountability?
     – if yes: the harmonization measure suggested by economic analysis (see questions 3–6) may be taken.
     – if no: no harmonization.

REFERENCES

Buchanan, J.M. (1991), 'An American perspective on Europe's constitutional opportunity', *Cato Journal*, **10**, 619–29.
Centre for Economic Policy Research (1993), *Making Sense of Subsidiarity: How Much Centralization for Europe?*, London: CEPR.
Easterbrook, F.H. (1983), 'Antitrust and the economics of federalism', *Journal of Law and Economics*, **26**, 23–50.
European Commission (1999), *Green Paper Liability for Defective Products*, COM 396 final.
Frey, B.S. and R. Eichenberger (1996), 'To harmonize or to compete? That's not the question', *Journal of Public Economics*, **60**, 335–49.
Frey, B.S. and R. Eichenberger (1997), 'FOCJ: Creating a Single European Market for Governments', in D. Schmidtchen and R. Cooter (eds), *Constitutional Law and Economics of the European Union*, Cheltenham: Edward Elgar, pp. 195–215.
Jans, J.H. (1994), *European Environmental Law*, The Hague: Kluwer.
Kirchner, C. (1997), 'Competence catalogues and the principle of subsidiarity in a European constitution', *Constitutional Political Economy*, **8**, 71–87.
Markusen, J.R., E.R. Morey and N.D. Olewiler (1993), 'Environmental policy when market structure and plant locations are endogenous', *Journal of Environmental Economics and Management*, **24**, 69 et seq.
Markusen, J. R., E.R. Morey and N.D. Olewiler (1995), 'Competition in regional environmental policies when plant locations are endogenous', *Journal of Public Economics*, **56**, 55 et seq.
Neven, V.D., R. Nuttall and P. Seabright (1993), *Merger in Daylight. The Economics and Politics of European Merger Control*, London: CEPR.
OECD (1995), *Recommendation of the Council on Improving the Quality of the Government Regulation*, OECD.
Ogus, A.I. (1994), *Regulation. Legal Form and Economic Theory*, Oxford: Clarendon Press.
Ogus, A.I. (1999), 'Competition between national legal systems: a contribution of economic analysis to comparative law', *The International and Comparative Law Quarterly*, **48**, 405–18.

Revesz, R. (1992), 'Rehabilitating interstate competition: rethinking the "race to the bottom" rationale for federal environmental regulation', *New York University Law Review*, **67**, 1210 et seq.

Romano, R. (1998), 'Empowering investors: a market approach to securities regulation', *Yale Law Journal*, **107**, 2359 et seq.

Slot, P.J. (1996), 'Harmonisation', *European Law Review*, **21**, 382–6.

Tiebout, C.M. (1956), 'A pure theory of local expenditure', *Journal of Political Economy*, **64**, 416–24.

Van den Bergh, R. (1994), 'The subsidiarity principle in European community law: some insights from law and economics', *Maastricht Journal of European and Comparative Law*, **1**, 337–66.

Van den Bergh, R. (1998), 'Subsidiarity as an economic demarcation principle and the emergence of European private law', *Maastricht Journal of European and Comparative Law*, **5**, 129–52.

Van den Bergh, R. (1999), 'Self-Regulation of the Medical and Legal Profession: Remaining Barriers to Competition and EC Law', in B. Bortolotti and G. Fiorentini, *Organized Interests and Self-Regulation*, Oxford: Oxford University Press, pp. 89–130.

Van den Bergh, R. and P. Camesasca (2000), 'Irreconcilable principles? The Court of Justice exempts collective labour agreements from the wrath of antitrust', *European Law Review*, **25**, forthcoming.

Van den Bergh, R., M. Faure and J. Lefevere (1996), 'The Subsidiarity Principle in European Environmental Law: An Economic Analysis', in E. Eide and R. Van den Bergh (eds), *Law and Economics of the Environment*, Oslo: Juridisk Forlag, pp. 121–66.

Vaubel, R. (1992), 'The political economy of centralization and the European Community', *Journal des Economistes et des Etudes Humaines*, **3**, 11–48.

Winter, R.K. (1977), 'State law, shareholder protection, and the theory of the corporation', *Journal of Legal Studies*, 6, 251–92.

2. How to predict the differences in uniformity between different areas of a future European private law? An evolutionary approach

Jan M. Smits

2.1 INTRODUCTION

In this chapter, it is investigated whether it is possible to predict the evolution of (parts of) national European private law systems toward a uniform private law. In doing so, insights of evolutionary theory, economic analysis of law and (socio)biology are taken into account in what is essentially an interdisciplinary approach toward the evolution of European private law. One of the characteristics of the now rapidly emerging discipline of European private law is after all that it is still so much in its infancy that it is very fertile to try to profit from neighbouring disciplines in establishing the foundations of this discipline.[1] Whether it is possible to predict the measure of uniformity in European private law is, of course, of great scholarly and practical interest. From a scholarly point of view, it may give us insight into the differences in types of legal rules and types of private law areas with regard to their resistancy to harmonization. From a practical viewpoint, insight into the measure of uniformity to be attained tells us what public policy should be regarding decisions on the introduction of European Directives on specific fields of private law. Drafters of European 'Principles',[2] and other projects aiming at being a 'soft law' precursor to some European Civil Code,[3] may also benefit from these insights.

This chapter presupposes a specific theoretical framework that is made explicit in Section 2.2. In Section 2.3, the insights comparative law studies have provided us with regarding the possibility of legal unification, are surveyed. From there, the perspective changes to some other disciplines and their experience in the domain of evolution of norms and to what has been attained in Law and Economics scholarship (Section 2.4). After that, we are allowed to make some explanatory predictions on the future of European private law and its penetration into the different areas private law consists of (Family law, Contract law, Tort law, Property law and so on).

2.2   THEORETICAL FRAMEWORK ON THE POSSIBILITY OF UNIFORMITY IN EUROPEAN PRIVATE LAW

The theoretical framework this paper presupposes[4] is that uniformity of law in most of the cases cannot be created by just imposing rules through public policy. Private law is – at least partly that is – more than rules and may in this respect and in some cases be considered as (legal) *culture;*[5] in those cases, public policy consequently cannot have a severe influence on private law. Would this be different, there would be no need to assess any organic evolution of legal norms, other than the evolution of legislation itself;[6] law would then be nothing but a positivist artefact of some sovereign. Moreover, it would not be a question any more whether it is possible to predict uniformity because uniformity would then follow automatically from the famous 'berichtigende Worte des Gesetzgebers' (von Kirchmann, 1848). Two different claims are immanent in this presupposition.

The first one is that the mere drafting and enacting of Principles of European Private Law or the mere searching for a common core[7] does not in itself lead to uniformity. Private law is to a certain extent harmonization-resistant, even when confronted with centrally imposed rules. To what extent this is the case (is it true for all areas of private law and for all types of legal rules?), is a question this chapter intends to illuminate. However, the contention of Pierre Legrand (1996, pp. 61–2) that 'legal systems . . . have not been converging, are not converging and will not be converging' appears to be too radical. His idea of law as entirely embedded in the society and culture of a specific country has not been recognized as insightful.[8] Moreover, Legrand's idea of comparative law would by many comparative lawyers not be identified as falling within the limits of that discipline at all. F.H. Lawson, for example, once stated that comparative law in itself 'is bound to be superficial' and linking law to other societal and cultural phenomena of a specific country would be impossible (Lawson, 1949, p. 16).

The second claim I implicitly make is that a greater extent of legal uniformity than exists right now *is* possible, but should to a large extent come about in an *organic* way. This opens up a whole variety of research themes, related to other disciplines than the law and aiming at the study of cases where organic, spontaneous, orders have originated through evolution and not by creation. More specifically, I previously defended that the best way of unification of law in Europe would be through the competition of legal rules (Smits, 1998, p. 328). In transplanting legal rules from one country to another on a 'market of legal culture' (compare Mattei, 1994, p. 3), the best European legal rule may survive. this does not automatically imply that *any* rule glorifies: in some instances, diversity of law may be just as good as uniformity as long as there is this free movement of legal rules, at least creating the *possibility* of legal change. Some of the questions this theory poses (When will uniformity prevail? Which rule is the best to survive? Is that rule the result of a 'race to the bottom' or not? Are there differences in the extent that various areas of a discipline are touched by the evolutionary process?) may be provided with a preliminary answer in this chapter, partly building upon other disciplines. Taking Alan Watson's famous saying that 'most changes in most systems are the result of borrowing' as a starting point (Watson, 1974, p. 95), it is important to see which conditions favour or hamper the legal development through transplants.

2.3 TRADITIONAL POINTS OF VIEW ON LEGAL CHANGE

It is surprising to see how little *comparative law* study has been made of the process of legal change in private law. Anyone interested in the process of unification of law in Europe should, however, be aware of the historical evidence that is present within legal systems and that shows us how a legal system copes with changes in society as a whole and which rules are better prepared for those changes than others. The explanation for this lack of interest is undoubtedly caused by the positivistic stance that private law studies have taken in Europe ever since the enactment of national Civil Codes (which may also explain why the evolutionary tradition is much stronger in Anglo-American jurisprudence, where codes are mostly lacking). Since then, private law is merely looked at as a design *choice* of a creator, not as an organism shaped by its environmental conditions. Now that the tendency in Europe is moving away from national private law systems and toward harmonization, it is no more than logic that evolutionary ideas are becoming more important again in law.

The evolutionary tradition in law that does exist is mainly related to authors opposing codification (like Von Savigny) or authors from the Anglo-American tradition. It is, however, sad to see that the most prolific application in law of evolution theory on the European continent still is the work of Von Savigny and his Historical School, propagating an organically progressive jurisprudence', law being part of the *Volksgeist* (Von Savigny, [1814] 1967). Von Savigny's view is, however, much too vague to be regarded as a true scientific theory of legal change.[9] Maine does offer such a theory,[10] although he looks at the evolution of the legal system as a whole and not so much to the evolution of legal rules *within* that system. Several other authors – influenced by the publication of Darwin's *The Origin of Species* in 1859 or not – have offered theories on the evolution of legal institutions,[11] without, however, taking advantage of the insights of other disciplines.[12]

The most prolific comparatist, emphasizing the need for study of 'the nature of legal development' is undoubtedly Alan Watson.[13] He stresses the historical dimension by looking at the evidence that the historical study of law provides us with. Evolutionary theory – or any theory whatsoever – he however denies as being too general for his purpose.[14] 'There is no equivalent of the "invisible hand" of economics that under perfect conditions would keep a balance between supply and demand' (Watson, 1974, p. 108). Yet, one need not go so far as to contend that a theory of general legal development should be applicable to *all* societies for *all* time and then reject such a theory as being too theoretical to explain the evidence that is present; I regard it possible to develop some general theory for Europe. That theory should go beyond the commonplace that it is much more difficult to come to harmonization in property law (compare Gambaro, 1997, p. 497) or family law (compare Steenhoff, 1999, p. 1) than it is in the law of contract or in the law of torts. When Koopmans (1997, p. 543) states that:

> There is . . . agreement that we should not include family law and the law of succession. In these areas, patterns of social behaviour tend to resist to the introduction of new rules. Besides, religion plays a certain role, and moral choices must be made, which are not necessarily the same in the whole of Western Europe.

he uses a rather rough argument. Counterarguments are of the same generality (compare Rieg, 1990, p. 58; Martiny, 1995, p. 419). Moreover, the evidence Watson provides us with on legal transplants that have taken place in the past (also in the field of family law) seems to contradict this general idea.[15] Neither are the traditional comparative law efforts to explain *why* legal transplants take place of a very precise nature. It is mostly just the 'prestige' of a specific legal rule that is mentioned (compare Mattei, 1997, p. 124). One should have a look at the interdisciplinary analysis of the process of change to reach better results. In the following, a sketch is given of some evolutionary disciplines with a view to the process of legal change. I will emphasize what to my idea is important for a better prediction of where uniformity will prevail.

2.4   EVOLUTIONARY BIOLOGY, ECONOMICS AND LAW AND ECONOMICS

The most well known application of evolutionary theory is, of course, to be found in biology.[16] According to classical Darwinism, evolutionary changes take place through natural selection. The individual members of a species organize their lives to produce the most surviving offspring and in doing so, they necessarily adapt themselves to changing circumstances (Rodgers, 1998, p. 451). The descent of one or more trees of life thus leads to a diversity of species through speciation, extinction and the evolving of new characteristics within these species. In Darwinism, this process of evolution by natural selection presupposes three ideas (Sober, 1993, p. 9). First, there must be variation in the species (otherwise there would be no species that could better survive than others); second, the variation must concern variation in fitness (understood as the ability to survive and reproduce, some species being more able to adapt themselves to changing circumstances than others), third the characteristics that are constituent for the fitness of the species must be inherited (otherwise, there could be no evolution of the species as such). Only with these three constituents, can a 'struggle for life' originate.

As to the evolution of legal rules in Europe, it is possible to 'transplant' the first two of these requirements: in European private law too, different rules exist as to the solving of identical cases and presumably not all of these rules are as 'fit' as others to carry out their task. Much of the present day rules in the various European countries are the result of a long evolution, adapting them to the environment these rules had to operate in. According to evolutionary theory, other rules that once existed in these countries must have been eliminated in this process of natural selection and any change of the environment in the future would – again – lead to adaptation of the present rules. The third requirement of Darwinism (the inheritability of characteristics) is more problematic in the context of law because of the simple fact that descendants that take over the genes of the previous species do not exist. As we shall see, however, other disciplines that make use of evolutionary analysis (in particular economics) solve this problem by identifying analogues of genes.

Apart from these constituents of evolution, theoretical biology distinguishes between the different possible causes of evolution. In this respect, natural selection is only one of them, alongside with mutation, migration, recombination and mating (Sober, 1993, p. 18). What is important for the purpose of this chapter is the discussion about what *actually* causes evolution ('Why do polar bears have white fur and other bears brown fur?'). This discussion on what is called *adaptationism* is about the importance of natural selection in the process of evolution. What is actually the power of natural selection? (See Sober, 1993, p. 119.) The question is important for the evolution of law because it may give us insight into the question why it is that some legal rules survive and others do not. Biology teaches us that as to the direction of the evolution, *adaptation* is the main principle. Organisms fit themselves 'into niches of viability offered by their environments'. They have to, in order to survive the pressure of elective competition from other organisms. What may be of interest for the study of law is that the direction of adaptation is usually toward simplicity, in particular when homogenization of the environment reduces the number of distinct niches available. The movement is toward complexity when there are only a few species that proliferate within a new environment with many unfilled niches (Hirshleifer, 1993). I will come back to this point later on.

Theoretical biologist Sober provides us with a good insight into another discussion (Sober, 1993, p. 119). To predict what the mechanism of evolution leads to, it is possible to make use of simple models of the selection process – for example in the case of the evolution of running speed in zebras, fast zebras may survive over slow zebras – taking into account only natural selection and not mutation nor other evolutionary processes and abstaining from the fact that running speed may not evolve independently of other characteristics the zebra has. Adaptationists would say that any refinement of the simple model does not affect the prediction of how the running speed would evolve. If this were also true for the law, it would mean that selection of legal rules is a straightforward process, not hampered by other factors than the pursuit of finding the best rule available. As we shall see, this is not the case in the real world.

As Darwin intended a theory on how life evolves, other theorists have expanded his theory to other disciplines. Among these are chemistry, history (Shaw and Pomper, 1999), sociology, psychology (Plotkin, 1997), political sciences (Hayek, 1973–1979), history of science (Popper, 1979), sociology,[17] ethics,[18] economics and linguistics.[19] In this section, I will focus on evolutionary economics.[20] In this application of evolutionary theory too, the idea of an unalterable human nature or of a conscious design is abandoned for the idea that 'selection by the environment' (Elliott, 1985, p. 60) should be the starting point for any analysis of a social or economic order. It is a programmatic contention that some patterns have survived because they were able to be adapted to environmental circumstances (see Vromen, 1997, p. 45). There is, however, dispute as to the existence of real evidence for this idea. In neoclassical economics, this evidence is, for example, provided in the sense that only those firms that maximize profit survive the process of market selection. Neoclassical analysis – excluding uncertainty anyway (see Hodgson, 1999, p. 40) – assumes this is the case because of deliberate choices made by these firms,[21] and usually adds to this that in evolutionary theory the natural selection process mimics rational decision making.[22] 'Market selection will produce rational market behaviour even if firms display irrational behaviour.'[23]

Would this be true for the law as well, it would be an important point for legal analysis of European private law. The rough transplantation of this idea to law would mean that even if the legislature decides to enact legislation by deliberate choice, subsequent selection of rules on the market of legal culture would produce the same results. It is, however, very much disputed if neoclassical analysis is right at this point. Evolutionary theory makes clear what is the significance of 'path dependence' in evolutionary processes, Roe (1996, p. 643) has applied this idea to law.

The future time path the evolution is bound to take depends on the 'adaptive landscape' in which various factors such as environment conditions (like natural constraints) are at work. What should be the case to have a true spontaneous order evolve is to have the external environmental conditions prevail. Often, however, there are also internal materials (in organisms these would be the genes) that have been shaped by transformations in the past that are now irreversible. These were once responsive to the environment of those days, but are now constraints upon adaptive change (Hirshleifer, 1993, p. 205). The future development is thus affected by the path it has traced out in the past. In economic terms, it would mean that an equilibrium will not originate, and this – as Hodgson puts it – is in contrast with the view that 'real time and history could be safely ignored' (Hodgson, 1993, p. 204). In biology, especially, Gould (1989) has pointed out that evolution often depends on 'accidents', leading to an eccentric path, like in an economy where the most efficient organizations may not come out on top because, for example, of the fact that early factories to a large extent originated in times of war (in the time of Napoleon in Britain, in the time of the civil war in the US), thus promoting a militaristic and hierarchical organization (Hodgson, 1999, p. 204). The lesson to be learnt from this for the law is that evolution of legal norms may not under all circumstances lead to the best result. The task that lies ahead is to find out where this strong path dependency has had a formative influence on the law of the various European countries.

Another insight evolutionary economics provides us with is that as to the third requirement of natural selection (the inheritability of characteristics), some analogy to genes is possible. Notably Nelson and Winter use *routines* as playing the same role in firms as genes do in organisms (Vromen, 1997, p. 52). The routines of a firm establish a *stable identity* of the firm that endures over time *and* – just like genes – they *programme* the behaviour of the firms. As long as the routine is profitable, firms stick to these. Here, again, it goes without saying that firms are usually not able to change these routines too fast. Vromen points out that this is consistent with evolutionary game theory, which says that agents have fixed, unalterable behavioural strategies (rules of conduct restrain the behaviour of agents), but inconsistent with neoclassical economics which says that economic agents are able to respond in an optimal way to changes of circumstances (Vromen, 1997, p. 53).

Some of the insights of the previously mentioned disciplines have been incorporated into standard Law and Economics scholarship. Of course, the standard hypothesis there is that since people have a desire to eliminate costs, the law evolves toward legal rules that minimize social costs and thus increase economic efficiency (Rubin, 1977, p. 51; Priest, 1977, p. 65). This thesis on the evolution of legal norms then follows from the more general assertion that the whole of the common law is efficient (Posner, 1998). Rubin and Priest point out[24] that since inefficient rules are more likely to be disputed in court, these rules change in the re-examination by the court, while other rules survive. Cooter and Kornhauser (1980, p. 139) have added to this that evolution does not necessarily lead to only one surviving efficient rule, but to some equilibrium of best and worst legal rules, constantly competing for survival. This would be in accordance with modern biology, in which it is recognized that nature may have very different solutions for one and the same problem (Elliott, 1985, p. 70). The problem of path dependency, however, does not play an important role in present Law and Economics scholarship. Roe[25] may be right that this is due to the important role that policy plays in this discipline: evolutionary ideas do not direct us toward some policy direction.

In the following section, I will try to make use of these – admittedly eclectic – insights in trying to establish the factors that are decisive for the development of uniform private law in Europe.

2.5 PREDICTING DIFFERENCES BETWEEN AREAS OF PRIVATE LAW

2.5.1 General Observations

What is the relevance of the above for the venture of European Private Law? The way I see it, uniform law in Europe primarily comes about through an evolution of legal norms. If this is an apt qualification of the unification process, it is subject to the more general mechanisms and principles of evolution as just described. At first, some general observations that stem from the previous survey seem to be appropriate for the purpose of this chapter. Then, I will elaborate some points in more detail.

First, the question should be put to what extent Darwinist requirements for a survival of the fittest are applicable in European private law. In an evolutionary theory of European unification, the various national rules to solve similar problems may be regarded as the necessary variety of species. This variety has come about through differentiation that started from one 'tree of law' (most probably some general concept of 'fairness' from which the various rules originated). The second requirement as to the variation in fitness is met as well as long as it is presumed that not all the legal rules are as 'fit' as others to carry out their task. Some rules may have been eliminated by the environment in which they had to operate; others may have survived because of their ability to adjust themselves to changing circumstances. The third requirement (inheritability of characteristics) can be met if legal institutions are looked at as the 'genes' of a legal system: the content of these institutions may differ as the identity of the institution as such remains the same (as in economics routines establish a stable identity of a firm). Just as new routines of firms are seldom entirely new, but most of the time combinations of old ones that guarantee that the specific identities of these firms are maintained (Vromen, 1997, p. 53), the institutions that programme the behaviour of the rules in response to the changing environment maintain their specific identities as well. This idea calls for an application in the field of private law (Section 2.5.2).

Secondly, evolutionary theory enlightens us as to the possibility of the best rule surviving in the 'struggle for life'. This is definitely not a straightforward mechanism. To predict which rules survive and which do not, one cannot just take efficiency or any other mono-explaining mechanism (the 'simple model') as a key concept. Two different sorts of barriers to the emergence of the best legal rule should be taken into account. First, historically, the rule that has emerged may have been best adapted to the environment in which it had to function in the past. The consequence of this is that some rules may have been responsive to that past environment, at the same time eliminating rules that were not adaptive in those days, but may have been the best rule for present times had it not been for their elimination. Selection on the market of legal rules in this sense does not produce the best available rules. Second, there is a future oriented aspect of this approach as well. Even if one is able to 'reinvent' the rule that disappeared (and legal history can play an important role in doing so), it may be too costly to have that other rule prevail over the one we have become accustomed to. This so-called *path dependency* (the future development is affected by the path it has set out in the past) prevents an equilibrium from evolving. 'Accidents' may thus be just as important to explain the past and the future development of law. I will elaborate this idea with a view to the harmonization process in different areas of private law (Section 2.5.3).

Thirdly, it is fruitful to look at legal rules as having a desire to reproduce themselves. This analysis may explain why it is that the *same* legal rules over time are often used for different goals. 'Funktionswandel' of a rule may indeed happen more frequently than the clear-cut elimination of a rule. As we saw that organisms fit themselves into 'niches of viability offered by their environments', legal rules want to survive as well in a changing society. It, then, is only because of the use of the same terminology or the embedding within the same institution that a stable identity remains (this point is related to the one discussed in Section 2.5.2). Legal transplants may – at least partly – also be explained by this mechanism (Section 2.5.4). Moreover, it is interesting to find out to what extent the adaptation process in legal rules follows the same principle as in biology. If the direction of adaptation were indeed toward simplicity in case of homogenization of the environment, it would be an indication of the direction private law would take in a unified Europe (that is, the environment of a highly uniform economy). This biological idea is – as I see it – very much related to the famous *race to the bottom* argument. Unlike the present debate about that argument – that is merely on a *normative* level – evolutionary theory is able to show us that this process may be *inevitable* in a changing economic environment (Section 2.5.5). This argument may even be somewhat generalized with a view to the discussion on mentality as preventing a uniform European private law from coming about.

2.5.2 About the Way Private Law Rules Adapt to Changing Circumstances

For the enterprise of creating a uniform law in Europe, it is interesting to see what *form* this law is bound to take. Evolutionary theory predicts that the external identity of institutions may very well stay the same while their contents may differ. This result is consistent with what legal history shows us: concepts like contract, tort, property and marriage may *in name* remain identical, their content on the level of rules differs to a great extent in the various periods of time. This combination of an 'inherited' element and an element of variation guarantees that the adaptation of a rule to a new environment takes place in a not so overt way. To be more precise: a true *elimination* of one rule for another is not as likely as the *adaptation* of existing rules. Moreover, this adaptation or *mutation* of rules is not likely to happen in a stable evolutionary way. In biological evolution, the genes of a species are stable until there is a crisis (like an asteroid hitting the earth). It is only then that the species begins to mutate rather quickly and then either dies or adapts itself to the changed circumstances (Roe, 1996, p. 663). The species then may be extremely well adapted for the period of crisis (having the characteristics to survive that crisis), but not for the period thereafter.

This theory can be substantiated with the following. The environment in which most of the present legal rules in Europe have survived has been an environment of a *national* legal system that was most of the time embedded within a *mixed market economy*. Most of the private law rules in continental Europe were able to survive because of their ability to adapt themselves to these characteristics. It is thus not much of a surprise that the surviving rules are the exponents of a liberal and individualist model: in particular, they were extremely well adapted for the 'crisis' of the French Revolution; these rules have subsequently been laid down in national civil codes. Freedom of contract, the liability for damages in case of fault and the absoluteness of property – including the rules originating from these concepts – thus have survived. To say that these concepts are well adapted for the present-day environment is, however, hard to maintain. The many amendments that have been made to the rules emanating from these – indeed still under the same institutional heading – but in particular the importance that is attached to open-ended norms (good faith, reasonableness, negligence) in my view indicates that the present rules are now much less *normative* (and thus prescribing their future application) than they were at the time of the crisis they have survived.

A good example of this phenomenon is the elimination of mechanisms to decide which promises are binding and which are not. *Causa* and *laesio enormis* served this particular purpose in the law of contract of the continental European private law systems before the great codifications (on this see Gordley, 1991). They were eliminated in the codification process or in the time period immediately after the codification because they were useless in a system that put so much emphasis on the absolute bindingness of contracts. It would, however, have been fruitful to have these concepts available in a later period of time, when contract law had to find a mechanism for deciding which contracts had to be binding upon the parties and which not. But in most European legal systems, courts were not able to refer to that concept any more: they now had to use other legal concepts (good faith, the reliance principle in contract law and so on; see Smits, 1997, p. 280) to reach the same result. It was only in the common law that the requirement of 'consideration' still could play the role of distinguishing between promises that were enforceable and those that were not.

The coming into being of a common European market may very well be a new evolutionary 'crisis'. It is highly likely that – again – legal institutions will get a different content while keeping their identity in a process of adaptation. The new environment that is now emerging at high pace is the *European* environment of a *common* market, in contrast to the *national* environment of a *national* market that most of the rules have adapted themselves to. Joerges (1995, p. 179) rightly points out that market integration leads to a rationalization process in which all national law that constitutes an obstacle to the functioning of the internal market is under a pressure to change. This calls for a survey of which areas of private law will be most affected by this process.

2.5.3 Path Dependence and Areas of European Private Law

It is usually held that the process of emergence of a common market only calls for the unification of those parts of the law that are vital to that market, namely contract law and parts of the law of property (in particular the security interests) (see Gambaro, 1997, p. 497; Bonomi, 1998, p. 497; Zwalve, 1995, p. 391). From the evolutionary perspective that is chosen in this chapter we should, however, not be concerned with which parts are from a normative perspective *to be* unified, but – more descriptively – which parts are *most likely* to be affected by the changing environment.[26]

To decide to what extent uniformity of private law can come about in Europe, it is at first useful to follow Roe (1996, p. 646) in his concept of – what he calls – *weak-form path dependence*. This form of path dependence only *explains* what has survived; it does not entail that the survivor is better than another: 'a society chose between two institutions and the choice became embedded, but the chosen institution functions as well as the one discarded would have (ibid., p. 647). A road may be built on the left bank of the river or on the right bank of the river, but the left bank is not any 'better' than the right bank.

In case of this weak-form path dependence, there are no obstacles for harmonization. The types of rules one would think of as touched by this form of path dependence are those related to the more technical aspects of the law. Whether prescription periods or other time-related devices in the law are two years, five years or ten years is usually arbitrary. On the other hand, an evolution towards some 'best' rule is not really feasible here either. Courts usually are not willing to reconsider these types of legal norms. Harmonization would therefore only be possible through the imposition of a rule by some sovereign (European) authority. In other words: the framework as described in Section 2.2 (uniformity as far as legal culture allows) is not inconsistent with a centralistic imposing of law upon the various European countries.

It is not so easy to identify the type of rules just described from other types of rules. Watson (1974, p. 96) seems to see a much more important place for these 'arbitrary rules':

> The truth of the matter seems to be that many legal rules make little impact on individuals, and that very often it is important that there be a rule; but what rule actually is adopted is of restricted significance for general human happiness.

As far as the substantive parts of contract law, tort law and the law of property are concerned, I would rather not qualify these as examples of weak-form path dependence. The idea that it is indifferent which rule to adopt and that any evolution toward rules better suited for some environments than others is impossible, is not in line with the idea of these disciplines evolving to more efficient rules to the extent that this is possible.

This is not to say that path dependency does *not* play a role in the traditional private law disciplines. On the contrary: other forms than weak path dependency[27] are certainly present. If we assume that the Europeanization of private law presents a 'crisis' in the evolutionary sense, the path already taken may thus prevent the best possible rules for the new European environment from evolving. That evolution leads to a great amount of uniformity is least probable where it is only possible to change the present rules at the expense of high costs. The least uniformity is likely to be the case with rules that many people rely upon; on the other hand, the amount of uniformity to be attained should theoretically be the most in the case of rules that are only of use for the parties that set these rules themselves. Gambaro, for example, states the following about the law of real property:

> When one considers the nature of various property rights (obligations between neighbours, riparian rights, condominium law, rights of superficies, servitudes, and the like), it becomes rather clear that much property law is deeply rooted in locally developed legal traditions. And, for this reason it is better left to those local legal traditions which for hundreds of years have addressed these issues in the manner most adapted to the locality. (Gambaro, 1997, p. 497)

Gambaro is certainly right, but the reason why these rules are looked at as most adapted to the locality has, in my view, much more to do with the investments that have already been made in the path of property law, and from which it is too costly to deviate, than with 'the nature' of property rights. To change the national law in the areas mentioned by Gambaro would mean that third parties' interests would have to be reconsidered on a very large scale. The reliance of the parties involved on the existence of 'absolute' rights that have effect *erga omnes* would be violated if the applicable rules on, for example, the establishment of limited rights and the registration of these would be eliminated or even changed. The taking into account of so many different interests has led to delicate static systems of property law with – most of the time – a *numerus clausus* of limited real rights (see Smits, 1999, p. 246). Moreover, to get to know the ins and outs of property law in a specific system is far more difficult than to get to know a country's law of contract: the information costs of the former are much higher.[28] In this sense, property law is 'stuck in a local equilibrium'. In the bigger part of property law, this does not pose a true problem: any need to have uniform law is virtually absent. It is a problem, however, where there *is* a need, namely in the field of security interests: here, the *desire* and the *present practice* as it has evolved in the past (adapted to national systems of law) are the most divergent. Accordingly, it is the most difficult to come to uniformity in this area of law.

This is all different in case of the law of contract. The parties to a contract would not be truly hampered by a change of the law because of their ability to set the rules for their relationship themselves. The law of contract's dynamic character guarantees the elimination and survival of rules that are respectively the least and the most suited for their new environment. Benson (1998, p. 90) quotes Rubin as he says:

> If conditions change . . . and two individuals decide that, for their purposes, behaviour that was attractive in the past has ceased to be useful, they can voluntarily devise a new contract stipulating any behaviour that they wish. That is, old custom can be quickly replaced by a new rule of obligation toward certain other individuals without prior consent of or simultaneous recognition by everyone in the group (or of some legal authority).

This evolutionary thesis is backed up by evidence from both economic analysis of law and comparative law.

Economic analysis of law shows the need for a distinction between default and mandatory rules. This type of analysis makes clear that rules should be mandatory when any other rule that the parties would adopt would be violating third parties' interests. Mattei and Cafaggi (1998, p. 348) rightly point out that the amount of mandatory rules should decrease in a system where alternative means of protection of third parties are available. They mention, for example, the lesser amount of mandatory rules in contract law if the tort system protects third parties. It is obvious that property law is much more related to these mandatory rules than contract law. The economic reason for property law being more mandatory runs parallel with the evolutionary idea of property law being less able to change when confronted with a changing environment.

Comparative law also provides us with evidence on the evolutionary thesis. Legal transplants in the field of contract law are far greater than in the field of property law. This may partly be due to private international law's *lex rei sitae* (accordingly there is no need to incorporate foreign property rights into one's own legal system), but it is certainly also due to the high costs of transplanting from another system in the case of property law and the much lesser costs in the case of contract and tort law. In the latter, legal transplants have been vigorous; the relative uniformity that already exists in the field of European contract law is undoubtedly caused by these transplants. In particular English law was to a great extent influenced by the civil law of the nineteenth century (see Reimann, 1993), as continental European law is influenced in the late twentieth century by the law of financial transactions on, for example, swaps, lease and franchising, coming from the common law world. I will elaborate the comparative law evidence for an evolution of law that is more or less easy by looking at legal transplants.

2.5.4   Legal Transplants and the Desire of Legal Rules to Reproduce

To look at the amount of legal transplants from one system to another is fruitful in order to discover which areas of private law are more or less touched by the evolutionary process. The mere fact that a rule is transplanted is already informative as to the low costs of introducing that rule into another legal system. If that same rule would also have the same effect as it has in the 'mother country', the rule would be even neutral to considerations of national morality. Not much systematic research has yet been done to find out to what extent there are differences between the various areas of law being influenced by legal transplants. A preliminary investigation that I undertook in the traditional mixed legal systems clearly shows, however, that the amount of legal transplants has been far greater in the field of contract law and tort law than it has been in the field of property law.

Contract law in South Africa, for example, seems to a high extent to be a true mix of civil law and common law elements. It has, for example, rejected the requirement of consideration but has developed a system of contractual remedies that is to a large extent comparable to English law. In the field of tort law, it has also mixed in a fruitful way the general civil law approach with the protection of specific interests in English law. Any true influence of English property law on the Roman-Dutch system is, however, absent: South African private law has kept its system of a *numerus clausus*. In Scottish law, the same tendency can be identified (compare Smits, 1999, p. 189).

Putting this into evolutionary terms: legal rules have a desire to reproduce themselves in other countries, but in doing so adjust themselves most of the time to the new environment. This gives them the best chance of surviving. If this new (socioeconomic) environment is comparable to that of the mother country, the rule can be expected to remain more or less identical to the one operating in that country. It follows from this behaviour of rules that legal transplants only lead to uniformity in countries that have a comparable socio-economic constellation. Thus, in the case of the European Union, the rules that are directly related to the coming into being of a common market can be expected to remain the most uniform.

2.5.5   The Race to the Bottom Argument and Evolutionary Theory

Finally, I will investigate whether evolutionary theory gives us some insight into the famous problem of the 'race to the bottom', particularly of interest in company law. The idea of competition of legal systems,[29] instead of a central-istic harmonization by the state, has the consequence that companies are free to move from one state (or country) to another. In doing so, they will choose the state (or country) with the lowest standards (in the case of American company law that would be the state of Delaware). The 'home country control principle' subsequently guarantees that this low standard is exported to other states as well. What will evolve in the end is a uniform law of the lowest stan-dard. The race to the bottom (or 'social dumping') may thus be said to arise when, 'in a deregulated internal market, a state unilaterally lowers its social standards in an attempt to attract business from other states'.[30]

The present debate on the race-to-the-bottom argument is mostly norma-tive: usually, concerns are expressed about the lowering of standards through jurisdictional competition. The enactment of mandatory social legislation by the European Union even has as an explicit goal to avoid social dumping (Barnard, 2000, p. 66). This chapter addresses the problem from a somewhat different angle: evolutionary theory may be able to show us to what extent a race to the bottom is *inevitable* in a changing economic environment.

As we saw in biology (Section 2.4), the direction of adaptation of a species is toward simplicity in case of homogenization of the environment and toward complexity when the environment still has many unfilled niches. If this were true for the evolution of private law as well, it would mean that homogenization of the economic environment (that indeed originates within the European Union) leads to simple rules. This seems to confirm that the 'race' is indeed to some common *legal* denominator. Barnard (2000, p. 70) shows, however, that there is little evidence so far of this phenomenon in Europe. She identifies six conditions that need to be met for a race to the bottom to emerge. Among these conditions are a wide choice of different jurisdictions (like more than 50 legal systems in the United States) and full knowledge of each jurisdiction's characteristics. These requirements are not being met in Europe, where there are only 15 jurisdictions with often not so great differences and sometimes great difficulties in obtaining the necessary information about the respective legal systems.

From the evolutionary perspective, a race to the bottom is, however, likely to emerge if these two requirements will be met in the future. As to the first requirement, the enlargement of the European Union with Eastern European states would imply that the differences between the various systems could very well increase. A migration of companies toward systems with lesser standards than the present member-states is then likely to occur. In order to meet the condition of full knowledge of all the European jurisdictions, there is a need for more comparative law study. The only barrier for a true race to the bottom would be constituted by the minimum standards of law, set by the European Union's Directives and Regulations. However, the fact that these standards would be a barrier to evolution can also be explained from evolutionary theory: the path that has been traced out in the past, has – in Europe – been one of not only giving economic considerations the upper hand. A social policy has always been part of the whole European venture. In this sense, the investments already made in this policy would be too costly (maybe even not only in a social or cultural sense, but also in a financial sense in that it would entail large costs of changing the present legal position of workers, unemployed, and so on) to deviate from.

That not all of the present social guarantees in the European legal systems (namely those that guarantee *more* than the European minimum standards) will be kept intact is, however, inevitable. Hayek is right when he stresses that legal rules may have come into being through historical accident, but that natural selection decides which rules are to survive. The natural selection process then chooses between competing groups of humans, letting those groups survive whose cultural norms and rules are more suited to efficiently coordinating social interations.[31] The European venture of creating a common market then necessarily implies that it is the group of those who are best able to operate on that market whose rules will eventually survive. Worries about some 'mentality' being strangled in this process are then not relevant anymore: that would be the irreversible consequence of an internal market coming about.

2.6 CLOSING REMARKS

To predict to what extent the different areas of private law will evolve toward some uniform system is not an easy job. If anything should have become clear from this chapter it is that whatever way one wants to travel, a strictly legal perspective does not suffice. In this chapter, I tried to develop an evolutionary perspective on unification, taking from evolutionary biology and economics whatever I found useful to adopt. I do not contend that evolutionary theory is the only framework that provides us with explanatory predictions on how a European private law will develop, but it does provide us with some fruitful insights on the way legal rules adapt themselves to changing circumstances, on path dependence, on legal transplants and on the probability of a race to the bottom. That not all areas of private law appear to be touched to the same extent by the unification process is insightful for what public policy should be in this field. To adopt some European Directive or Regulation in the field of property law appears, for example, to be much too costly because of the strong path dependence in this area of law.

What is perhaps the most important outcome of evolutionary theory applied to the law is that the coming into being of a uniform law for Europe will to a large extent be the result of the emergence of a *spontaneous order* that has not so much to do with a deliberate enactment of law by some sovereign, but much more with a 'cultural evolution'. As Hayek puts it: culture is not rationally designed, but a tradition of 'rules of conduct' that are passed on through cultural transmission in a process that is not consciously planned. A system of rules should primarily be looked at as a spontaneous order that emerges in response to its environment. In this sense, the whole venture of creating a common European market automatically invokes a new, partly unintended, legal system.

NOTES

1. For an elaboration of this programmatic manifesto see Smits (2000). A recent overview of the European Private Law debate is given by Schmid (1999, p. 673).
2. The now most well known set of principles is the Principles of European Contract Law (Lando and Beale, 2000). Compare Hayton, Kortmann and Verhagen (1999).
3. See for an extensive survey of these other initiatives Smits (1999, p. 51).
4. An elaboration of this framework can be found in Smits (1999, p. 19 and 1998, p. 328).
5. For the most outspoken defence of this thesis see Legrand (1999).

6.   As has been investigated by Clark (1977, p. 90, and 1981, p. 1238).
7.   On common core projects such as the Trento Project see Bussani and Mattei (1997–1998, p. 339).
8.   Although Legrand has some illustrious predecessors. I refer to F.C. von Savigny's idea of the *Volksgeist* and of civil law as characteristic for the people of a country (von Savigny [1814] 1967 and to Lord Cooper of Culross, cited in Watson (1974, p. 22): 'law is the reflection of the spirit of a people, and so long as the Scots are conscious that they are a people, they must preserve their law'.
9.   Compare Elliot (1985, p. 43): 'by modern standards Savigny's work seems hopelessly metaphorical and unscientific'.
10. Sumner Maine (1861). What Maine does do, however, is predict as the dominant evolutionary trend the change from family responsibility to individual obligation.
11. For an excellent overview see Elliott (1985, p. 38). Compare Stein (1980).
12. See, however, the writings of Clark and Roe, cited hereafter.
13. Watson (1974, p. 7). Compare Watson (1977, 1978, p. 313) and Sacco (1991, p. 1).
14. Watson (1974, p. 13, and 1985). Compare, however, the general reflections (Watson, 1974, p. 95), stemming from his survey of evidence.
15. Watson (1974, p. 98): 'no area of private law can be designated as being extremely resistant to change as a result of foreign influence'. He mentions the import of Swiss family law into the Turkish Civil Code of 1926.
16. On evolutionary biology see Sober (1993), Maynard Smith (1993) and Futuyma (1998).
17. On the influence of Herbert Spencer see Hodgson (1993, p. 81).
18. On sociobiology and the claims it makes about explaining morality see Sober (1993, p. 202); see notably the groundwork laid by Wilson (1975) and Alexander (1987).
19. For an overview see Maynard Smith and Szathmary (1999), Maynard Smith (1982) and Beckstrom (1993).
20. The extensive literature on evolutionary economics includes Hodgson (1993, 1999) and Witt (1993). On the relationship with biology see Foster (1994, p. 23) and Nelson and Winter (1982).
21. Compare the Coase theorem that leads to the conclusion that regardless what the initial assignment of property rights was, there is a trend toward the efficient use of resources. If there are no transaction costs, the outcome of the mutually advantageous exchanges will be efficient.
22. See Vromen (1997, p. 45) on this discussion.
23. Becker (1962, p. 1); compare Vromen (1997, p. 46), who mentions more literature. Hodgson (1999, p. 177): 'the assumption of maximizing behaviour by individual firms is not necessary for the scientific purposes of prediction'.
24. For an overview see the excellent survey by Elliot (1985, p. 62).
25. Roe (1996, p. 667). It does, however, in Comparative Law and Economics; see Mattei and Cafaggi (1998, p. 346).
26. I leave aside the view of Epstein (1980, p. 665), who defends the sociobiological thesis that those who follow rules of conduct have a better chance of surviving than others who do not. Epstein does not see this mechanism operate in each category of law. He regards four categories having evolutionary roots: (a) prohibition of using force against strangers in the same species; (b) first possession of an unowned thing as the root of title; (c) obligations of parents to their children; (d) promissory obligations.
27. Roe (1996, p. 648) distinguishes between semi-strong path dependence (leading to inefficient paths that were once satisfactory but are now worth changing; they are left intact because of the inefficiency to change these). In case of strong-form path dependence, the situation is now inefficient, it would be efficient to change it, and yet we do not do that. Political pressure groups or a lack of information about 'the other way' prevents any change.
28. See Dreher (1999, p. 109): 'Da Wissen und Kosten eng miteinander verbunden sind, stellt Unwissenheit zumindest vor Informationskosten und begrenzt so auch die Faktormobilität ganz entscheidend.'
29. Literature mentioned in Reich (1992, p. 861), Kraus (1997, p. 377), Dreher (1999, p. 105) and Barnard (2000, pp. 57–78).

30. Barnard (2000, p. 57). This 'jurisdictional competition' should be well distinguished from the idea of *free movement of legal rules* (compare Smits 1998, p. 328). The former is concerned with choosing some legal *system*, the latter with choosing some legal *rule*.
31. Hayek (1979; 1967, p. 66); compare Introduction, in Witt (1993, p. xxii) and the critical assessment by Vanberg (1993, p. 482).

REFERENCES

Alexander, R. (1987), *The Biology of Moral Systems*, New York: Aldine de Gruyter.

Barnard, Catherine (2000), 'Social dumping and the race to the bottom: some lessons for the European Union from Delaware', *European Law Review*, **25**, 57–78.

Becker, G.S. (1962), 'Irrational behavior and economic theory', *Journal of Political Economy*, **70**, 1f.

Beckstsrom, John H. (1993), *Darwinism Applied: Evolutionary Paths to Social Goals*, Westport: Praeger.

Benson, Bruce L. (1998), 'Evolution of Commercial Law', in *The New Palgrave Dictionary of Economics and the Law*, Vol. I, London: Macmillan, pp. 90f.

Bonomi, Andrea (1998), 'La nécessité d'harmonisation du droit des garanties réelles mobilières dans le marché unique européen', in F. Werro (ed.), *l'Européanisation du droit privé*, Fribourg: Editions Universitaires, pp. 497f.

Bussani, M. and U. Mattei (1997–1998), 'The common core approach to European private law', *Columbia Journal of European Law*, 339f.

Clark, R.C. (1977), 'The morphogenesis of subchapter C: an essay in statutory evolution and reform', *Yale Law Journal*, **87**, 90f.

Clark, R.C. (1981), 'The interdisciplinary study of legal evolution', *Yale Law Journal*, **90**, 1238f.

Cooter, Robert and Lewis A. Kornhauser (1980), 'Can litigation improve the law without the help of judges?', *Journal of Legal Studies*, **9**, 139f.

Dreher, Meinrad (1999), 'Wettbewerb oder vereinheitlichung der rechtsordnungen in Europa?', *Juristenzeitung*, **54**, 105f.

Elliott, E. Donald (1985), 'The evolutionary tradition in jurisprudence', *Columbia Law Review*, **85**, 38f.

Epstein, Richard (1980), 'A taste for privacy? Evolution and the emergence of a naturalistic ethic', *Journal of Legal Studies*, **9**, 665f.

Foster, John (1994), 'Biology and Economics', in Hodgson, Samuels and Tool (eds), *The Elgar Companion to Institutional and Evolutionary Economics A–K*, Cheltenham: Edward Elgar, pp. 23f.

Futuyma, Douglas J. (1998), *Evolutionary Biology*, 3rd edn, Sunderland: Sinauer.

Gambaro, Antonio (1997), 'Perspectives on the codification of the law of property: an overview', *European Review of Private Law*, **5**, 497f.

Gould, Stephen J. (1989), *Wonderful Life*, New York: Norton.

Gordley, James (1991), *The Philosophical Foundations of Modern Contract Doctrine*, Oxford: Clarendon Press.

Hayek, F.A. (1967), 'Notes on the Evolution of Systems of Rules of Conduct', in *Studies in Philosophy and Economics*, London: Routledge, pp. 66f.

Hayek, F.A. (1973–1979), *Law, Legislation and Liberty*, London: Routledge.

Hayton, D.J., S.C.J.J. Kortmann and H.L.E. Verhagen (eds) (1999), *Principles of European Trust Law*, The Hague: Kluwer.

Hirshleifer, Jack (1993), 'Evolutionary Models in Economics and Law', reprinted in Witt (ed.), *Evolutionary Economics*, Aldershot: Elgar, pp. 205f.

Hodgson, Geoffrey M. (1993), *Economics and Evolution*, Cambridge: Polity Press.

Hodgson, Geoffrey M. (1999), *Evolution and Institutions: On Evolutionary Economics and the Evolution of Economics*, Cheltenham: Edward Elgar.

Joerges, Christian (1995), 'The Europeanisation of private law as a rationalisation process and as a contest of disciplines – an analysis of the Directive on Unfair Terms in Consumer Contracts', *European Review of Private Law*, **3**, 175f.

Kirchmann, Julius von (1848), *Die Wertlosigkeit der Jurisprudenz als Wissenschaft*, Berlin.

Koopmans, T. (1997) 'Towards a European Civil Code?', *European Review of Private Law*, **4**, 543f.

Kraus, Jody S. (1997), 'Legal design and the evolution of commercial norms', *Journal of Legal Studies*, **26**, 377f.

Lando, Ole and Hugh Beale (eds) (2000), *Principles of European Contract Law, Parts I and II Combined and Revised*, The Hague: Kluwer.

Lawson, F.H. 'the field of Comparative Law', *Juridical Review*, **LXI**, 16f.

Legrand, Pierre (1996), 'European legal systems are not converging', *International and Comparative Law Quarterly*, **45**, 52f.

Legrand, Pierre (1999), *Le Droit Comparé*, Paris: PUF.

Martiny, D. (1995), 'Europäisches familienrecht – utopie oder notwendigkeit?', *RabelsZeitschrift*, **59**, 419f.

Mattei, Ugo (1994), 'Efficiency in legal transplants: an essay in comparative law and economics', *International Review of Law and Economics*, 3f.

Mattei, Ugo (1997), *Comparative Law and Economics*, Ann Arbor: The University of Michigan Press.

Mattei, Ugo and Fabrizio Cafaggi (1998), 'Comparative Law and Economics', in *The New Palgrave Dictionary of Economics and the Law*, Vol. I, London: Macmillan, pp. 346f.

Maynard Smith, J. (1982), *Evolution and the Theory of Games*, Cambridge: Cambridge University Press.

Maynard Smith, J. (1993), *The Theory of Evolution*, Cambridge: Cambridge University Press.

Maynard Smith, John and Eors Szathmary (1999), *The Origins of Life: From the Birth of Life to the Origin of Language*, Oxford: University Press.

Nelson, R. and S.G. Winter (1982), *An Evolutionary Theory of Economic Change*, Cambridge: Harvard University Press.

The New Palgrave Dictionary of Economics and the Law, London: Macmillan 1998.

Plotkin, Henry (1997), *Evolution in Mind: an Introduction to Evolutionary Psychology*, London: Allen Lane.

Popper, Karl R. (1979), *Objective Knowledge: an Evolutionary Approach*, rev. edn, Oxford: Oxford University Press.

Posner, Richard (1998), *Economic Analysis of Law*, 5th edn, Boston: Little Brown.

Priest, George (1977), 'The common law process and the selection of efficient rules', *Journal of Legal Studies*, **6**, 65f.

Reich, Norbert (1992), 'Competition between legal orders: a new paradigm of EC law?', *Common Market Law Review*, **29**, 861f.

Reimann, Matthias (1993), *The Reception of Continental Ideas in the Common Law World 1820–1920*, Berlin: Duncker & Humblot.

Rieg, A. (1990), 'l'Harmonisation européenne du droit de la famille: mythe ou realité?', in *Conflits et Harmonisation (Liber amicorum Von Overbeck)*, Fribourg: Editions Universitaires, pp. 58f.

Rodgers, William H. (1998), 'Law and Biology', in *The New Palgrave Dictionary of Economics and the Law*, Vol. II, London: Macmillan, pp. 451f.

Roe, Mark J. (1996), 'Chaos and evolution in law and economics', *Harvard Law Review*, **109**, 641f.

Rubin, Paul (1977), 'Why is the common law efficient?', *Journal of Legal Studies*, **6**, 51f.

Sacco, R. (1991), 'Legal formats: A dynamic approach to comparative law', *American Journal of Comparative Law*, **39**, 1f.

Savigny, F.C. von ([1814] 1967), *Vom Beruf unsrer Zeit für Gesetzgebung und Rechtswissenschaft*, reprint Hildesheim: Olm.

Schmid, Christoph U. (1999), 'The emergence of a transnational legal science in European private law', *Oxford Journal of Legal Studies*, **19**, 673f.

Shaw, David Gary and Philip Pomper (eds) (1999), *The Return of Science: Evolutionary Ideas and History*, Middletown: Wesleyan University.

Smits, J.M. (1997), 'Van wil, causa en verrijking; over een alternatieve route naar de contractuele gebondenheid', *Stellenbosch Law Review*, **8**, 280f.

Smits, Jan (1998), 'A European private law as a mixed legal system', *Maastricht Journal of European and Comparative Law*, **5**, 328f.

Smits, Jan M. (1999), *Europees Privaatrecht in wording*, Antwerpen-Apeldoorn: Intersentia.

Smits, Jan M. (2000), *The Good Samaritan in European Private Law*, Deventer: Kluwer.

Sober, Elliott (1993), *Philosophy of Biology*, Oxford: Oxford University Press.

Steenhoff, Gert (1999), *Een zoektocht naar Europees familierecht*, Deventer: Kluwer.

Stein, P. (1980), *Legal Evolution: The Story of an Idea*, Cambridge: Cambridge University Press.

Sumner Maine, H.J. (1861), *Ancient Law*, London.

Vanberg, Viktor (1993), 'Spontaneous Market Order and Social Rules', reprinted in Witt (ed.), *Evolutionary Economics*, Aldershot: Elgar, pp. 482f.

Vromen, Jack J. (1997), 'Evolutionary Economics: Precursors, Paradigmatic Propositions, Puzzles and Prospects', in Jan Reijnders (ed.), *Economics and Evolution*, Cheltenham: Edward Elgar, pp. 41f.

Watson, Alan (1974), *Legal Transplants*, Edinburgh: Scottish Academic Press.

Watson, Alan (1977), *Society and Legal Change*, Edinburgh: Scottish Academic Press.

Watson, Alan (1978), 'Comparative law and legal change', *Cambridge Law Journal*, **37**, 313f.

Watson, Alan (1985), *The Evolution of Law*, Oxford: Basil Blackwell.

Wilson, E.O. (1975), *Sociobiology: the new Synthesis*, Cambridge: Harvard University Press.

Witt, Ulrich (ed.) (1993), *Evolutionary Economics*, Aldershot: Elgar.

Zwalve, W.J. (1995), 'De zekerheidsrechten van het Noord-Amerikaanse recht en hun belang voor het Europese privaatrecht', *Weekblad voor Privaatrecht, Notariaat en Registratie*, (6185), 391f.

3.   Legal culture as (natural?) monopoly

Anthony Ogus

3.1   INTRODUCTION

Comparative lawyers have become increasingly obsessed by notions of 'legal culture'.[1] By this, they mean 'those historically conditioned, deeply rooted attitudes about the nature of law and about the proper structure and operation of a legal system that are at large in the society'.[2] Some authors have drawn on the idea to argue that harmonization between two fundamentally different legal cultures (such as those of the civil law systems of continental Europe on the one hand and those of the common law systems of the Anglophone world on the other) is inherently impossible: 'transplants' will be rejected.[3] And, of course, such views have important practical implications in an age when considerable efforts are being made to integrate legal systems, particularly in the European Union.

Undeniably there are problems of mutual adaptation between legal systems with different traditions but the views of the 'culture' theorists ought to be treated with caution. This is not only because they exaggerate the problems, but also, and more importantly, because they fail to recognize the economic forces which lie behind the phenomena they are describing. The very language of culture might seem to invoke values which defy assessment in terms of willingness-to-pay and which therefore transcend conventional market processes.[4] But, however elevated the discourse, its opacity should not be allowed to conceal the fact that there are groups who stand to profit materially from treating resources as culture. In this chapter, I argue that legal culture should be construed as a situation in which monopoly power is enjoyed by those supplying law and legal services within a particular tradition. Given that, as well as leading to other undesirable consequences, such power confers rents on the suppliers, they are resistant to changes which will undermine it.

The reasoning thus provides an explanation for the observed problems of accepting transplants. But at the same time, normatively it also challenges the view held by some that integration of foreign legal ideas is impossible or wrong. It is true that, under certain conditions, a dominant legal culture may properly be regarded as a natural monopoly. That, of course, suggests that while its existence may be tolerated, its adverse effects should be controlled.

In Section 3.2, I outline the notion of competition between legal orders which provides the context for the ideas presented in this paper. I then provide, in Section 3.3, an economic interpretation of legal culture, arguing that practitioners are able to enhance their income through formalism, complexity and the linguistic and conceptual structure of the law, all of which are inherent features of legal culture. In Section 3.4 I consider whether, and in what circumstances, it is appropriate to treat legal culture as a natural monopoly. I draw a distinction between jurisdictions which have a single dominant culture and those – so-called 'hybrid jurisdictions' – which involve some competition between cultures. I also investigate the circumstances in which external competition can render the natural monopoly unsustainable.

3.2   COMPETITION BETWEEN LEGAL ORDERS

The present chapter is part of a broader enterprise in which I seek to show how an economics perspective can contribute to an understanding of the relationship between legal developments in different jurisdictions. In a recently published paper,[5] I argued that the chief engine for change is competition between national legal orders. The opening up of international markets, the mobility, particularly of firms, between jurisdictions and the adoption of more liberal choice-of-law rules or of principles of mutual recognition all serve to broaden the range of legal regimes applicable to transactions or sets of transactions. Competition should thus influence the behaviour of those demanding, and those supplying, law reform.

One of the main predictions emerging from this analysis is that competition should exert pressure for a convergence of legal principles in those areas of law (for example, contract, property and corporate law) which are predominantly facilitative.[6] That is, because there is a homogeneity in the legal product being demanded, actors will search for the legal means of reaching desired outcomes at lowest cost, and if the domestic legal system does not provide what is demanded it will risk losing some of the actors to another jurisdiction. In this model, lawyers act as 'transaction cost engineers', designing the mechanisms which most cheaply meet their clients' needs.[7] In contrast, it is difficult to predict the impact of competition in relation to interventionist law (for example, tort and regulation). Here the legal product is heterogeneous, because in different jurisdictions it is likely that different preferences will exist as to the levels of protection to be supplied and of the costs which must be incurred.[8]

In my earlier paper I nevertheless recognized that the forces for change generated by competition may be thwarted, to a greater or lesser extent, by key players in the law reform process.[9] Professional lawyers are the most prominent in this category; inside or outside government, they can exert a huge influence on outcomes, in particular by their evaluation of what is legally 'feasible'. To be sure, some lawyers may benefit from the increased demand for their services following migration to their jurisdiction or adoption of it under a choice-of-law clause. That would suggest a strategy of supporting cost-reducing law reform as a response to the pressure of competition from other legal systems. On the other hand, it is perhaps equally likely that the majority of lawyers would benefit from resisting the competitive processes, maintaining their control over the supply of domestic legal skills and deriving increased income from unreformed and more costly legal principles. One efficacious way of opposing reform proposals is to argue that they are anathema to the jurisdiction's legal culture.[10] But this begs the question, what is 'legal culture'?

3.3 LEGAL CULTURE: TOWARD AN ECONOMIC EXPLANATION

The generally accepted notion of 'legal culture' described above has provided a powerful explanation of why legal ideas may not be transplanted from one jurisdiction to another with a different tradition. We ought also to note the affinity between the concept and Hayekian notions of how rules of conduct emerge and spread spontaneously.[11] I nevertheless consider that the importance attributed to legal culture in this sense may be exaggerated and that there are other, more potent, reasons why there may be a lack of convergence between legal systems.

Functional Aspects

Let us first recognize that, judged by its functional capacity, it may not be very significant that a given legal system fails to integrate a particular, foreign legal device if it effectively provides an equivalent solution formulated in terms of its own legal language and concepts. Legal concepts, we may need to be reminded, are simply convenient linguistic expressions for linking particular outcomes to particular factual situations.[12] Thus, even if the English common law does not explicitly recognize 'good faith' as a requirement for a valid contract,[13] if the courts will set aside an agreement which in other legal systems would be held unenforceable for a failure in this respect, the outcome will be the same and there is an effective convergence. So also French property owners may not care that their domestic legal system does not have the 'trust', if alternative legal concepts can ensure the same degree of management of resources as the Anglo-Saxon concept.[14]

Productive Efficiency

Nevertheless, corporations and other major actors in the market for legal reform will be concerned with what we may describe as the productive inefficiency (the ratio between input and output) of a particular set of legal rules. If the juristic link between the factual situation and the desired outcome is, for one reason or another, more costly to interpret or apply in the domestic legal system than elsewhere, there will be a demand for adaptation of the native legal concept. Why would it be cheaper in some jurisdictions to reach desired outcomes by legal means? That is a broad and difficult question on which comparative lawyers have expended much labour. It may be, as the Turin School has proposed, that different legal systems are capable of adapting to technological, social and economic developments with greater or lesser friction, according to the interaction between the different sources of law (legislature, judiciary, bureaucracy, *doctrine*, and so on) – what they refer to as 'legal formants'.[15] Here I wish to focus on an alternative, economic explanation which, though it has been around a long time, seems to have been relatively neglected in modern times. It is based on the simple proposition that there is a class of persons who benefit when law is unduly costly – and that is obviously practising lawyers.[16]

Mystification of Law

About two centuries ago Jeremy Bentham wrote stringent criticisms of the then state of English law.[17] He was particularly reproachful of its obscurity and complexity. He found court procedures to be artificial and irrational. He made a detailed study of the formalities and technical language used by lawyers and observed how different the latter was from the language used in ordinary social and commercial intercourse. He saw all this as the 'mystification' by lawyers, designed to create for themselves an atmosphere of awe, to set themselves apart from other professionals and, most importantly, to enable them to engage in depredation, by the creation of business and the securing of substantial fees.

   Now, of course, jargon can lower, as well as increase, the legal costs of transacting, simply because, when used by experts, language of this sort can facilitate communication. One should note too that the degree of divergence between legal and lay language may vary over time. It was a worthy goal of the *Code Napoléon* to render the main principles of French law comprehensible to the ordinary citizen. And in modern times there is a welcome effort in many countries to make legal procedures more accessible to the general public. Nevertheless, the core of Bentham's allegations, effectively that of rent-seeking, remains valid and it provides an excellent source of understanding to some of the key features of legal culture.

If, according to Legrand, legal culture is 'the framework of intangibles within which an interpretative community operates, which has normative force for this community . . . and which, over the *longue durée*, determines the identity of a community *as community*',[18] a corollary is that the process of the culture evolving is facilitated by the creation of a special language and other attributes which distinguish it from those used by other 'communities'. The first step must be to differentiate the product from other systems designed to settle disputes between citizens – what in modern parlance we refer to as 'alternative dispute resolution'. Formalization of procedures, combined with doubtless some pomp and ceremony, serves very well for this purpose, but adequate demand for the more expensive product will not be secured unless they are seen to be effective and that means, in particular, ensuring that the state's police power can only be exercised through these procedures. One further, but also crucial, step is to obtain, no doubt by capture of the sovereign power, monopoly power to regulate, or rather self-regulate, the supply of services connected with the procedures, typically through a professional association. That can ensure the easy construction of barriers of entry to the supply of services by closely controlling the conditions for entry into the profession and for modes of delivery of the services.[19] Professionalization has been described by one sociologist as 'the process by which producers of special services sought to constitute *and control* a market for their expertise'.[20]

Legal professional groups can thus acquire and retain for themselves monopoly power over the supply of expert services which most corporations and many citizens within a jurisdiction will require. And as usual with monopolies, we can envisage consequences adverse to the public interest, including the overriding of consumer preferences and the securing of rents. If, for example, the self-regulatory professional agency deems that certain procedures or formalities (such as the wearing of a wig and gown) are necessary on certain legal occasions, the client has no option, but must pay for these. The example may be regarded as a trivial one, but there are others which equally well serve as part of 'legal culture' and have a more profound impact on costs. I deal in turn with procedures, complexity and the linguistic and conceptual structure of the law.

Legal Procedures

A legal system may over-indulge in formalism. All legal rights and remedies have procedural dimensions, mainly formalities, which serve principally to reduce errors in the adjudication process.[21] It follows that there is, in theory, an optimal level of formality, where its marginal cost is equal to its marginal benefit, measured by the reduction in error costs. Now since legal practitioners take most of the benefit of the formalities – they must be paid to do what is necessary – but incur little of the costs, they are strongly motivated to insist on an excessive, non-optimal level of formalities.

Legal Complexity

So far I have focused on the procedural aspects of legal culture and it is invariably the case that the legal profession determines, or at least strongly influences, the nature and details of procedural law. What about the content of substantive law and the language or concepts in which it is expressed? As we know from the public choice literature, professional associations, because of the relative homogeneity of interest and the relatively low costs of coordination, can also prove to be a highly effective force in influencing the policy and detailed provisions of relevant areas of law.[22] Certainly it is not difficult for lawyers to persuade legislatures or governments on the desirability of complex, as opposed to simple, statutory provisions. Laws, they will argue, should be 'accurately' formulated, exceptions to a given proposition should be explicitly prescribed and any ambiguity should be removed. Nor is it difficult to understand lawyers' motivations for increased complexity. The situation is almost identical to that of procedural requirements. More detailed laws reduce the quantity of errors[23] that judges and other interpreters of the law will make; and there is an optimal level of complexity, where the marginal costs of additional complexity equal the marginal benefits, in terms of reduced errors.[24] But again, it is largely the lawyers who benefit from increased complexity, since the phenomenon increases the demand for their services.

Linguistic and Conceptual Structure of Law

I come finally to the least tangible, but arguably the most significant, feature of legal culture: the linguistic and conceptual structure of the body of law administered within the jurisdiction. This is more properly the domain of legal historians and comparative lawyers, but some generalizations will be uncontroversial. First, this dimension of a legal system is largely the consequence of historical roots which may be very deep. Secondly, the most formative part of the historical evolution is typically connected to key political factors. Thus the acceptance of the Roman model of law in continental Europe was not unconnected with the Holy Roman Empire;[25] the widespread imitation of the French civil code, as well as its constitutional structure, had much to do with the Napoleonic conquests;[26] members of the Soviet bloc faithfully followed Russia in attempting to adapt civil codes to Marxist principles;[27] and there are many examples in the nineteenth and twentieth centuries of colonialist powers imposing their legal order in Africa and Asia, notwithstanding sometimes sharp clashes with native traditions.[28] A third, but equally important, generalization for our present purposes is that though most legal systems have established their core legal concepts and language through borrowings from other systems, legal practitioners always play a key role in the process.[29]

Where do these generalizations take us? Changes in rules and ultimately systems can be forced on legal professionals by external circumstances but once they have been assimilated and coloured to meet 'local needs', they become irretrievably associated with the professionals themselves. And the latter will be concerned to mould them in such a way as will best preserve their own power exclusively to provide services in relation to them and thereby extract rents.[30]

Conclusions

Legal culture then is, or at least supplies, monopoly power and this helps to explain why it so often has proved to be an obstacle to reforms which are desirable because they meet social preferences. This is not, as some comparative lawyers have maintained, because there is something inherent in legal culture which makes it resistant to transplants or adaptation. It is rather because those who derive profits from legal systems adopting certain language, forms and traditions do not wish to lose them. The normative question then arises, how best to deal with this type of anti-competitive behaviour. To address this issue requires some consideration of how the strength of the monopoly will endure against countervailing forces of competition and of the extent to which it can be regarded as 'natural monopoly', in the sense of it being desirable for there to be single legal culture. This is my task in the remaining sections of this chapter.

3.4   LEGAL CULTURE: A NATURAL MONOPOLY?

If my arguments that legal culture should be considered a monopoly are accepted, a further question arises whether it has the characteristics of a *natural* monopoly. That issue has important normative implications. A natural monopoly is, by definition, one that it is appropriate to sustain because in the circumstances competition will generate welfare losses. But of course that does not imply that the monopoly should go unregulated; controls are necessary to eliminate the harmful effects.

Characteristics of Natural Monopoly

In general, a natural monopoly exists where the average costs of production decline in the long run, as output increases.[31] This typically occurs when fixed costs are high relative to demand, a classic instance being where there is inter-dependence of demand. With traditional telephony, requiring fixed link networks, where one person wishes to speak to another and/or receive calls from that same person, both must subscribe to the same network, and there is clearly an economy of scale in a single network.[32] That network requires an enormous initial investment before even the smallest demand can be met. And the same obviously applies to railways.

The question whether a natural monopoly exists in a given situation and the extent to which it is sustainable as the costs of supply and the demand curve change are more complex than the simple description in the preceding paragraph implies and economists have developed sophisticated models to address these issues.[33] For present purposes, it is sufficient to mention some key aspects of which account should be taken. First, in relation to even the most capital-intensive product, the cost curve will not decline indefinitely; rather it will flatten out after a certain level of output is reached. Secondly, over time technological developments are likely to have a major impact on the cost curve and thus it is difficult to envisage a natural monopoly being permanent. Thirdly, it is important to consider economies of scope as well as scale. And this involves an investigation of the nature of the product or service being considered. A long-distance call or train service may be considered a separate product from a local call or a local train and the declining cost function may be applicable to the latter but not the former. On the other hand, where there is a high degree of interdependence between two products, it may well be cheaper, even in the long run, for a single firm to provide both.

Let us now see how these concepts can be applied to legal culture, drawing where appropriate on the railway and telephony analogies.

Economies of Scale

Take first a jurisdiction in which, over a period of time, a dominant single legal culture has become established. The scale economies may then become pronounced and there are parallels in the way other, more conventional, instances of natural monopoly developed. When railways were first introduced into advanced industrialized nations, there were, in terms of technical specifications, competing systems and also competing suppliers, in particular between those called 'standard' and 'broad' gauge, respectively.[34] The need for intercommunication between systems typically led to a dominant set of specifications, first within national boundaries and subsequently to accommodate transboundary traffic.[35] In less developed countries, a system based on foreign technical specifications was generally imported, without there being any prior competition.[36] In relation to legal culture, a dominant set of 'specifications' might emerge either spontaneously or else as a consequence of foreign occupation. In either case, the single network, relying on the same set of specifications, enables lawyers to communicate with one another in highly specific terms that each is familiar with.

Now, there is no magic – or at least not much – in a particular set of specifications, used in one country rather than another. Although there may be some advantages pertaining, say, to the gauges used in the Paris metro compared to the London underground, the crucial requirement is that all who use the same network have the same specifications. But when one set of specifications has been adopted it may be hugely expensive to substitute, or adapt to, another;[37] in other words the cost of entry to suppliers with other sets of specifications is prohibitively high. That is the basic economies of scale argument for treating legal culture as a natural monopoly.

Economies of Scope

The economies of scope argument is less clear. It seems appropriate to treat a legal system as a multiproduct, but there are different ways of dismantling it. Take first the distinction between procedural and substantive law. Here the railway system might seem to provide the analogy: the system of tracks can be regarded as a different product from the services that run on them, with the former, but not the latter, satisfying the conditions of natural monopoly.[38] But in the case of the law, there are surely economies of scope in the same legal culture embracing both substance and procedure since the degree of interdependence is considerable. However, if the legal system is disassembled in another way, with reference to the area of law, the economies of scope argument may falter. Take the familiar distinction between private law and public law. Here, particularly in continental Europe, it does not distort reality to suggest that the legal cultures between the two are markedly different, such that they can be regarded as being based on separate specification sets.[39] And the same may be true of certain highly specialist areas, such as taxation or social welfare law. It is then possible to envisage an alternative legal culture being supplied in sectors of the law which are relatively discrete and, as such, are not significantly dependent on the main framework of the legal system.

Implications of Natural Monopoly for Legal Change

Assuming the conditions for a natural monopoly are fulfilled, what are the implications for changes? As regards the technological changes relevant to railways and telephony, we can note that, up to a certain threshold, it will be cheaper for adaptations to be made to the dominant specification set. But the point may be reached where the basic framework of the specification set will have to be revised or replaced if further change is to be accommodated. So, too, it may be argued, with the essential structures of most legal systems.

We can observe cases where a legal culture is able to accommodate a new, more productively-efficient legal concept within its dominant specification set. At the present time, English administrative law is showing signs of adopting the concept of 'proportionality', a major feature of continental public law systems, because there is a perception that it can achieve the desired goal of administrative rationality more effectively (cheaply) than traditional English public law concepts.[40] But there may also be instances where it is cheaper to retain the less efficient domestic concept. Although the foreign legal concept is productively more efficient in its own environment (that jurisdiction's dominant set of specifications) than the functional equivalent in the domestic setting, the cost of accommodating it within the dominant specifications set is too great. So, for example, it may be cheaper *within an Anglo-Saxon legal system* to employ the trust concept to achieve certain complex property transactions than it is for identical aims to be achieved in (say) France using the nearest equivalent in French law to the trust concept.[41] But that does not mean that there is an economic case for incorporating it into French law where the basic structure of property law does not admit of a distinction between legal and equitable ownership. With colossal investment (legislation, caselaw, training) in a particular legal culture, the cost of the substantial change to the basic structures necessary to admit the foreign element will be massive.

The Exceptional Case: Competing Networks

In the preceding sections we considered the economic argument for maintaining a single legal culture and for resisting certain reform proposals that would be too costly to accommodate within the specifications set of that culture. Before proceeding to consider the implications (the need to regulate and what degree of competition to entertain), we should note that some legal systems do not conform to this model because, for historical reasons, they are not subject to a single, dominant culture. These are those systems that are referred to by comparative lawyers as 'hybrid', 'mixed' or 'pluralistic' jurisdictions.[42] Broadly speaking they fall into three categories. First, there are those where a culture was imposed by a colonialist power, but where a native culture persisted to some degree and 'competes' with the imposed culture; such a situation prevails in many African countries.[43] Secondly, there are some countries which have experienced successive colonialist or other occupations, each having a major impact on the legal culture and therefore give rise to some competition between them: Quebec and Louisiana (both involving a clash between French and English systems) and South Africa (English v Roman-Dutch) are good examples.[44] The third category comprises countries which experienced industrial and commercial development relatively late and where rulers recognized the need to look elsewhere for more sophisticated legal input than the domestic system could provide.[45] Japan, Turkey and Greece are good examples of cases where there were effectively 'tenders' from several major legal cultures to supply the necessary set of specifications.[46] In somewhat different circumstances, the recent efforts to use Western systems as models for legal reform in Eastern Europe also fall into this category.[47]

What would we expect to happen in jurisdictions of this kind? Although there will be significant variations between the three categories, some common characteristics which set them apart from the systems with a single dominant culture can be predicted. In the first place, the incorporation of foreign legal concepts should be easier (cheaper) because the existing system already contains more than one specification set and adaptation costs are lower. Secondly, inefficient levels of formalism and complexity are likely to be less evident. In a single-culture jurisdiction, lawmakers can be easily captured by the legal profession able to persuade them that a high degree of formalism is desirable. The same may arise in a hybrid jurisdiction if there is collusion (cartelization) between the professionals representing the different cultures; but some degree of rivalry can be expected. If, and to the extent that, such competition exists, lawmakers – and indeed consumers (firms and individuals using the law) – will be able to compare the performance of the areas of law subjected to the different specification sets. This is analogous to 'yardstick' competition, used by utility regulators to exert pressure for efficiency on suppliers of localized natural monopolies.[48]

On the face of it, then, we might expect hybrid jurisdictions to be more efficient, and adapt more readily to changing external variables, than those with a single dominant culture; and there is some evidence produced by comparative lawyers to support this.[49] But much will depend on how the processes of competition actually work. Take the identified third category of hybrid jurisdictions. The fact that there will be a choice for the domestic lawmaker between the different tenders does not necessarily mean that the optimal selection will be made. There will, again, be a possibility of capture. Those lawyers trained in a particular foreign system will, of course, envisage the rents to be enjoyed should 'their' system be adopted. So also firms engaged in trade between the jurisdiction and one of the tendering countries will want to exert its influence to minimize its future legal costs. This is not necessarily inconsistent with an efficient outcome if all such firms can exert influence, but it may be too easy for a few powerful multinationals to dominate the lobbying process.

Regulation or (Some) Competition?

Let us now return to the standard case of a dominant legal culture and the problems to which it gives rise. The traditional solution adopted to deal with natural monopolies is regulation. I have already indicated the reasons why that is unlikely to be very successful in the present context. Although, in theory, legislatures ought to be able to impose on the legal systems and those that operate it such constraints as are in the public interest, practising lawyers are a very powerful pressure group, able to capture the legislative process with regard to what is, and what is not, legally 'feasible'. Nor should it be forgotten that a significant proportion of the members of the legislature in many countries are lawyers with continuing professional affiliations. And capture is all the easier if, as is also often the case, the legal profession is largely self-regulated, thereby enabling the homogeneity of self-interest to prevail.

So, as with other natural monopolies, the question arises whether some forms of competition might if not replace, then at least complement, the regulatory controls. Let us first note the value of some form of internal competition. In the sphere of utilities, this has taken several forms, including the fragmentation of suppliers into smaller entities with regional monopolies, the admission (at a regulated price) of alternative suppliers to the single network, and awarding of monopoly rights by competitive franchising.[50] I have already argued elsewhere for the merits of forcing different professional associations to compete for the exercise of self-regulatory powers – thus a form of competitive franchising; and this could curb the excesses which result from professional regulation.[51] Another form of competition would arise from permitting and encouraging the growth of alternative dispute resolution. This could include enabling ADR practitioners to make use of the facilities of the ordinary judicial process (and thus have access to the dominant infrastructure of the system). To this may be added the merits, often argued,[52] of some form of competition between different lawmakers, notably the legislature and judges.

However, external competition is likely to be more effective than internal competition. Transfrontier trade will have a profound impact. That impact will, of course, be direct where to accommodate international communications specifications on one side of the boundary, or on both sides, have to be modified. Transport and telecommunication systems involving international connections provide good examples of this.[53] But so also do legal systems. Elsewhere, I have shown how freedom of choice of law in governing an international transaction, because it involves competition between national legal orders, should positively influence legal systems towards efficient solutions.[54] Economic agents may, nevertheless, find that no one set of legal principles sufficiently meets their preferences and an (informal) autonomous legal order may emerge. This was the origin of Law Merchant (*lex mercatoria*) which was developed in the medieval period as a system of customary law governing interstate commercial transactions and generating a legal culture of its own.[55]

How will all this affect the sustainability of the single dominant legal culture? A key proposition can be formulated: as the volume of international communications relative to purely domestic communications increases, so also will the benefits of harmonizing the specifications sets, since these will become (relatively) cheaper. As a consequence, the natural monopoly characteristics of the domestic legal culture will fade. So long as the dominant set of specifications are applicable totally or primarily to domestic transactions as a single product, the economies of scale justifications for the monopoly may prevail. But in the multiproduct case, where those specifications become applicable also to transactions with a foreign connection, and with an increasing degree of interdependence between the two products, so there are *diseconomies* of scope which are likely to outweigh the economies of scale.

Conclusions

On the basis of the analysis in this section, we can reach some general conclusions. Single legal cultures which are dominant in particular jurisdictions are likely to have the characteristics of a natural monopoly, a predictable consequence is that practising lawyers will exploit the situation, generating rents for themselves by, for example, promoting formalism and complexities and other features which enhance their income. Such rent-seeking behaviour is difficult to constrain by regulatory means because lawyers constitute a powerful pressure group, adept at influencing the law-making machinery.

The competition provided by other legal cultures is likely to be a more effective method of dealing with the problem: the greater the competition, the less sustainable the natural monopoly. Legal business with an international connection is an important variable in this respect since it is the source of much effective external competition. We can predict, therefore, that a *jurisdiction* where, for historical or geographical reasons, international trade makes a relatively high contribution to the gross domestic product, will be less vulnerable to a single legal culture, less prone to excessive formalism and complexity and more susceptible to efficient adaptations to legal reforms. We can also argue that within a particular jurisdiction those *areas of law* more likely to involve an international connection (notably, commercial and corporate law) will have similar features and as such contrast with others areas (for example land law) having a much stronger connection with the jurisdiction.

Internal competition between legal cultures, where it exists, should be no less effective and here we should recognize the importance of 'hybrid' or 'mixed' jurisdictions, where no single legal culture is dominant. Such legal systems should, unless obstructed by private interest groups allied to a particular culture, adapt more readily to efficient legal reform.

NOTES

1. See especially: C. Varga (ed.), *Comparative Legal Cultures* (1992); D. Nelken (ed.), *Comparing Legal Cultures* (1997); P. Legrand, *Fragments on Law-as-Culture* (1999).
2. J.H. Merryman and D.S. Clark, *Comparative Law: Western European and Latin American Legal Systems* (1978), 29.
3. P. Legrand in several papers, notably 'European Legal Systems are Not Converging' (1996) **45** *International and Comparative Law Quarterly* 52. For less extreme but broadly similar views see O. Kahn-Freund, 'On Uses and Misuses of Comparative Law' (1974) **37** *Modern Law Review* 1; G. Teubner, 'Legal Irritants: Good Faith in British Law or How Unifying Law Ends Up in New Divergences' (1998) **61** *Modern Law Review* 11.
4. The French government has always attempted to justify subsidising European and particularly French cinema on this basis. See, for example, 'La règle du jeu', *The Economist*, 18 March 1995.
5. 'Competition between National Legal Systems: A Contribution of Economic Analysis to Comparative Law' (1999) **48** *International and Comparative Law Quarterly* 405 (a shorter version of this paper appears as 'Economic Analysis and Comparative Law' in *Mélanges en L'Honneur de Denis Tallon: D'Ici, D'Ailleures: Harmonisation et Dynamique du Droit* (1999), 169).
6. Ibid., 410–12.
7. R.J. Gilson, 'Lawyers as transaction cost engineers' in P. Newman (ed.), *The New Palgrave Dictionary of Economics and the Law* (1998), vol. 2, 508.
8. Ibid., 412–15.
9. Ibid., 411–12. A. Watson in his monograph, *Society and Legal Change* (1977) argues that legal rules are often out of step with the needs and desires of society and he attributes this phenomenon to the fact that professional lawyers have an interest in resisting change. See also 'Sources of Law and Legal Culture' (1983) **131** *University of Pennsylvania Law Review* 1121.
10. For example, what was perceived to be the most powerful criticism of the proposals for increased judicial management of the litigation process contained in the Woolf Report was that they might undermine the adversarial approach so cherished in the English legal tradition: Lord Woolf, *Access to Justice: Final Report* (1998), 14.
11. F.A. Hayek, *Law, Legislation and Liberty*, vol. 3 (1979), 155–61.
12. H.L.A. Hart, 'Definition and Theory in Jurisprudence' (1954) **70** *Law Quarterly Review* 37; A. Ross, 'Tu-tu' (1957) **70** *Harvard Law Review* 812.
13. Compare M. Bridge, 'Does Anglo-Canadian Law Need a Doctrine of Good Faith' (1984) **9** *Canadian Business Law Journal* 385, 426; and Teubner, above. n.3.
14. D.B. Walters, 'Analogues of the Trust and Its Constituents in French Law from the Standpoint of Scots and English Law', in W.A. Wilson (ed.), *Trusts and Trust-Like Devices* (1981), 117.
15. R. Sacco, 'Legal Formants: A Dynamic Approach to Comparative Law' (1991) **39** *American Journal of Comparative Law* 1, 343.
16. M.J. White, 'Legal Complexity and Lawyers' Benefit from Litigation' (1992) **12** *International Review of Law and Economics* 381.
17. The following paragraph is derived from H.L.A. Hart, 'Bentham and the Demystification of the Law' (1973) **36** *Modern Law Review* 2.
18. Legrand, above n.1, 27 (author's italics).
19. For evidence for this in relation to the legal profession in different countries, see M. Faure, J. Finsinger, J. Siegers, and R. Van den Bergh (eds), *Regulation of the Professions: A Law*

and Economics Approach to the Regulation of Attorneys and Physicians in the US, Belgium, the Netherlands, Germany and the UK (1993).

20. M.S. Larson, *The Rise of Professionalism: A Sociological Analysis* (1977), xvi–xvii (author's italics), cited in R. Dingwall and P. Fenn: 'A Respectable Profession? Sociological and Economic Perspectives on the Regulation of Professional Services' (1987) **7** *International Review of Law and Economics* 51.
21. See J.S. Johnston, 'Legal formalities' in Newman, above n.7, vol. 2., 254.
22. M. Olson, *The Logic of Collective Action* (1965); and see M. Trebilcock, 'Regulating Service Quality in Professional Markets' in D. Dewees (ed.), *The Regulation of Quality* (1983), ch. 4.
23. 'Errors' in this context mean divergences from the policy intention.
24. I. Ehrlich and R. Posner, 'An Economic Analysis of Legal Rulemaking' (1974) **3** *Journal of Legal Studies* 257.
25. J.H. Merryman, *The Civil Law Tradition* (1969), 10.
26. K. Zweigert and H. Kötz, *An Introduction to Comparative Law* (3rd edn, 1998), ch. 8.
27. J.N. Hazard, *Communists and their Law: a Search for the Common Core of the Legal Systems* (1969).
28. R. David, C. Jauffret-Spinosi, *Les Grands Systèmes de Droit Contemporains* (10th edn, 1992), 454–61.
29. A. Watson, *Legal Transplants: An Approach to Comparative Law* (1974).
30. 'A change that made the law simpler or less ambiguous or reduced the volume of disputes, actual or possible, could have an adverse effect on [lawyers'] income . . . the stock-in-trade of a practising attorney is his or her knowledge of the *existing* law', Watson (1983), n.9 above, 1153.
31. R. Baldwin and M. Cave, *Understanding Regulation* (1999), 203–5.
32. W.K. Viscusi, J.M. Vernon and J.E. Harrington, *Economics of Regulation and Antitrust* (1992), 457.
33. W.W. Sharkey, *The Theory of Natural Monopoly* (1982).
34. G. Hawke and J. Higgins, 'Britain' in P. O'Brien (ed), *Railways and the Economic Development of Western Europe 1830–1914* (1983), 181–2.
35. R.L. Wedgwood, *International Rail Transport* (1946), 15–17.
36. O.S. Nock, *Railways of Asia and the Far East* (1978).
37. O. Williamson, *The Economic Institutions of Capitalism* (1985), 52–6.
38. The privatization of UK railways was structured on this basis: D. Helm, 'Putting the Railways Back Together Again: Rail Privatisation, Franchising and Regulation', in M.E. Beesley (ed.), *Regulating Utilities: A Time for Change?* (1996), ch. 7.
39. David, Jauffret-Spinosi, above n.28, 67–8.
40. J. Jowell, 'Is Proportionality A Dangerous Concept?' (1996) **2** *European Public Law* 1.
41. Walters, above n.14, 124–33.
42. T.B. Smith, 'The Preservation of the Civilian Tradition in "Mixed Jurisdictions"', in A. Yiannopolous (ed.), *Civil Law in the Modern World* (1965), ch. 1; E. Örücü, E. Atwooll and S. Coyle (eds), *Studies in Legal Systems: Mixed and Mixing* (1996); M. Guadagni, 'Legal Pluralism' in Newman, above n.7, vol. 2, 542.
43. M.B. Hooker, *Legal Pluralism: An Introduction to Colonial and Neo-Colonial Laws* (1975).
44. Smith, above n.42.
45. E. Buscaglia, 'Law and Economics of Development' in B. Bouckaert and G. De Geest (eds), *Encyclopedia of Law and Economics*, 0580.
46. E. Örücü, 'Critical Comparative Law: Considering Paradoxes for Legal Systems in Transition' (1999) **59** *Nederlandse Vereniging Voor Rechtsvergelijking* 1, 80–117.
47. G. Ajani, 'By Chance and Prestige: Legal Transplants in Russia and Eastern Europe' (1995) **43** *American Journal of Comparative Law* 97.
48. J. Vickers and G. Yarrow, *Privatization: An Economic Analysis* (1988), 115–18.
49. See, for example, H.L. MacQueen, *Scots Law and the Road to the New Ius Commune* (2000).
50. Viscusi et al., above n.32, 337–49.
51. A. Ogus, 'Rethinking Self-Regulation' (1995) **15** *Oxford Journal of Legal Studies* 97.

52.   For example Sacco, above n.15.
53.   Wedgwood, above n.35, and for modern developments in relation to the European Union, see C. degli Abbati, *Transport and European Integration* (1987).
54.   Ogus, above n.5, 408.
55.   L.E. Trakman, *The Law Merchant: The Evolution of Commercial Law* (1983); B.L. Benson, 'Law Merchant' in Newman, above n.7, 500–505.

4. Judicial competition, legal innovation and European integration: an economic analysis*

Sophie Harnay and Isabelle Vigouroux

4.1 INTRODUCTION

European legal integration has deeply transformed the nature of the European Community (EC). Repeated decisions by the European Court of Justice (ECJ) in the direction of the constitutionalization of the initial set of European Treaties, the so-called 'judicial activism' of the fifteen judges of Luxembourg, and the growing importance of the European jurisprudence have gradually affected not only the content of domestic law of member states but also the legal enforcement process by their national courts. In this respect, one of the major questions posed by the evolution of the Community relates to the relationship between the European Court of Justice and national judges. The trickiness of the issue stems from the possible contradiction between the empowerment of the former and the preservation of the latter's role. In particular, the national courts' acceptance of the European legal integration, their willingness to enforce European law within national legal orders, even if widely investigated by legal scholars and political scientists, have received (to our knowledge) relatively few echoes among lawyer economists, although it is an issue about which economic tools may prove their relevancy.

The problem that has to be explained is the influence of coexisting judiciaries on the European integration process. A usual analysis refers to the respective *empowerment* of national and European judges. The emphasis is put on the vested interest of national judges to promote EC law. Once they have become aware that European integration could help them to increase their power and control, they agree to actively participate in the construction of

*Earlier versions of the paper were presented at seminars in Reims (CERAS-EDJ), Paris 1 (LAEP) and Marseille (IDEP), at the 2000 annual meeting of the European Public Society in Siena (IT), and at the First Corsica Workshop in Law and Economics, Corte, May 2000. We thank all participants in these conferences for their valuable comments. We especially thank Pierre Salmon and Sophie Delabruyère for very helpful suggestions. Remaining errors are ours.

European law. Thus, both European and national judiciaries have an incentive to cooperate since the cooperation results in larger competence[1] (Stein, 1981; Weiler, 1991). In this perspective, European integration then is a result of the complicit relationship between national and European judges. In contrast to this cooperative theory, we advocate for a competitive perspective on European integration. Judicial empowerment is also at stake – national judges are still assumed to search for more power. However, the choice to participate in the implementation of the EC law is supposed to be the consequence of the competition with European judges. In this perspective, European legal integration is shown to result from competition between national courts and the European Court of Justice. We also depart from standard law and economics perspective on European legal integration analysed as the outcome of a more or less regulated *horizontal* competition among courts of the various member states (Ogus, Smits, Van den Bergh, this volume). Indeed, we insist on the idea that *vertical* competition may also take place among national and European judges and may therefore influence the scope and pace of the integration process. Our argument refers to the link between legal innovation and European integration. More precisely, we refer to a prominent result put forward by the economics of innovation, according to which innovation not only leads to an increase in profit for the successful innovator but also helps to prevent entry by potential competitors (Gilbert and Newbery, 1982; Reinganum, 1985; Beath, Katsoulacos and Ulph, 1989; Tirole, 1995). We develop the idea that vertical competition as a mechanism rests on a political assignment of judicial rights. Within such a framework, national and European judges compete for these rights on the domestic legal markets. Judges have to innovate to signal themselves to political decision makers. As a consequence, innovation is a way to gain jurisdiction rights. Doing so, they find themselves in a legal innovation race where each tries to achieve the rights for himself and adopts a pre-emptive behaviour toward the competitor.

This chapter is organized as follows. Section 4.2 shows that legal innovation is linked to judicial empowerment and monopoly rights. Section 4.3 outlines a model of competition between two courts. Section 4.4 presents the interpretation of the competition between national and European courts along the lines of our model.

4.2   JUDICIAL EMPOWERMENT AND LEGAL INNOVATION

A judicial decision is enforceable on the legal market on the condition that the corresponding right of production was formerly assigned to the court that made it. In other words, the achievement of specific property rights, that we label jurisdiction rights, is a prerequisite for the production of legitimate decisions. When this condition is not satisfied, the decision can be contested and overturned, on the grounds that the court was not competent. Therefore, judges, either national or European, are granted with a franchise, or licence, that is to some extent, a monopoly right – there cannot be various suppliers of alternative laws in one jurisdiction, or two courts cannot hear the same case at the same time. The rationale behind this is the need for legal certainty, or the prevention of the risk that two courts give opposite solutions to a unique case.

At the European level, such monopoly rights are politically allocated. Member states, not pure market mechanisms, determine the assignment of rights. The citizens – litigants – are not allowed to bring litigation before the court they prefer but are constrained to respect and follow the current distribution of rights applying among courts. In other words, competition between national and European judges is regulated. We thus assume here that member states choose to grant a jurisdiction right to the 'most appropriate' level of jurisdiction. This does not mean, however, that the assignment of rights is decided on subjective, non-technical, rent-seeking criteria. Appropriateness here simply means consistency with the political objective of the decision makers, according to the neo-functionalist conception of EC institutions as agents of the member states.[2] That does not imply that courts are dependent on politicians. Indeed, the implicit contract between them does not provide the court with binding instructions nor restrict its set of possible choices. In that view, the political selection of the fittest agent among different contenders in the race for production rights can simply be explained by the interest of political principals in ensuring the production of high-quality decisions, whatever their reasons[3] (democratic control exerted by constituents, uncertainty about their situation in the future, and so on). In other words, we focus here on the political assignment of jurisdiction rights as a means of regulation of the judicial market, without questioning political motives further.

However, the assignment of rights is not immutable but may still be reversed by the political decision makers. Two reasons can be put forward. First, the contract linking politicians and courts is incomplete. New developments or unforeseen changes in the environment may lead to the breach of the existing contract. Consequently, whenever a new assignment of rights is expected to produce superior outcomes, rights are susceptible of being transferred from their current owner to a new performer. Secondly, judges presumably derive positive utility from the judicial realization of jurisdiction rights, in terms of power, prestige and reputation. According to the fact that the greater the extent of the jurisdiction rights, the higher the judicial utility, judges as rational utility-maximizers have an interest in developing their jurisdiction rights. Therefore courts belonging to different levels of jurisdiction have a strong incentive to engage in competition in order to gain production rights. Again, then, the current distribution of rights may be modified by the relative efforts of competitors. Thus, while 'competition within the field' and simultaneous production by different courts are precluded by the grant of monopoly rights, 'competition for the field' provides a mechanism for a competitively determined allocation of the right to operate the monopoly.

The major consequence is that a court may enjoy only temporary monopoly power since the monopoly conferred by the grant of a jurisdiction right is always threatened by entry. As both competitors try to achieve the right for themselves, the challenger, or the potential entrant on the market (namely the court that has not been granted with the right – or not yet) aims to induce a transfer from the decision makers. On the other hand, the current monopolist, or incumbent (namely the court currently entitled to produce decisions) tries to prevent the potential entrant from entry. Consequently, both engage in a "patent race" whose aim is ultimately the achievement or the protection of judicial rights.[4] The crucial point is now to determine how competing courts can influence the assignment of rights in the absence of any explicit price or auction systems.

We argue that legal innovation proves to be a means for competitors to obtain or defend disputed jurisdiction rights. As the franchise is awarded to the contender that seems to offer the fittest decision, both monopolist and potential entrant have an incentive to innovate, so as to signal themselves as the most appropriate level of jurisdiction to the decision makers. Deriving inspiration from the imperfect market analysis, we distinguish two incentives to innovate. The first incentive, that is very similar to the pure profit incentive put forward in the R&D literature, is a power incentive and depends only on the expected power from the legal innovation. It derives directly from the judicial exercise of additional rights achieved through successful innovation. The second incentive to innovate, usually known as 'strategic incentive', derives from the potential entry of a competing supplier of judicial decisions on the market. Accordingly, the monopolist is not induced to innovate for the expected power *per se* (or not only) but also to pre-empt the right, so as to prevent entry from the competitor.[5] In short, courts behave like legal entrepreneurs differentiating their offers on the market of judicial decisions. In that view they develop a sequence of innovations. Potential competition has here implications very similar to those underscored by Schumpeter as well as in the theory of disputable markets. As a consequence, the initial assignment of rights may evolve according to the inventive characteristics of competitors.

The next section is devoted to a more formal presentation of the arguments.

4.3   A MODEL OF COMPETITION BETWEEN TWO COURTS

We concentrate on a model with two courts. Court A denotes the monopolist, or incumbent. Court B denotes the potential entrant, or challenger. The latter has an incentive to innovate to gain a jurisdiction right from the decision maker, while the former has an incentive to innovate to preclude the latter from entry. A measure of their incentives to innovate is given by the respective value of innovation for both.

We denote x_A (x_B) the probability that the court A (B) successfully innovates in the interval $(t, t + dt)$, conditional upon B (A) not having discovered it by t. We assume x_A and x_B to be solely functions of the legal innovation expenditures currently engaged in by A and B but not to depend on the accumulated amounts of previous expenditures. This assumption is justified by the consideration that the former innovations have still been embodied in the current market structure.[6] π_A^s is the flow power derived by the court A from a successful innovation. π_A^{ns} is the flow power for A in the reverse case (for example, when B successfully innovates before A). Obviously, $\pi_A^s > \pi_A^{ns}$. Symmetrically, π_B^s denotes the corresponding flow power for the court B when it innovates successfully. p_A is the current power exerted by the monopolist A at the time the innovation is realized, that is, under the current assignment of rights. But while the monopolist, as an incumbent, already derives some power from the existing assignment of rights, the potential entrant does not, for by definition he has not yet entered the market at that time. The discount rate, r, is assumed to be common to both courts. Both courts face the same innovation technology. $c(x_i)$ denotes the cost of effort. We denote V_i the present discounted value of the expected profit associated with the participation to the legal competition for each court i. For the monopolist (A), this value is given by:

$$V_A(x_A, x_B) = \frac{x_A\left(\dfrac{\pi_A^s}{r}\right) + x_B\left(\dfrac{\pi_A^{ns}}{r}\right) + p_A - c(x_A)}{x_A + x_B + r}$$

For the challenger B, it can be written as:

$$V_B(x_A, x_B) = \frac{x_B\left(\dfrac{\pi_B^s}{r}\right) - c(x_B)}{x_A + x_B + r}$$

The formulation allows us to distinguish two effects playing in opposite directions. The first effect provides the monopolist with an incentive to remain in a monopoly position. The monopolist gains a net flow profit of $\pi_A^S - \pi_A^{nS}$ by innovating first (the difference between the flow profit he derives from a successful innovation minus the flow profit he derives when the entrant innovates successfully before he does). The entrant gains π_B^S (the flow profit he gets when he innovates successfully). Moreover, according to the efficiency effect in the monopoly theory, it can be reasonably assumed that a monopolist does not make less profit than two non-colluding duopolists, for if he wishes, the monopolist can always duplicate the situation of duopoly. Hence, $\pi_A^S \geq \pi_A^{nS} + \pi_B^S$ or $\pi_A^S - \pi_A^{nS} \geq \pi_B^S$. Therefore, the incentive of the monopolist to remain a monopolist is greater than the entrant's incentive to become a duopolist. Within our legal framework, this signifies that the incumbent court's incentive to innovate to protect his monopoly right is greater than the challenger court's incentive.

The second effect provides the monopolist with the incentive to allow the entry of the outsider to occur. This is because the marginal return of his innovation expenditures decreases with the initial profit (p_A), as shown by the derivatives below.

$$\frac{\partial V_A(x_A, x_B)}{\partial x_A} = \frac{1}{(x_A + x_B + r)^2} \left[\left(\frac{\pi_A^S - \pi_A^{nS}}{r} \right) x_B \right. \\ \left. + \pi_A^S - p_A + c(x_A) - c'(x_A)(x_A + x_B + r) \right]$$

$$\frac{\partial(\partial V_A / \partial x_A)}{\partial p_A} < 0$$

When the monopolist increases his innovation expenditures, he moves the innovation date forward and hastens his own replacement by himself. To the contrary, the entrant does not forgo any flow profit when he innovates successfully, as he starts from scratch anyway. As a consequence, this effect reduces the incumbent court's incentive to innovate, whereas it increases it for the challenger.

Two main conclusions may be drawn from these effects. First, the monopolist's effort at legal innovation could be higher in a competitive system than in a single-court system where the court has no strategic incentive to innovate. This straightforward result leads to some interesting implications for European integration, as we will see below. Secondly, the innovating behaviour of courts clearly affects the market conditions in which they operate and is in turn affected by them. Indeed, the sense of the general effect is indeterminate, depending on whether the first or the second effect dominates. This is likely to result either in the persistence of the monopoly or to lead to the entry of the challenger, depending on the predominant effect. In the first case, the monopolist court has been able to successfully influence the assignment of jurisdiction rights, so as to put institutional barriers to the challenger's entry. Still, this does not imply that the monopolist forever retains his monopoly gains and is protected against any competitive pressure. On the contrary, even if unsuccessful, the outsider may continue to exert a competitive pressure to turn the unfavourable assignment of rights into a more favourable one. In the second case, the challenger's entry occurs as a consequence of some winning innovation. However, this does not mean the end of the innovation race, since the situation provides the basis for further legal innovations. In this view, legal evolution can merely be seen as a sequence of successful judicial innovations.

In practice, the process of legal evolution in Europe is more complicated, due to the scope and number of jurisdiction rights, to various interactions between courts and other institutional actors, and to the emerging hierarchical order among levels of jurisdiction. Nevertheless, the relationship between the ECJ and the national courts of member states strongly supports the theoretical framework developed above, as illustrated in the following section.

4.4   AN APPLICATION TO THE COMPETITION BETWEEN THE NATIONAL COURTS AND THE EUROPEAN JUDGES

The European integration process provides a clear illustration of the judicial strategies mentioned above. At the beginning, national judges were strict monopolists in their domestic legal market, defined as the national territory in which they operate. The emergence of the European Union and the creation of the European Court of Justice brought about important changes in the legal environment. Although the European Court of Justice was initially a strict monopolist in its own legal market, defined by A.164 of the EEC Treaty, it gradually engaged in a series of legal innovations enhancing its power, potentially at the expense of national courts. It forced them to adapt their production, so as to protect their current market position and preclude entry from the ECJ. Competition between both judiciaries has thus strongly affected legal production and legal processes, whether domestic or European. We highlight this point now through a few illustrations collected from evolutions empirically observed in the EC.

4.4.1   The Behaviour of the ECJ

As laid down in A.164 of the EEC Treaty, the task of the ECJ is to 'ensure that in the interpretation and application of this Treaty the law is observed', by institutions as well as member states and their nationals. In addition, a number of more detailed provisions confer upon the Court specific heads of jurisdiction. Under this line, its activity is supposed to be limited to the jurisdiction expressly conferred upon it by the Treaties and some later measures, among others the Protocol on the interpretation by the ECJ of the Brussels Convention on jurisdiction and the enforcement of judgements in civil and commercial matters. With respect to this chapter, the implications of these dispositions are twofold. First, the Court supposedly exercises exclusive jurisdiction. That is, no other court is allowed to make decisions in the fields expressly conferred upon the ECJ. In this respect, the ECJ, Simon (1997, p. 308) writes, 'has always devoted much attention to the defence of the jurisdictional competence it is granted with by Treaties'. Secondly, a naïve or textual interpretation of the role of the ECJ suggests that it has no jurisdiction to entertain actions which do not fall within the (narrow) scope of its power such as it was defined by the Treaties. Yet, according to a wide interpretation of the expression 'the law is observed' in A.164, this strict interpretation of the wording of the Treaty has clearly been challenged and gradually replaced by an alternative conception of the role of the Court. Progressively, wider jurisdiction has been conferred upon the Court, including fields where it was initially not expected to have jurisdiction (Arnull, 1990, pp. 684 et seq.). In other words, as 'new problems developed and opportunities opened up as a result of past achievement', the ECJ behaved like a 'purposeful opportunist' (Wincott, 1995, p. 585), generally giving, 'a broad interpretation to provisions of Community law relating to its own power' (Arnull, ibid.). Thus, the ECJ behaved in a way perfectly consistent with the theoretical framework developed in the previous sections. At any rate, it behaved like a legal entrepreneur grasping opportunities supplied by litigation (the so-called 'accidents of litigation').

With the expanded conception of the role of the ECJ, inevitably, competition with national judges was bound to arise. And indeed, in *Van Gend & Loos v. Nederlandse Administratie der Belastingen* (26/62, 1963, E.C.R. 1), the European Court of Justice states that the Community is 'a new legal order of international law for the benefit of which the States have limited their sovereign rights, albeit within limited fields and the subjects of which comprise not only the Member States, but also their nationals'. Moreover, it adds that 'Community law has authority which can be invoked by ... nationals [of member states] before their courts or tribunals'. A few months later, the *Costa v. ENEL* decision (6/64, 1964) consolidated *Van Gend*, stating that 'the EEC has created its own legal system which ... became an integral part of the legal systems of the member states and which their courts are bound to apply'. Through these decisions, thus, the Court clearly innovates (as emphasized in the expression 'a *new* legal order'). It proclaims two new doctrines, respectively the doctrine of the direct effect and of the supremacy of EC law over conflicting provisions of national law. Thereby, it fundamentally alters the legal character of the Community. It also alters its own former relationship with national courts such as it had been negotiated and established by the member states in European Treaties. Namely, the two aforementioned decisions resulted in a shift in the existing jurisdictional boundaries, since the combination of the doctrines of the direct effect and of the supremacy made it possible for the ECJ to claim and exert jurisdiction on a wider range of competence. Furthermore, arguing that Community law has to apply uniformly within each member state of the Union, the Court took advantage of the new situation to establish monopoly rights, therefore depriving national judiciaries of some part of their former monopolistic competence and even turning them into its agents. Finally, as long as the new jurisdictional boundaries remain unchallenged by a 'better' innovation of national judges that would put them into the position of recovering their domestic market, or in the absence of any political choice that would explicitly confer the transferred competence on the national courts again, the new assignment of rights can be considered enforcing. In this respect, thus, judicial activism by European judges proves to be a rather successful strategy of legal innovation oriented toward the entry on national markets of member states.

4.4.2   National Courts' Responses

As a logical consequence of the empowerment of the ECJ with respect to the national courts, a hierarchical conception of the judicial organization in Europe emerged that led to the marginalization of national courts within the 'new legal order'. Against the corresponding decrease in their prerogatives, the latter have engaged in an innovation strategy aimed at protecting threatened markets, proving then to conform to the results of our former section. In short, this strategy can be depicted as the national production of European decisions. Indeed, since national courts had no escape but participate in the 'Eurolaw game', they have been compelled to signal their ability to apply Community law at least as efficiently as their competitor. Antitrust law provides an obvious illustration of such strategic innovations, as shown by the evolution of the French administrative jurisprudence on the matter. In this regard, Caillosse (2000) recalls that most radical transformations in the French jurisprudence have been undertaken under European pressure, in order to avoid a shift of litigation toward the ECJ. Thus, in this case as in many others, the national courts have proved to be responsive to the requirements of Community law. This responsiveness, however, does not seem – solely – to be due to some kind of intrinsic European conviction but somewhat to the threat exerted by the ECJ.

However, that is not to say that the national courts have immediately agreed to enforce EC law or that any judicial resistance against legal integration has been bound to fail. On the contrary, such resistance, when successful, has led to the situation of persisting monopoly analysed in the third section. In this regard, one might argue that the doctrine of direct effect applied to the EC directives has been frequently challenged by national courts, among others French, Italian, German, that have objected to various stages of its development (Wincott, 1995, pp. 592–3). Concerning the supremacy of Community law, objections by national courts in France, the UK, Germany and Italy have also been observed, since '[C]ourts in these states variously declined to test national legislation to see if it conflicted with EC law, refused to acknowledge the direct effect of directives and proved reluctant to make Article 177 references to the ECJ' (ibid., 1995, p. 593). In this respect, constitutional courts have appeared to be particularly reluctant to enforce EC law to that extent that it would possibly undermine their own jurisprudence and power.

Despite such signs of obvious non-compliance, the question of the viability of domestic monopoly in most legal fields nevertheless remains. In the third section we argued that the persistence of monopoly is a function of the relative strengths of competing courts' incentives to innovate, provided that legal innovation is costly. Obviously, where the expected return from innovation is high, judges have a strong incentive to innovate, either to achieve a right or to protect it. It is not the purpose of this chapter to determine which fields are most likely to be affected by strong competition. However, from the past evolution of the relationship between European and national judiciaries, from the ongoing reinforcement of European institutions, and from litigation possibilities opened up by past achievements, we may infer that European judges will continue to challenge domestic prerogatives and that fields untouched by judicial competition are very unlikely to expand.

4.4.3   The Application of A.177

Furthermore, our competitive interpretation of judicial behaviour is confirmed by the way the ECJ and national courts apply A.177. Briefly, this article provides that when Community law is material to the resolution of an ordinary lawsuit before a national court, that court is permitted to request the ECJ for an interpretation of the law – and even in some circumstances, *must* ask for a preliminary ruling.[7] This process is supposed to enable the ECJ to advise the national court of the proper interpretation of Community law. This interpretation is expected to be only a guideline for the national court in the solution of a particular case, but in no way an explicit decision by the ECJ. In other words, the ECJ is not expected to enforce Community law directly in the national law of member states.

In actual practice, however, the ECJ frequently tends to provide the national judges with rather directive rulings, leaving them with limited free-dom and flexibility. This widely recognized behaviour led Mancini and Keeling (1994, pp. 184–5, quoted in Wincott 1995, p. 597), among other authors, to confess that 'A.177 [has] been transformed in the course of the years into a quasi-federal instrument for reviewing the compatibility of national laws with Community law'. Therefore, as a combination of direct effect and of the increasing accuracy of the rulings provided by the ECJ, A.177 procedures have resulted not only in a wider range of cases before the ECJ and enhancement of its authority, but also in the erosion of control and jurisdiction for national judges.

As for the national judges, consistent with the behaviour pointed out above, they attempt to maintain the scope of their discretion threatened by A.177 procedures. In this view, they do not refer to the ECJ as often as litigated cases would require, so as to avoid a possible loss of discretion that could occur from the Court's ruling and would presumably undermine their own jurispru-dence. The judicial doctrine developed by the French *Conseil d'Etat* and labelled 'theory of the *acte clair*' epitomizes the setting of entry barriers for the challenger, since it enables the Supreme Administrative Court not to require further interpretation from the ECJ whenever it considers it unneces-sary. Not surprisingly, this doctrine has been applied quite frequently, and in a way so as to maintain the discretion of the national judges.

4.4.4   Competition Among National Courts on Domestic Legal Markets

As a consequence of the general legal evolution stated above, the conception of judicial organization in Europe has become hierarchical. Indeed, the ECJ behaves more or less like a further jurisdictional level within the existing national systems. Thus, its judicial activism affects not only its relationship with national courts, but also the competitive conditions applying to national courts on domestic legal markets. In this regard, the practice of preliminary references based on A.177 highlights behavioural differences among national courts, according to their rank in the domestic judicial hierarchy. Namely, national courts of high rank, especially constitutional courts, appear very reluctant to invoke A.177, for the reasons mentioned above. To the contrary, inferior courts prove to be much more willing to refer to the ECJ. The refer-ring process enables them to increase their autonomy within the national hier-archy and gives them 'powers that had been reserved to the highest court in the land' (Weiler, 1991, p. 2426). In this view, the existence and activity of the ECJ is a tool within the context of domestic competition among courts of vari-ous ranks. This tool is likely to be used by inferior courts against the interests of their own national supreme courts, so as to increase or protect their own jurisdiction rights against the national hierarchy. As a consequence, a further role for the ECJ in regard to its relationship with national courts is to provide inferior courts with a protection against possibly pre-emptive behaviour exerted by higher courts. This again is consistent with the competitive logic that is central to this chapter. This at first sight unexpected role simply corresponds to a shift in the jurisdiction level where competition occurs.

4.4.5   The Consequences of Judicial Innovation on European Integration

Altogether, judicial behaviour appears as a forward-thrusting force toward increased European integration. That result is also pointed out in judicial empowerment theory.[8] In the latter, courts adopt cooperative strategies leading to their 'reciprocal empowerment' (Burley and Mattli, 1993, p. 64). By contrast, in our framework, the movement toward legal integration does not derive from such collusive strategies, nor from any 'complicit relationship between the ECJ and the national courts', as Stone Sweet and Brunell (1998, p. 69) put it. On the contrary, it results from competition for judicial rights on domestic legal markets. There, the incentive structures facing national and European judges push them to innovate so as to adapt their production. As long as the demand is in favour of integration, the judicial strategies will strengthen the integration process.

CONCLUSION

We have developed an analysis of European integration based upon judicial innovation. Whereas the mainstream law and economics literature concentrates on individual incentives to produce decisions, we focus on the courts' incentive to innovate in order to gain jurisdiction rights, according to whether they are in a monopoly or in a challenger position in the legal market. We highlight the effects of the market structure on innovating strategies. More precisely, the analysis points out that the innovating behaviour of courts affects the market conditions on which they operate and is in turn affected by these market conditions. Moreover, the analysis indicates that under some conditions the judicial competition occurring between the European Court of Justice and domestic courts pushes in the direction of enhanced integration.

NOTES

1.   Courts could be assumed to compete for rents. Such a rent-seeking approach is nevertheless not entirely convincing. As most of these models still consider the rent as exogenous, they fail to take the process of judicial innovation into account. They presumably could be made more

relevant by considering the judicial innovation as an available instrument for competing courts to increase the size of the rent. This point is close to the argument developed in the chapter.

2. Neo-functionalism assumes that the European integration process has been mastered by the European Community and has resulted in a transfer of competence from the member-states to the European institutions. See a presentation in Stone Sweet and Brunell (1998) and Stone Sweet (2000).

3. Breton (1996) emphasized the importance of legitimacy and support (chapter 5) in his analysis of governmental systems. According to Salmon (1995), the increase in the European Commission's responsibilities at the expense of national governments and bureaucracies may be explained by the preferences of a majority of voters, since 'democratic governments cannot depart over extended periods of time and on essential issues from the wishes of a majority of voters' (p. 292).

4. Behaviours intended to preserve existing production rights are close to the rent-defending principle analysed in some rent-seeking models. Despite the very different context, they also present an analogy with the situation in France during World War Two. Indeed, the competition between the German authorities and the French bureaucracy still in place despite the occupation of the country led 'some high-level bureaucrats to insist in doing jobs that the German were offering to do themselves, and in particular to participate actively in the arrest and deportation of Jews'. This 'genuine and somewhat absurd concern, verging on the obsessional' of some French bureaucrats intended to '[safeguard] as much as possible of the sovereignty of the French State over the whole French territory, even or especially when that territory was occupied by German troops' (Salmon, 2001).

5. However, in contradiction to some practices that can be observed on traditional markets, the jurisdiction rights must be realized and exerted. In practice, thus, the counterpart of the prohibition to make decisions in the absence of the relevant production right is the obligation to make the decision when granted with it. In other words, when seized by a litigant, the competent court must make a decision on the case. This judicial obligation prohibits 'sleeping patents'.

6. However, this assumption of no accumulation of knowledge (or no learning by doing) contrasts with the assumption made in most of the models dealing with the production of precedents, according to which there is an accumulation of former legal capital (the current outcome depends on the past experience). See for example Landes and Posner (1976) for an analogy with capital formation models.

7. See Stone Sweet and Brunell (1998) for a statistical analysis of preliminary references. See also Weiler (1991, pp. 2419 et seq.), Shapiro (1992) and Arnull (1994).

8. For a presentation of the judicial empowerment theory, see Burley and Mattli (1993), Shapiro and Stone (1994), Stone Sweet and Caporaso (1998), Stone Sweet (2000).

REFERENCES

Arnull, A. (1990), 'Does the Court of Justice have inherent jurisdiction?', *Common Market Law Review*, **27**, 683–708.

Arnull, A. (1994), 'Judging the new Europe', *European Law Review*, **19**(1), 3–15.

Beath, John, Y. Katsoulacos and D. Ulph (1989), 'The game-theoretic analysis of innovation: a survey', *Bulletin of Economic Research*, **41**(3), 163–84.

Breton, Albert (1996), *Competitive Governments: An Economic Theory of Politics and Public Finance*, Cambridge: Cambridge University Press.

Burley, Anne-Marie and Walter Mattli (1993), 'Europe before the Court: a political theory of legal integration', *International Organization*, **47**(1), 41–76.

Caillosse, Jacques (2000), 'Le droit administratif français saisi par la concurrence?', *L'Actualité Juridique – Droit Administratif*, 20/2/2000, 99–103.

Gilbert, R.J. and D.M. Newbery (1982), 'Preemptive patenting and the persistence of monopoly', *American Economic Review*, **72**(3), 515–26.

Keohane, Robert and Stanley Hoffman (1990), 'Conclusions: Community Politics and Institutional Change', in W. Wallace (ed.), *The Dynamics of European Integration*, London: Pinter.

Landes, William M. and Richard A. Posner (1976), 'Legal precedent, a theoretical and empirical analysis', *Journal of Law and Economics*, 249–313.

Reinganum, J.F. (1985), 'Innovation and industry evolution', *The Quarterly Journal of Economics*, Feb., 81–99.

Salmon, Pierre (1995), 'Nations Conspiring Against Themselves: An Interpretation of European Integration', in A. Breton, G. Galeotti, P. Salmon and R. Wintrobe (eds), *Nationalism and Rationality*, Cambridge: Cambridge University Press, pp. 290–311.

Salmon, Pierre (2001), 'Extremism and Monomania', in A. Breton, G. Galeotti, P. Salmon and R. Wintrobe (eds), *Political Extremism and Rationality*, Cambridge: Cambridge University Press, forthcoming.

Shapiro, Martin (1992), 'The European Court of Justice', in *Euro-Politics. Institutions and Policy Making in the 'New' European Community*, Washington, DC: Brookings Institution, pp. 123–56.

Shapiro, M. Martin and Alec Stone (1994), 'The new constitutional politics of Europe', *Comparative Political Studies*, **26**(4), 397–420.

Simon, D. (1997), *Le Système Juridique Communautaire*, Paris: PUF.

Stein, Eric (1981), 'Lawyers, judges and the making of a transnational constitution', *American Journal of International Law*, **75**, 1–27.

Stone Sweet, A. (2000), *Governing with Judges: Constitutional Politics in Europe*, Oxford: Oxford University Press.

Stone Sweet, Alec and Thomas L. Brunell (1998), 'The European Court and the national courts: a statistical analysis of preliminary references, 1961–95', *Journal of European Public Policy*, **5**(1), 66–97.

Stone Sweet, Alec and J. Caporaso (1998), 'La Cour de Justice et l'intégration Européenne', *Revue Française de Science Politique*, **48**(2), 195–244.

Tirole, Jean (1995), *The Theory of Industrial Organization*, Cambridge, MA; London: MIT Press.

Weiler, Joseph H.H. (1991), 'The transformation of Europe', *Yale Law Journal*, **100**, 2403–83.

Wincott, Daniel (1995), 'The role of law or the rule of the Court of Justice? An 'institutional' account of judicial politics in the European Community', *Journal of European Public Policy*, **2**(4), 583–602.

PART TWO

Harmonization in Practice

5. European Union and public utility: a virtuous grouping? Lessons from the reorganization of Corsican external transport

Thierry Garcia and Xavier Peraldi

The structure of the European Union is often perceived as one that questions the principle of public utility, at least in the way it is traditionally viewed in France, where the phrase 'French public utility' (Valette, 2000) has a recognized, different meaning. In its public report of 1994, the Council of State stressed that 'Europe does not institute proceedings against public utility: it does worse; it obfuscates the concepts of public utility and the existence of the public utilities'. The fears expressed by the Council of State were founded on conflicting differences in the French and European approaches toward public utility. The two approaches seem to be basically opposed to each other concerning their priorities in criteria for fairness and efficiency in how the missions of public utility are determined. This resulting antagonism affects not only the objectives of public utility, but also the practical methods of achieving them.

In spite of these obvious differences, an analysis of the French and European approaches toward public utility in the transport sector seems likely to correct this perception of conflict. In fact, by observing the way in which the two approaches have developed during recent years it is possible to detect a marked convergence in their approaches.

This chapter supports an attenuation of the disparities of the two approaches toward equity and efficiency, and proposes appropriate action that can be taken by authorities and the public. Such action would not be uniform, as it would be subject to the characteristics of the transport sector and on the influence of European Union regulations with which it is associated. However, it shows that compromises can be made to define a European model of public utility based on the principle of citizenship (Section 5.2).

The reorganization of Corsica's external public transport provides an excellent practical illustration of the convergence of the French and European approaches to public utility. Following the restructuring of air transport in

1999, the regional public authorities turned their attention to maritime transport during 2000. Its restructuring involved the change from a system structured around public action and the monopolistic principle of exploitation, to a system based on the market and competition. However, it does not seem to address the issue of quality of service, which until then had been asked of the users, particularly the internal users. At the same time the new organization appeared able to reduce the collective cost of the services of Corsican external transport. Far from rejecting public utility, the reorganization in process seems to perpetuate it.

5.1 SYSTEMS OF PUBLIC UTILITY IN OPPOSITION

The basic requirement of a public utility activity is that it meets a need considered to be essential for the public, and that this is satisfactorily available to the whole of the population. Thus the activities of public utility are of a common interest to all members of the community and surpass the concerns of the individual. On this basis the recognition of an activity as a public utility depends in part on objective factors: the intrinsic characteristics of the activity and the needs that it aims to satisfy. But for another, undoubtedly more significant part, this recognition depends on the way society thinks of the State and collective action. More precisely, the relationship between the individual and their community conditions the nature, and the extent, of the effort that the community will agree to engage in for the benefit of its most underprivileged members.

Historical, cultural, political and even technological contexts are essential determinants of the contents of public utilities and the methods to implement them, as Le Mestre (2000) remarkably showed. In fact, they will condition the way in which society conceives the common interest, how it arbitrates between the criteria of equity and efficiency and how it defines the respective missions of the state (Section 5.1.2) and the market (Section 5.1.3). When the first steps toward closer European union began more than 40 years ago the various elements of these contexts were very different among the partner States. In fact, the international community in gestation had specific characteristics that distinguished it from its member States. Consequently it is hardly astonishing to note that the French and German systems of public utility are based on different, even opposite, founders' principles (Section 5.1.1).

5.1.1 Different Conceptions of the Common Interest

The will to satisfy common interest constitutes the foundation of public utility, but the concept of common interest is difficult to appreciate. Without saying it is flimsy (Wolfelsperger 1996), we must recognize that it does not have a precise and stable definition. Admittedly, it refers to the utility or the satisfaction of the whole of the components of the society (consumers, producers, State), but it does not say anything about the way in which this interest must be evaluated, or on the manner that conflicts of interest between the various components must be settled. As Laffont says about the European approach to public utility: 'According to the significance which one wants to put behind the vague words of common interests of the Community and service of common economic interest, one can justify all and anything' (1994, p. 345).

For the sake of clarity one usually associates the supply of public utility with several practical requirements: continuity, mutability and equality. Though these principles have a relatively easy perception, they lend themselves only with difficulty to an operational interpretation. Thus, as Henry notes: 'Interpreted in a literal way, these principles would mean for example, that at any place a train must stop any time and that it must be for free' (1994, p. 28). For these reasons the integration of activities in the field of public utility cannot be based on objective criteria. In fact, the concept of common interest constitutes a social compromise and as Bauby and Boual (1993) indicate 'Each public utility is the result of a particular historical, political, and social process original'. This social compromise is necessarily dependent on temporal and geographical contexts, and the current perception of common interest is consequently quite different from that which prevailed at the beginning of the century. Also, at a given time, the perception of common interest in one country is not identical to that held in another.

Not long ago, Martinand (1995) noted that in the political culture of the European Community, the 'common will' is a concept without meaning. In the absence of a distinctly European definition of the concept of common interest, those principles that do exist are based on the conceptions retained in the member States. As Gazin (1998) specifies, 'the formation of the Community common interest is carried out in two steps: collected at the national level, the common interests will have to go through the Community filter of the article 90§2 to become interests recognised by Community legislation'. This 'communautarization' of the separate national philosophies rejected the more extreme conceptions of the common interest followed in some member States, and European logic moved toward an intermediate course between the minimalist and the maximalist approaches to the common interest.

Although being strongly inspired by it, the European system is not completely comparable with the Anglo-Saxon tradition, which trusts the private economic actors to determine what common interests conform to their own interest, and uses the invisible hand to get this behaviour and the common interest to coincide (Gazin 1998). European logic seems to recognize that satisfying the needs of private actors will not fulfil the more general socially useful needs. It also clearly marks its distance from the French concept, which entirely trusts the State to define the common interest and to undertake the necessary action to satisfy it. Justification and strict measurements of control must systematically accompany public action when it is deemed necessary.

5.1.2 The French System: the State in the Name of Equality

Traditionally the French system of public utility is based on the extensive involvement of government authorities in the organization of the activities concerned. This approach reflects a cultural vision of social relations: the community of citizens is embodied in the Republican State, which has sole responsibility for the legitimacy of the indivisible common will. Public authority is legitimized through the services it renders (Martinand 1995, p. 25) and, within this framework, public utility is regarded as an instrument of national sovereignty (Chaltiel, 1998). The market, which is based on the interests of the individual, is presumed to be indifferent to the interests of society at large and thus is weak when it deals with developing non-profitable, although socially useful, activities. As Rachline (1996, p. 99) indicates, the market is the place for the expression of short-term interests and therefore reveals the collective preference rather than the common interest. The collective preference fulfils the wishes of the consumers at a given time, without automatic consideration of future evolutions.

Public intervention is justified first for reasons of equity. Because their purpose is to satisfy needs considered fundamental to society, public utilities must be provided to the entire population under equitable conditions. This refers to considerations of social justice and, in a broader sense, to the expression of solidarity between all constituents of the society. In such instances, the supply of public utilities is considered a means of fighting exclusion and reinforcing social cohesion. Very often, the principle of equity is interpreted as providing equal treatment for the users, i.e. whatever their individual situation, the members of a society should benefit from identical operating conditions – the same quality of service and same level of costs.

To satisfy these conditions the French system creates or chooses companies through public statute to run the public utility and places them in a monopolistic situation. The use of public statute is warranted by economic as well as political considerations, in that the State must appease its need for legitimacy at the same time as it secures total control of the public utility. Justification of the monopoly centres in particular on its ability to authorize a tariff system of equalization, allowing a redistribution between users (cross subsidies). A monopoly also prevents competing companies from exploiting, or 'creaming off', the most profitable segments of the market, and depriving the government appointed provider of the public utility of the resources to follow a policy of equalization (Perrot, 1998).

From a theoretical point of view, a public utility is also supposed to offer guarantees of efficiency. When the activities in question are considered natural monopolies characterized by important economies of scale and economies of scope, the supply of service by only one operator can be more efficient and less expensive than if it were carried out by several companies. It is generally estimated that the activities of networks show the characteristics of natural monopoly (Laffont, 1994). Traditionally, public authorities were led to adopt this point of view through several economic considerations such as the weight of investments, the existence of increasing outputs and the complementarity of the activities.

The idea of providing territorial continuity to Corsica as it exists in continental France corresponds perfectly to this concept of public utility, in which the islanders would be able to travel to the continent without obstacles, and at costs comparable to those on the continent.[1] Moreover, it aims to reduce the burden of transport costs in supplying the island with goods. According to this logic of intervention, the territorial continuity was extended to Corsica to enable a monopoly to exploit the links between it and the French mainland. Government authorities entrusted public companies with the responsibility to provide transport as a public utility according to a schedule of conditions.[2] Thus, government defined the frequency of service, the seat capacity offered, the level of tariffs and the amount of financial compensation offered to the transport companies in return for the administrative costs of exploitation. The monopoly services provided by Air Inter and later by CCM for air transport, that of the SNCM for the maritime transport of passengers and CMM for the maritime transport of freight, were formulated to help the transport companies make their fleets as profitable as possible.

5.1.3   The European System: The Market in the Name of Efficiency

The French concept of public utility is in radical opposition to the general European conception. Certainly the latter is not easy to define since it is determined by the actions of multiple entities, in particular the European Commission and the European Court of Justice, the first being more restrictive than the second due to its role of protector of European Union treaties. Beyond this disparity, the EU approach tends to lean toward the principle that a free market constitutes the best possible organization. This economic logic is perfectly coherent with the idea of the large European market and its corollary, the removal of intracommunity barriers to exchanges. According to this prospect, any public intervention in the economy, or any regulation (particularly one that would establish a monopoly), constitutes a distortion of competition. In fact, compared to the French concept, there is a kind of inversion of the presumption of efficiency. Today, competition profits from a presumption of efficiency and the obstacles and exemptions from competition suffer, on the contrary, from a presumption of inefficiency.

Companies responsible for the services of a common economic interest are subject to the rules of the Treaty of Rome, in particular to the rule of competition. Exemptions to these rules are only possible when the latter is likely to become an obstacle to achieving the mission of public utility. In the transport sector, the logic of competition adopted by the Community authorities orders the management of these activities in an increasingly precise way. In air transport policy (rule 2408/92) as well as in maritime transport policy (rule 3577/92) the process of liberalization, although having different degrees of development, is now relatively well established. In both areas, the European approach affirms its confidence in the efficiency of competitive play and defends the idea of a free access to markets. Since 1 April 1997 for air transport and 1 January 1999 for maritime transport, all EU-based transport companies can compete for business on any European domestic travel route. Profits resulting from competitiveness between companies, lower costs and prices to users, and increases in the frequency of the provision of transport are many potential effects associated with the suppression of monopolies.

Compared with government regulation of a public utility, free action in the market has an undeniable advantage with regard to efficiency, especially if one considers that the profits of efficiency result from the economies of scale and scope, technical innovations, performance of the management and commercial dynamism. By departing from the imposition of monopolistic policies on an activity, it is supposed that the arrival of competitors must constitute a strong incentive for lowering the costs and thus lowering the prices (Perrot 1998). Free competition is also supposed to reveal relevant information and to direct the choice of the economic actors correctly. In a broader way, the requirement for profitability incumbent on competing companies prevents them from obtaining undue advantages or disguised revenues for the benefit of a privileged few: consumers, shareholders or salaried employees (Martinand 1995, p. 34). From this perspective one can argue that the control of public utilities by the State is accompanied by many factors of high inefficiency and cost overruns. These can also come from the failure of the public authority in its capacity of regulation and of output. The theory of Economic Regulation (Stigler 1971) and that of bureaucracy (Niskanen 1971) provide numerous arguments likely to support this analysis.

With regard to equity, free competition can be less satisfactory. The market operates on principles of decentralized decisions that cater to the needs of the individual. According to Puel (1995), one can argue that this also encourages social solidarity, since it multiplies the wealth in order to facilitate growth of the economy, to satisfy the consumers and to meet the needs of the population (ibid., p. 101). In a more convincing way, one must note that the market ensures distribution of wealth on a coherent and transparent basis. Thus, contrary to the concept of equalization, which can produce regressive redistributive effects (the application of the same tariff to customers in different social conditions, in fact, penalizes the customers with weaker purchasing power), the market tends to bring the tariff closer to its cost of supply. Thus the tariff applied to each user of public utility can be perfectly justified on an objective basis.

It is accepted that if free competition is allowed it cannot satisfy the requirements for equity in all circumstances. Thus, in transport it admits that on certain routes there is a need to impose obligations of public utility (OPU) and even the need for a monopolistic[3] offer. But in each instance the acceptance of distortions to free exploitation is conditional on precise and rigorous arguments by the national authorities.[4] Within this framework, the EU authorities accept the public financing of certain services of transport by national authorities with the express condition that this does not produce a distortion in the competition.

In terms of collective cost, the organization of Corsican external transport seems to have been, during the past 25 years, particularly expensive. From 150 million francs in 1976, the public cost of territorial continuity exceeded more than 950 million francs in 1999. The extent of the public utility activities and the high costs of operating some of the transport services can explain some of the rise in the public contribution (Peraldi 1999). After introduction of territorial continuity to Corsica the supply of transport services continuously increased, with many links not proving financially viable due to a frequency of service exceeding demand and tariff reductions to the residents. At the same time, the costs of supplying the transport service were not well controlled, with prohibitive operating costs and some irrational investment choices.[5] As a consequence, a reorganization of the public utility of Corsican external transport became necessary. Its evolution allows us to discern a convergency of French and European Union concepts of public utility.

5.2 CONCEPTIONS OF PUBLIC UTILITY IN A PROCESS OF CONCILIATION

If one examines the recent evolution of the French and European regulations on public utility, a process of convergence can be discerned, especially in the transport sector. It is partly due to the way EU authorities regulate the sector. The regulation of public utilities comes simultaneously from the general measures of the European Community and from measures specific to the sector activities. Implementation of controls was at a variable pace according to the type of activity. The telecommunications sector was subject to, at the European level, an important and relatively early legal evolution. On the other hand, the transport sector was the subject of more limited action by EU authorities.[6]

Beyond sectoral specifics it is possible to see a conciliation between the French and European approaches to public utility in the form of a double convergent evolution. The French regulations on public utility, which were largely unchanged between 1970 and 1980, have been altered during the past few years (particularly in telecommunications) in a way that indicates the French attitude is gradually relinquishing its policy on the omniscience of the State and tends to be inspired more by the concerns of economic efficiency (Section 5.2.2). At the same time, the EU approach expresses much less distrust towards public intervention and tends to recognize some of its social virtues (Section 5.2.3). Since the decrees of Corbeau (ECJ/19/5/1993) and Commune of Almelo (ECJ/27/4/1994), the European system allows restrictions of competition when the economic equilibrium of a company responsible for common interest is compromised. In fact, the bringing together of the French and European systems seems to be based on an increasingly similar definition of the common interest,, rather than the former national specificities (Section 5.2.1).

5.2.1   A Convergent Perception of the Common Interest

Increasingly, EU logic considers the concept of common interest by disassociating it from references to the States and by linking it to the position of the citizens. As a result, in the concept of public utility the user moves from being a simple purchaser of goods to the role of an individual having basic rights. The progressive formation of an EU principle of common interest (Pignon 1998) freed from national references seems to be explained by several wide-ranging phenomena from the various fields already mentioned regarding the determination of the principle of common interest. They are economic, political and technological, and relate equally to the worldwide context as to the more strictly European context.

From the economic point of view, one cannot ignore that evolution of the international context is marked by the geographical diversification of markets and the worldwide expansion of the economy. This implies that it is now necessary to conceive the markets and their functions globally and also implies that the majority of companies can no longer be restricted to development only in the domestic market. On this basis, suppliers of public utilities have sometimes driven official authorities at national level to reform the institutional framework in which they evolved. Their argument has been that, in the European and world economic context, this framework constituted a yoke which was extremely prejudicial and thus, in the long term, dangerous (Thatcher 1997).

From a political perspective, the process of economic and monetary integration constrained EU member states to adopt more harmonious and coherent economic policies. Important disparities still exist in this field, but requirements such as those relating to the pact of stability, impose a convergence of the various States' positions. Thus the need to control public deficits requires authorities to control the cost of financing public utilities.

Accordingly, and in a more general way, one can argue that the treaty of Maastricht offers new opportunities for convergence (Bauby 1997; Bauchet 1996), organized around the ideas of European citizenship, consumer protection, economic and social cohesion or opening up of peripheral regions. In this spirit, it suggests the launch of joint projects such as the development of trans-European networks. These elements contribute to greater consistency in a unified Europe and allow it to develop its own values gradually, integrating national differences. In such a way, it can lead the process of rebalancing the system of competition and to establishing a European concept of public utility.

Finally, from a technological point of view, innovation has transformed the organization of certain activities, in particular networks. Technological progress has encouraged the appearance of new products and services to meet changing market needs, to increase productivity in the supply of considered goods and services, and to introduce flexibility in management and regulation. In the air transport sector, the development of computerized reservation systems contributed to the growth of agreements between service providers and the creation of new spoke and hub transport networks. Equipment processing also made a greater diversification in the tariffs possible. In maritime transport, the introduction of high speed ships supported the supply of systems of modulation because of the increased frequency in traffic.[7]

Even if a precise evaluation of each of these evolutionary factors is not possible, it clearly seems that within Europe, despite some national diversities that persist, a common approach on the concept of public utility is emerging. It is built on the idea that certain activities must be accessible to everybody for the economic, social, territorial and cultural cohesion of the society. This manner of thought rises directly from the belief in a European citizenship and from the will to forge EU solidarity. Support for convergence lends itself to the idea that these activities must be an exception to commercial logic and must be managed according to specific criteria. The idea has gradually emerged that public utility activities can be complementary to both the State and the market if the criteria of equity and efficiency are taken into account. In the European approach, public utility is no longer the instrument of state power, but an expression of the needs of its citizens.

5.2.2 Complementarity between the State and Market

The organization of European public utilities that is developing appears able to combine the action of the State and the market in a harmonious way. EU authorities seem to have become aware, particularly from the point of view of social cohesion, that the market is not a panacea. Alone, it cannot act in favour of the common interest and sometimes its actions need to be supplemented by means of public intervention. While affirming free access to the market, the European Commission estimates that this principle should not be an obstacle to the application by member states of certain restrictive clauses, in so far as their need is clearly proven. French authorities have become aware of the benefits of competition in terms of dynamism and good economic information. The softening of what were previously opposing positions makes it possible to consider a European scheme of organization or public utility based simultaneously on the State and the market. In such an agenda, the goal of public utility should not be to replace the action of the market but rather to compensate for its gaps. This scheme can be outlined by using the principle of obligations of public utility, by defining its contents and by specifying the means of financing it.

When a market cannot satisfy the needs of the citizens by itself, its operation can be constrained by obligations of public utility (OPU) which are based on the principle of subsidiarity. Member states are authorized to manage the supply of public utilities with respect to certain criteria. This imposition of OPU can be inserted into a concessionary system (and thus a monopoly of public utilities) and also into an open market system. In the case of a concession, the European Commission requires that there be an obstacle to achieving the service of common interest either because its operation becomes materially impossible, or because the financial balance of the service is threatened by competition. To allow the establishment of a monopoly of public utility the Court of Justice specifies that it must take account of the economic conditions in which the company is placed, in particular the costs it must bear and the regulations to which it is subjected. In addition such agreements must conform to certain principles of organization decided by the European commission.[8] In the case of a market opened to competition, competitive play remains the rule, but before being able to enter the market companies must submit a preliminary request revealing various facts, including those relevant to OPU.

In each area considered, intensive public intervention does not completely eliminate competition. To some extent the OPU replaces the laws of the market by determining the conditions of prices and quantities to be proposed, without changing them completely. In situations where a monopoly of public utility is created, though competition is no longer practised in the market, its effect is considered prior to setting up the market. The selection of the public utility supplier involves invitations to tender, where the candidates to produce the public utility propose how they will formulate the service based on the market while it was competitive (Jacquemin 1994). The principles of free entry to the market and free exploitation within legal limits are thus preserved, each potential supplier being able to try to exploit his comparative advantages as well as possible.

When considering the financial aspect of public action, it is important to recall that the treaty establishing the European Union prohibits aid granted by individual States when it affects exchanges between member states. The prohibition includes aid in any form that distorts or threatens to distort competition by supporting specific companies or production. However, in the emerging European approach, public aid is compatible if it aims to refund certain constraints inherent in the concept of public utility. In such cases, the determination of the compensation must be made on the basis of expenses and receipts. In a complementary way, the EU approach authorizes payment to recipients of social aid, provided that it is granted without discrimination (as in aid to residents, to students or to handicapped people).

The reorganization of Corsican territorial continuity makes a broad use of the various methods of public intervention accepted by the EU authorities, and the use of a certain formula for one industry does not necessarily mean it will be used for another. Air links are now open subject to the constraints of the OPU whereas sea links require a concession of public utility for their basic service. Complementary services should remain open to competition but be subject to the OPU. The authorities have approved various types of government aid such as public subsidization of companies providing a basic maritime service and aid to the users of other services subject to the constraints of the OPU. In this latter case there are transport companies which receive a subsidy calculated on the number of passengers and which is reflected in the cost of transport.

5.2.3 Balance Between Equity and Efficiency

Often the questions relevant to the future of public utilities arise in arbitration when the criteria of equity and efficiency arise, and any concession to the second to the detriment of the first is perceived as an attack on the industry. The emerging policies seem able to refute the relevance of this kind of approach. Not only can the search for efficiency be carried out without neglecting the need for equity, but also to some extent, the search for equity cannot be completely appreciated by disregarding the financial considerations.

The analysis of an activity on the criterion of equity must also refer to considerations of justice. However, as Minc (1994) indicates, 'there is no more absolute justice that absolute equity. The universality of justice does not exist.

It depends on the 'historical moment', on perception of the moment and on the evolution of the society'. Though the French system of public utility considered equity in terms of equal treatment for many years, it now seems to consider this criterion in terms of discrimination. In other words, among the observable inequalities in a society, some are unjust and must be fought, but others are right and must be preserved. For example, by referring to Rawls' studies (1985), one can consider the inequalities that ultimately benefit the most underprivileged people and do not affect the basic rights of others are justifiable. The principle of equality that results from this is more a principle of absence of discrimination rather than a principle of absolute equality. 'It means that identical situations must be treated in the same manner, but not at all that two consumers who induce different costs to the producer of public utility must pay the same price' (Laffont 1994). The EU idea of public utility rests on this principle of non-discrimination between the users; it respects the right of access and, compared with the services provided, assures identical treatment for everybody.

In a complementary way it is appropriate to use the criterion of equity, and its relevance to social solidarity when considering the effort needed for a society to become engaged in helping its most underprivileged members. This principle necessarily leads to controlling the costs of the supply of public utilities. As Cohen and Henry emphasize (1997, p. 24) 'a public intervention in the name of the contribution of public utilities to the exercise of the basic rights of the person or in the names of the correction of inefficiencies of the market or in the name of social cohesion, is legitimate only as far as it uses means which are adapted to the aims in view and whose costs should be controlled'. From this point of view, one can even consider that research into equity and efficiency work in a complementary way. The more the supply of public utility is carried out under efficient conditions, the more the results of this action of social solidarity are amplified.

The reorganization of the system of territorial continuity seems able to reconcile both the requirements for equity and efficiency. In spite of a few inaccuracies which still affect the new system (especially in the field of maritime transport), it seems that it can guarantee a supply of satisfactory transport comparable to that which prevailed before under conditions of less cost. Indeed, in accordance with the various European regulations, the Corsican public authorities decided to define the OPU (i.e. the frequencies and tariffs) which seem close to what they were in the past. If strong competition became established on one or the other of the relevant transport links, the tariff levels set for the users could even decrease. As a condition for following the OPU, companies would receive a reduced public subsidy. Therefore, the collective cost of the system seems capable of decreasing compared to previous levels.

5.3 CONCLUSION

The progressive character of the European concept of common interest, freed from State control, makes it possible to consider the definition of a public utility as it relates to the principle of citizenship. Though the evolution we have observed in this chapter is incomplete and does not cover all areas, we have seen how it is strongly dependent on the characteristics of the transport sector and on the level of development of the European regulations that relate to it, in particular the rules of competition. One cannot ignore that in the Treaty of Rome the expression of public utility was only used for the activities of transport. However, events that have taken place in that industry make it possible to see how similar compromises can be reached in other sectors to define a European model of public utility that reconciles national and EU requirements. Such an evolution is possible only if certain obstacles can be removed, most of them of a political and institutional nature which requires standardization (Peraldi-Leneuf 1996).

The lack of a formal EU approach to public utility explains the need for standardization. Such an approach creates a balance between the position adopted by the European Commission and that defended by the Court of Justice. The dialectical game between the two European institutions requires a considerable degree of adaptability. According to the circumstances, the Court of Justice can be brought in to interpret and modulate any restrictive principles adopted by the Commission. The best illustration of this dual approach is provided by the coexistence of the concepts of universal public utility, taken in reference by the Commission, and that of the economic service of common interest, taken in reference by the Court of Justice. The first of these two concepts expressed a will to limit the field of the public utility activities to the supply of a minimal service defined at a certain level of quality and at an accessible price for any user (Debène 1998). This universal public utility seems to be both a transfiguration of public utility, and a formula for public utility since it reaches a compromise between the dictates of competition and the necessities of the common interest (Bailleul 2000). The second concept seems to consider a wider field, taking into account the collective needs, which are both economic and political, or social. It can be compared with innovations in public utility since it requires a clear organization and evidence of public utility (Rainaud 1999).

Such diversity in the perception of public utility appears to constitute a potential source of instability and inconsistency. Consequently, it is desirable that an effort of standardization is engaged at the European level to give a more rigorous base to the concept of public utility. In fact, one can consider that this standardization is all the more necessary since it seems to be the essential ingredient to the principle of subsidiarity adopted as the definition of public utilities. Indeed, the influence of special interest groups or lobbyists can lead the local public authorities to estimate incorrectly the need for public utility. Then, in order to produce accurate decisions, the principle of subsidiarity must be framed by specific regulation. The setting of precise standards of public utility by EU authorities must be able to support the requirements and to facilitate public decision making. The absence of such standards in the maritime transport sector makes it difficult to define clearly the public utility of Corsican transport. In order for standardization to be completely satisfactory, it should take into consideration the concept of common interest.

NOTES

1. The system of Corsican territorial continuity was set up in 1976. Initially it only applied to maritime transport, then from 1979 it was extended to air transport.
2. In its initial organization, the system of Corsican territorial continuity chose the principle of concession for a long time. Thus, from 1976, the maritime company SNCM obtained a concession for 25 years.
3. The links towards an airport serving a peripheral area or an area of development and the links towards a regional airport which are characterized by less important traffic can benefit from European principles of limited competition.
4. The arguments in favour of a restriction of free competition must be mainly based on the lack of importance of the traffic and on the vital character of links for the economic development of the areas concerned.
5. According to recent studies we can note that the maritime company SNCM suffered from employing too large a workforce, from not adapting the remuneration of the crew and from a fleet with an excessive capacity.
6. As Thatcher says (1997), 'because of the regulations adopted in 1962, the European Commission could not apply articles 85 and 86 to the sector of transport but was obliged to comply with detailed rules of competition which were specific to the transport sector'.
7. The high speed ships, introduced just five years ago, attract approximately 30 per cent of the maritime traffic of passengers between the French continent and Corsica.
8. Among the principles concerned with a concession of public utility are: the recourse to a European invitation to tender; the level of compensation such as the principal criterion of selection; the fact that the concession will be limited to three years; the clarity of the information provided by the companies.

BIBLIOGRAPHY

Bailleul, D. (2000), 'Le service universel, futur service public?', *Revue de la Recherche Juridique*, **XXV-83**, 2000-2, 561–75.
Bauchet, P. (1996), *Les transport de l'Europe*, Paris: Economica.
Bauby, P. (1997), 'Services publics: des modèles nationaux à une conception européenne', *Politiques et Management Public*, **15**(3), September, 107–22.
Bauby, P. and J.-C. Boual (1993), *Les Services Publics au Défi de l'Europe*, Paris: Editions ouvrières.
Becker, G.S. (1983), 'A theory of competition among pressure groups for political influence', *Quarterly Journal of Economics*, August, **3**, 371–400.

Caves, D.W., L.R. Christensen and M.W. Tretheway (1984), 'Economies of density versus economies of scale: why trunk and local service airlines costs differ', *Rand Journal of Economics*, **15**, 471–89.

Chaltiel, F. (1998), *'La souveraineté de l'Etat et l'Union européenne: l'exemple français'*, Thèse pour le Doctorat en droit, Grenoble II.

Cohen, E. (1996), 'Ne pas confondre service public avec service du public', *Chroniques Economiques*, 3, 15 March, 84–91.

Cohen, E. and C. Henry (1997), *Service Public, Secteur Public*, Conseil d'Analyse Economique, Paris: La documentation française.

Debène, M. (1996), 'Sur le service universel: renouveau du service public ou nouvelle mystification', *Actualité Juridique Droit Administratif*, 3, 20 March.

Eckert, G. (1998), 'Les Modes de Financement du Service Public dans l'Environnement Concurrentiel', in D. Simon and R. Kovar (eds) *Services Publics et Communauté Européenne: entre l'intérêt général et le marché*, Actes du colloque de Strasbourg: La documentation française.

Gazin, F. (1998), 'La Conception Communautaire de l'Intérêt Général dans le Droit des Services Publics', in D. Simon and R. Kovar (eds) *Services Publics et Communauté Européenne: entre l'intérêt gén´ral et la marché*, Actes due colloque de Strasbourg: La documentation français.

Grard, L. (1998), 'Les Obligations de Service Public et la transport Aérien', in D. Simon and R. Kovar (eds) *Services Publics et Communauté Européenne: entre l'intérêt général et le marché*, Actes du colloque de Strasbourg: La documentation française.

Hardy, J. (1996), 'Le service public en question', *Politiques et Management Public*, **14**(3), September, 45–66.

Henry, C. (1994), 'Concurrence et obligations de service public dans une perspective européenne', *Réalités Industrielles*, October, 27–30.

Henry, C. (1997), *'Concurrence et Services Publics dans l'Union Européenne'*, Paris: PUF.

Jacquemin, A. (1994), 'Compétitivité et Intérêt Général' in Ch. Stoffaës (ed.), *L'Europe à l'Épreuve de l'Intérêt Général*, ASPE Europe, Collection ISUPE, pp. 325–32.

Laffont, J.-J. (1994), 'Service Public et théorie Économique', in Ch. Stoffaës (ed.), *L'Europe à l'Épreuve de l'intérêt général*, ASPE Europe, Collection ISUPE, pp. 333–46.

Laffont, J.-J. and J. Tirole (1991), 'The politics of government decision-making: a theory of regulatory capture', *Quarterly Journal of Economics*, **106**, 1089–127.

Le Mestre, R. (2000), 'La notion de service public dans les systèmes juridiques des etats membres de l'Union européenne', *Revue de la Recherche Juridique*, **XXV-82** 2000-1, 199–221.

Maisl, H. (1998), 'Réflexions sur la régulation des réseaux de services publics', in D. Simon and R. Kovar (eds), *Services Publics et Communauté Européenne: entre l'intérêt général et le marché*, Actes du colloque de Strasbourg: La documentation française.

Martinand, C. (1995), *La Régulation des Services Publics*, Commissariat Général du Plan, Paris: ASPE Europe.

Miart, J. (1994), 'Libéralisme et service public: l'exemple des transports aériens dans la CEE', in J.-C. Nemery (ed.), *Le Renouveau de l'Aménagement du Territoire*, Paris: DATAR, Economica, pp. 143–60.

Minc, A. (1994), *La France de l'an 2000*, Rapport du Commissariat général du Plan, Paris: La documentation française.

Niskanen, W.-J. (1971), *Bureaucracy and Representative Government*, Chicago: Aldine Atherton.

Peraldi, X. (1999), 'Le système de continuité territoriale de la Corse: coûteux, forcément coûteux', *Revue d'Economie Régionale et Urbaine*, 2, 333–52.

Peraldi-Leneuf, F. (1996), 'La politique communautaire d'harmonisation technique et de normalisation. Etude d'une nouvelle modalité de régulation?' Thèse pour le doctorat en droit, Strasbourg.

Perrot, A. (1998), 'Déréglementation et Service Universel dans les Entreprises de Réseaux', in D. Simon and R. Kovar (eds), *Services Publics et Communauté Européenne: entre l'intérêt général et le marché*, Actes du colloque de Strasbourg: La documentation française.

Pignon, S. (1998), 'La prise en compte de l'intérêt général par le droit communautaire', Thèse pour le doctorat en droit, Nice.

Puel, H. (1995), 'Les paradoxes de l'économie: l'éthique au défi', Paris: Bayard Editions.

Rachline, F. (1996), *Services Publics, Économie de marché*, Paris: Presses de la Fondation Nationale des Sciences Politiques.

Rainaud, J.-M. (1999), *La Crise du Service Public Français, Que sais-je?*, 3482, Paris: Presses Universitaires de France.

Rangeon, F. (1986), *L'Idéologie de l'Intérêt Général*, Paris: Economica.

Rawls, J. (1985), 'Justice as fairness: political, not metaphysical', *Philosophy and Public Affairs*, **14**(3), 223–51.

Simon, D. (1996), 'Les Mutations des Services Publics du fait des Contraintes du droit Communautaire', in D. Simon and R. Kovar (eds), *Services Publics et Communauté Européenne: entre l'intérêt général et le marché*, Actes du colloque de Strasbourg: La documentation française.

Stigler, G.J. (1971), 'The theory of economic regulation', *Bell Journal of Economics and Management Science*, **2**, 3–21.

Stoffaës, Ch. J.-C. Berthod and M. Feve (1995), *L'Europe: Avenir de Ferroviaire*, Paris: Edition ASPE Europe.

Subremon, A. (1999), 'Les obligations de service public dans les transports aériens', *Revue du Marché Commun et de l'Union Européenne*, 432, October, 606-12.

Thatcher, M. (1997), 'L'impact de la Communauté européenne sur la réglementation nationale: les services publics en France et en Grande-Bretagne', *Politiques et Management Public*, **15**(3), September, 141–67.

Wolfelsperger, A. (1996), 'La contribution de la théorie économique à la définition d'un concept d'utilité publique', colloque cedece – irene, Strasbourg, October.

6. The economics of harmonizing law enforcement

Nuno Garoupa

6.1   INTRODUCTION

The economic analysis of crime and criminal law is now a well-established field within the economic analysis of law. If the large body of literature surveyed by Garoupa (1997a) and Polinsky and Shavell (2000b) is not suffi-cient demonstration, a quick look at the current textbooks of law and econom-ics justifies the observation.

The proposition that crime rates respond to risks and benefits is called the deterrence hypothesis. It is an application of the theory of demand to one of the most important issues in criminal justice. The hypothesis asserts that people respond significantly to the incentives created by the criminal justice system. If so, increasing the resources that society devotes to the arrest, conviction and punishment of criminals will reduce the amount, and social costs, of crime. As many scholars note, there is a competing hypothesis that holds that criminals are not deterred by variations in the certainty and severity of punishment. Rather, this hypothesis holds that crime is caused by a complex set of socio-economic and biological factors, and that the appropriate way to reduce the amount of crime and thus lower the costs of crime is to divert resources into channels that attack these root causes of crime.

Although recent public debate has tended to frame these two hypotheses as mutually exclusive, we argue that it is more sensible to view them as comple-mentary in which case the optimal public policy for reducing crime may be a mix of deterrence and policies directed at the root causes.

Suppose that there is a particular crime that we wish to deter, say, fraud. It might be possible to eliminate fraud, or very nearly eliminate it, by having severe punishment imposed with a high probability upon offenders. However, deterring fraud in this way may run into two kinds of difficulties.

First, very harsh penalties may violate the moral and constitutional rights of criminals. The second consideration, which is our direct concern, is cost. Apprehending, prosecuting, and punishing offenders can be expensive. Policymakers will want to balance these costs against the advantages of reducing crime when making policy decisions. The optimal amount of deterrence does not eliminate crime altogether. The reason for this is that eradicating crime is costly and has a declining social benefit. Policymakers will also want to allocate their limited resources so as to achieve any given level of deterrence at least cost, that is, they will seek to achieve their goal efficiently.

The economic theory of criminal law enforcement is recent. Gary Becker's seminal paper on law enforcement dates from 1968, and most of the papers surveyed by Garoupa (1997a) and Polinsky and Shavell (2000b) have been published in the last fifteen years. Becker posits that criminals are rational utility-maximizing decision makers choosing conditions of risk. The basis of the model is the specification of the potential criminal's preferences. A given offence is committed if and only if:

$$EU = pU(y + b - f) + (1 - p)U(y + b) > U(y) \qquad (6.1)$$

where p is the probability of capture and punishment, U is utility, EU is expected utility, $y + b$ is income if undetected, $y + b - f$ income if punished, y is the certain income, and b is the gain from committing the offence. All monetary gains include psychic components such as fear, excitement, pain which are assumed to be convertible to monetary equivalents.

Becker differentiated the left side of the expression with respect to p and f concluding that the negative partial differentials show that certainty and severity of punishment deter crime.

Will the individual accept the gamble? The answer depends upon the individual's attitude to risk, the sizes of b, f and p, and the utility of the certain income from honesty. Even if the individual is risk-averse he will accept the gamble if its expected value is sufficiently large (p and f are sufficiently low, and the gain in income if undetected is sufficiently high).

Brown and Reynolds (1973) take the individual's initial income as the reference point and present a slightly different functional:

$$EU = pU(w - f) + (1 - p)U(w + b) > U(w) \qquad (6.2)$$

where p is the probability of capture and punishment, U is utility, EU is expected utility, w is the initial income, b is the criminal gain and f is the sanction. It is easily seen that both functions are equivalent.

Having specified individuals' choice, we proceed to discuss optimal enforcement. Maximization of social welfare comes out as the natural objective of public policy. The specification of the government's objective function is of some controversy, in particular the inclusion of gains from committing offences. Nevertheless, a fundamental result is implied by any cost–benefit analysis: a monetary sanction (f) should be maximal because it is a costless transfer whereas detection is costly.

Becker's high-fine–low-probability result is a seminal contribution to modern understanding of crime. Recent papers have been stimulated by Becker's stark result to investigate the circumstances in which a maximal sanction may be non-optimal. These papers extend Becker's seminal model to a variety of aspects of criminal law and law enforcement.

6.2 WHY OPTIMAL LAW ENFORCEMENT IS CONTROVERSIAL

The application of economic analysis to criminal law is based on the proposition that economic efficiency is useful for examining and designing rules and institutions. Economic efficiency, in particular social welfare maximization, is controversial.[1] Applying economic efficiency is useful in two different roles. First, there is a positive role by explaining the actual behaviour of individuals and the structure of legal norms. The second role refers to a normative analysis by suggesting how rules and institutions could be improved. Although the positive and normative role of optimal law enforcement theory can have common features, we distinguish both for the purpose of this chapter.

On the modelling of criminal behaviour, the theory faces the usual criticism of the expected utility framework and the usefulness of the assumption of economic rationality. It assumes that the deterrence hypothesis (basically no more than an application of the theory of demand) is a reasonable explanation for some crimes: people respond significantly to the deterring incentives created by the criminal justice system.

The assumption that criminals are expected utility-maximizing decision makers has been particularly criticized. Empirical contradictions between expected utility predictions and actual decisions have been found. These recent findings tend to stress that expected utility theory is not a good predictor in experimental situations. However, that does not imply that the alternative theories perform better.

A second argument is that there is a task complexity: decisions are made in a decomposed fashion using relative comparisons. Potential criminals may find optimization impossible or unduly costly. They may solve a simpler approximate optimization problem. While economists assume that criminals are rational, most psychologists and criminologists prefer to accept that criminals are, at most, 'limited' rational. 'Limited' rationality is a weaker version of rationality by which criminals are sensitive to risk and payoffs but do not combine this information optimally.

A third argument is that people manipulate beliefs: individuals have not only preferences over states of the world, but also over their beliefs of those states. Cognitive assessment of gains and losses relative to a reference point may imply that the objective function is no longer the expected utility functional.

It is true that the current economic theory of crime and punishment only very recently has started to respond to these criticisms. A more promising approach is the one proposed by Jolls, Sunstein and Thaler (1998) and Harel and Segal (1999): the behavioural approach to law and economics. Their project is an ambitious one because it blends rational theory with a psychological twist enriching the economic model.

The successfulness of the theory as a positive valid analysis depends crucially on the empirical adherence. Most studies corroborate the hypothesis that the probability of punishment, and to a lesser degree also the severity of punishment, has a deterrent effect on crime. The bulk of empirical studies consists of cross-section analysis based on macro data. Time-series and panel-data analysis based on micro surveys are less numerous. The probability and severity of punishment (fines, length of sentence, or time served) are found to have a negative effect on crime. The magnitude of the negative sign is a matter of controversy depending on the estimation method and the data used. Most time-series studies give additional support to the hypothesis that the probability of punishment has a preventive effect on crime. The results concerning the severity of punishment are somewhat less conclusive: in some studies it is not statistically different from zero.

There has been severe criticism of the policy consequences of the Becker's type of models. It has been suggested that the models have a simplistic view of the actual process of law enforcement. As a consequence of the complexity of the actual process, law enforcement cannot be a set of policy rules but is a rather discretionary set of responses to negotiation and compromise.

A related point is if maximization of social welfare is the natural objective function of public policy. Kaplow and Shavell (2001) and Polinsky and Shavell (2000b) have insisted that within welfare economics, social welfare should be the normative criteria. Moreover, it is the only objective function that respects the Pareto criteria.

It has been suggested that social welfare maximization is not the adequate criteria because it overlooks fairness and does not contemplate the possibility that policymakers are not benevolent, but rather pursue their own agenda. Potential offenders, victims and enforcers are rational agents maximizing their selfish payoff. Friedman (1999) argues that so should politicians. Social welfare is not the natural payoff of politicians. Here the rational theory of law enforcement could find in the Public Choice movement the needed help to address this problem. A possibility is that people do care about the fairness of punishment, and so the objective function of policymaker must consider the issue of fairness. As Polinsky and Shavell (2000a) discuss, fairness should be included in social welfare because individuals care about it, and not because the policymaker decides to add it. Optimal deterrence (in the classical sense) is rejected because individuals reject it, and not because the policymaker rejects it.

Many sociologists have suggested that the current economic theory of criminal law prescribes politically conservative policies. The perception of a conservative bias derives from the observation that the current economic theory seems to be more of economics of enforcement than economics of crime.[2]

The economic theory of crime and criminal law has been above all a theory of deterrence and criminal prevention. If pursuing criminal deterrence is a conservative policy then the economic theory cannot escape such label. A related point is the economic theory of criminal incapacitation (eliminating opportunity for crime *ex post*), rehabilitation (eliminating criminal motivation) and retribution. As pointed out by Polinsky and Shavell (2000b) this is still a poor area in terms of output research but with a growing empirical literature.

6.3   LESSONS CONCERNING THE EUROPEAN CONTEXT

6.3.1   Harmonization of Law Enforcement

The Schengen Agreements are now fully operational after being beset for a long time by technical problems and political pressure.[3] The agreements aim at creating a common territory without internal border controls, harmonizing rules governing the crossing of common external frontiers (creation of a uniform visa) and favouring cooperation of law enforcement agencies. Each state keeps the direction and control of operations that take up within each jurisdiction, but a permanent working group has been created. After Britain opting out, the plans to develop Europol were finally approved.

In Garoupa (1997b), I have commented on the Schengen Agreements from an economic perspective. It is well known in economics that a cooperative solution asserts a larger surplus than a non-cooperative solution. One important determinant of the cooperative solution is the spillover effect; the more interdependent jurisdictions are (the lower are transportation costs), the more likely is the success of such an agreement. This observation suggests that islands or countries with geographical discontinuities within the union have less to gain.

The elimination of internal borders favours interjurisdictional criminal mobility. Rational offenders will commit their offences where the marginal cost of one more offence is lower. This marginal cost is determined by law enforcement policies and transportation costs. This effect should lead to competition among the different jurisdictions to have a tougher law enforcement policy in order to avoid immigration of offenders. This competition produces a waste of resources because each jurisdiction ignores the loss of welfare on other jurisdictions. Therefore, a cooperative solution internalizes this externality.

However, some observations should be taken into account when implementing a cooperative solution. On one hand, some countries may be worse off in a cooperative solution. On the other hand, there are incentives to 'free-ride behaviour'.

An important point is to understand why countries have different policies before harmonization. According to our rational theory of law enforcement, there are three possible explanations: (a) individuals have different preferences with respect to committing an offence, (b) individuals have different wealth, (c) enforcement technology is different. Even if the first two explanations are possibly true, I suggest the third explanation is the one we should study. A cooperative solution does not affect the first two observations, but plays an important role in the discussion of the third.

Technological differences across countries in Europe could be explained by the difficulty of police bureaucracies in adjusting to changes.[4] Cooperation could lower adjustment costs by making access to new technologies easier, by providing more information, and by creating internal incentives for police bureaucracies to be more flexible. In the future, interjurisdictional cooperation could create competition between police bureaucracies across the union making them more efficient.

A related problem is the eventual conflict between the supranational structure (the Europol) and the local bureaucracies. Currently, it is not the case of a hierarchy of different enforcement agencies. National police forces keep the monopoly in many activities, including the direction and control of operations that take place within their jurisdiction. Jurisdictional overlap is reduced to a small set of policies, essentially working groups. The existence of 'free-riding' supports the creation of a supranational structure, making policy decisions at a supranational level and enforcing decisions on its members. However, this benefit must be compared with the cost of federalizing police bureaucracies within the union.

The effects of the Schengen Agreements on criminal activities are an open empirical question. As to the effect of interjurisdictional cooperation, it will take quite a while to assess this question since most of it has been at the level of working groups, with a possible exception of a common visa policy. As to the elimination of internal borders, the issue of criminal mobility is certainly there. The Belgian and the French governments have complained more than once about the conditions at their borders with the Netherlands. However, most criminal organizations have considerable amounts of money and are in a position to take full advantage of communication facilities, independently of border controls.

6.3.2 Narcotics

Drugs policies in Europe have been subjected to intense debate. Although very large amounts of resources have been invested in fighting drugs, the effectiveness of these policies is far from clear. Conservatives have argued that the measures taken are too lenient, whereas liberals propose a less repressive approach, including some liberalization of the market. On the basis of different treaties, including the Schengen Agreements, there is a strong tendency for the unification of drugs policies in Europe. There are some differences in national policies, but they are not as deep as some might think. In all countries, supply-side activities in the drugs markets are subject to penal punishment; the penalties not being exactly the same. On the demand side, the three widely accepted policy instruments are prevention, repression and therapy. The distinguishing feature is not so much the repressive nature of the national policies, but the extensive use of therapy or medical approaches.[5] One possible indicator of this uniformity of policies is the average retail prices of drugs. The Netherlands is the only outlier, with a lowest average price. Further empirical evidence, however, does not seem to draw a firmer conclusion about the effects of different policy styles. As pointed out by Frey (1997), a homogenized European drug policy will probably result in a repressive approach. To the extent that such harmonization already exists, further effort will almost certainly be ineffective.

The economic argument for restricting drugs derives from some associated negative externality. Even though some controversy surrounds this remark (for example crimes committed by drug addicts should be punished as crime itself rather than the underlying motivations for that criminal act), most people seem to accept that drugs do cause a negative externality. The disagreement refers to how to regulate the drugs market to internalize the externality. Our rational theory of law enforcement tells us that the optimal policy is determined by the sensitivity of the drugs with respect to enforcement expenditure. Most empirical literature does not give a clear cut response, even though the general feeling seems to be that such elasticity is reasonably low.

A particularly controversial policy is liberalizing the drugs market. The welfare implications depend on how much the quantity of drugs will increase and how much the average price will go down. Nevertheless, these are not the only effects to consider. One important consideration relates to using enforcement expenditure in therapy and changing individual preferences, thus reducing demand for narcotics. On the supply side, another important factor relates to the change of the nature of the firm. When illegal, a criminal organization designs internal control mechanisms to adapt the firm to such environment. Fewer drug dealers are hired, but those hired could be better at their task since smaller firms are easier to manage. Moreover, violence supports self-enforcing contracts. When legalized, eventually more dealers (now legal employees) are hired, but they could be worse at their tasks. And more contractual conflicts could emerge since violence is not a legal mechanism.

With respect to the rational theory of law enforcement, the most critical remark seems to be that drug addicts are not rational. An alternative view is that drug addicts have a very high willingness to pay for drugs (eventually infinite), and they cannot be deterred by severe punishment or a high probability of apprehension. Empirical evidence seems to point out that most consumers of drugs are not addicts, but dabblers. Within our rational model, the marginal individual is necessarily a dabbler and not an addict. Consequently, most of the analyses focus on using law enforcement to deter dabblers, and not addicts.

The question of individuals not being sensitive to enforcement only makes sense when the individual at the margin is an addict, and not a dabbler. It is clear that such point has not been reached. It does make sense for criminal policies to spend more resources punishing dabblers and not addicts. Conversely, resources invested in alternative policies (for example, therapy) should target addicts rather than dabblers.

6.3.3 Corporate Criminal Law

In most European countries, the criminal justice system does not allow for criminal liability of legal corporations. Directors and employees, but not legal corporations, may be prosecuted for offences they have committed. In some particular cases, as in the money laundering directive (1991), the directors are criminally liable rather than the corporation when employees engage in money laundering. After a series of prominent cases (for example the collapse of Barings, the Drexel affair), governments have become increasingly concerned about internal control mechanisms and the growing incidence of large-scale frauds. One possible aspect has been the imposition of criminal penalties on senior management and on corporations.[6]

Most of the law and economics literature is not very enthusiastic about criminal penalties on corporations because it might create over-deterrence, and it could dissuade internal control mechanisms that would provide evidence to be used against the corporation later in court.

In fact, an empirical open question is how much different are European corporations from US corporations as a consequence of different criminal liability rules. It seems to be that these differences are less important than expected (Instefjord, Jackson, and Perraudin 1998). One explanation is that, since corporate criminal punishment is purely monetary, criminal and civil liability are substitutes: European civil liability could be as effective as US criminal liability. Another explanation is that corporations are more concerned with substantial punitive damages than with criminal sanctions. Thus, the relevant empirical question would be to investigate the magnitude and likelihood of punitive damages in the US and their equivalent in Europe.

Within our rational theory of law enforcement, one important remark is that since sanctions are constrained by wealth, penalizing a corporation permits a higher sanction coupled with a lower probability, saving on enforcement costs. However, the same cost argument justifies why criminal sanctions should be replaced by reputation sanctions. Reputation sanctions are less costly than monetary sanctions because forfeiture of a corporation's assets has an opportunity cost.

6.3.4 Tax Evasion

A consequence of harmonization of fiscal policy in the European Union is the need for coordination of enforcement policies against tax evasion. Therefore the European effort to control and reduce tax evasion is an important area of research.

The problem of tax compliance concerns equity and efficiency at the same time. It can be approached from different perspectives: public finance and tax harmonization, law enforcement, design of European tax authorities, labour supply, or a combination of all of these. Our direct concern is enforcement measures.

Our model predicts that sanctions should be large and the probability of auditing low. It is well known that the empirical adherence is not high (Andreoni, Erard, and Feinstein, 1998). With respect to the European context, it is of particular interest to explore the diverse psychological, moral and social influences. Also of importance is the relationship between tax bureaucracies, judicial authorities and European institutions.

A first observation is that the free movement of people and capital has not pushed governments to adopt similar enforcement policies across Europe. One possible explanation is competition between member states to attract capital gains that have evaded taxation elsewhere. Another explanation is a rent-seeking one. Those who can take advantage of the current loopholes are precisely those who have more influence in policymaking, precisely those who can easily move capital across Europe.

A second observation is that tax compliance seems to be higher in Northern Europe rather than in the South jurisdictions. Such a fact is a consequence of different audit programmes, enforcement policies and also social norms. Diverse social norms are important because it will be difficult to change them in a top-to-bottom policy such as harmonization of tax compliance.

An important factor is the taxpayer's perception of the fairness of the tax burden and the degree of satisfaction with government. Clearly taxpayers across Europe differ with respect to fairness perception and satisfaction. Also the 'democratic deficit' of the European Union could reduce shame and guilt from non-compliance.

A European tax compliance policy should start with governments sharing information and training truly European tax practitioners making detection and compliance easier. It is likely that sharing information would help governments detecting 'ghosts' more than tax evaders.

In my view the fundamental problem with enforcement of tax compliance in Europe (and not in the US) is the diversity and complexity of rules. Enforcement measures are difficult to design when even enforcers are bewildered by the complexity.

6.3.5   EU Corruption

Corruption is becoming an important issue in the context of the European Union. Within our rational theory, corruption is a natural consequence of over-regulation in Europe. There is a public monopoly of law enforcement and clear tendency for the use of public administrative agencies. Most European public agencies are centralized and monopolistic bureaucracies rather than competitive and open structures. Control mechanisms are usually very weak and judicial review of agency action is mild. It is not surprising that corruption emerges.

An important research area is how much over-regulation in Europe is caused by rent-seeking making corruption endogenous. That of course is a consequence of weak political control mechanisms and lack of financial and procedural accountability.

There are three areas that the European Union should target to reduce corruption. First, enforcement policies should be designed to deter corruption and severely punish corrupt bureaucrats, in particular at the top of the European bureaucracy. Second, salaries and wages to bureaucrats and enforcers should be high to increase the opportunity cost of corruption. Finally, European bureaucracies should be redesigned to be competitive and open, with clear financial and procedural accountability. Judicial and political review and control is important to enforce anti-corruption measures.

One possible mechanism to tackle corruption in Europe is to couple a bounty system with an amnesty. As shown by Cooter and Garoupa (2000), these two instruments would create a virtuous circle of distrust. An essential element of this approach is a fairly competitive judicial system that reduces the likelihood of collusion. That could be a fundamental problem within the European Union since there is a tradition of judicial and administrative centralization.

6.4   CONCLUSION

In this chapter we have reviewed the economic theory of optimal law enforcement within the context of European harmonization. We have argued that a better theory of enforcement institutions is needed to help policymaking in Europe.

Some lessons concerning the European context were discussed. The chapter adopts a non-enthusiastic view of harmonization of law enforcement across Europe. It is argued that the benefits are not clearly superior to the costs.

NOTE

1. Essentially Kaldor–Hicks efficiency.
2. For example, Posner (1998) uses the economic rationale for the right to counsel, the economic approach to the standard proof in criminal cases or the use of bail as examples to show that the theory can support politically liberal policies.
3. The Schengen Area includes Germany, Belgium, France, Luxembourg and the Netherlands by the 14 June, 1985 agreement; Italy by the 27 November, 1990 agreement; Portugal and Spain by the 26 June, 1991 agreement; Greece by the 6 November, 1992 agreement; Austria by the 28 April, 1995 agreement; and Denmark, Finland, Iceland, Norway and Sweden by the 19 December, 1996 agreement. The United Kingdom and Ireland are not part of the Schengen Area.
4. It would be useful to recall that most Schengen countries have been under the same enforcement policies in the past, for example the Napoleonic occupation or the German occupation in 1939 to 1945.
5. Prinz (1997) classifies drug policies into four categories: strictly repressive (Belgium, France, Norway, Sweden), repressive (Austria, Germany, Greece, Irish Republic, Luxembourg, Portugal, Switzerland, United Kingdom), less repressive (Italy, Spain) and least repressive (Denmark, the Netherlands).
6. In most countries, civil sanctions can be applied. The only exceptions in the European Union are the Netherlands, Ireland and the United Kingdom. In countries such as France and Denmark sanctions are seldom used (Instefjord, Jackson and Perraudin, 1998).

REFERENCES

Andreoni, J., B. Erard and J. Feinstein (1998), 'Tax compliance', *Journal of Economic Literature*, **36**, 818–60.

Becker, G.S. (1968), 'Crime and punishment: an economic approach', *Journal of Political Economy*, **76**, 169–217.

Brown, W.W. and M.O. Reynolds (1973), 'Crime and punishment: risk implications', *Journal of Economic Theory*, **6**, 508–14.

Cooter, R. and N. Garoupa (2000), 'The Virtuous Circle of Distrust: A Mechanism to Deter Bribes', Universitat Pompeu Fabra and University of California at Berkeley mimeograph.

Frey, B.S. (1997), 'Drugs, economics and policy', *Economic Policy*, **25**, 389–94.

Friedman, D.D. (1999), 'Why not hang them all: the virtues of inefficient punishment', *Journal of Political Economy*, **107** (Supplement), S259–S269.

Garoupa, N. (1997a), 'The theory of optimal law enforcement', *Journal of Economic Surveys*, **11**, 267–95.

Garoupa, N. (1997b), 'Optimal law enforcement and the economics of the drug market: some comments on the Schengen Agreements', *International Review of Law and Economics*, **17**, 521–35.

Harel, A. and U. Segal (1999), 'Criminal law and behavioral law and economics: observations on the neglected role of uncertainty in deterring crime', *American Law and Economics Review*, **1**, 276–312.

Instefjord, N., P. Jackson and W. Perraudin (1998), 'Securities fraud', *Economic Policy*, **27**, 587–603.

Jolls, C., C. Sunstein and R. Thaler (1998), 'A behavioral approach to law and economics', *Stanford Law Review*, **50**, 1471–550.

Kaplow, L. and S. Shavell (2001), 'Any non-welfarist method of policy assessment violates the Pareto Principle', *Journal of Political Economy*, 109, 281–6.

Polinsky, A.M. and S. Shavell (2000a), 'The fairness of sanctions: some implications for optimal enforcement policy', *American Law and Economics Review*, **2**, 223–7.

Polinsky, A.M. and S. Shavell (2000b), 'The economic theory of public enforcement of law', *Journal of Economic Literature*, **38**, 45–76.

Posner, R.A. (1998), *Economic Analysis of Law*, 5th edition, New York: Aspen Law & Business.

Prinz, A. (1997), 'Do European drugs policies matter?', *Economic Policy*, **25**, 373–85.

7. Product liability and product safety in a federal system: economic reflections on the proper role of Europe

Michael G. Faure

7.1 INTRODUCTION

In Europe it has been known for a long time that the domains of product safety and product liability are, for many years now, no longer subjected to only national legislation. Europe has issued many Directives harmonizing product safety standards. In addition there is the Council Directive 85/374/EEC of 25 July 1985 on the approximation of the laws, regulations and administrative provisions of the Member States concerning liability for defective products.

The question that will be addressed in this chapter is whether there are economic reasons for a harmonization of product safety standards and product liability. The fact that product safety standards have, to a large extent, been harmonized, can at first blush easily be understood as an important instrument to facilitate interstate trade. However, it is less clear why a harmonization of product liability law was also needed. This harmonization of product liability is all the more remarkable since Europe has so far taken in fact only one initiative with respect to tort law, which is precisely the domain of product liability. Other attempts, for example, to harmonize the liability for services, have failed (see Faure and Hartlief, 1996, pp. 241–2).

The European product liability Directive entered into force when there was not yet any talk about a subsidiarity principle. According to this principle, which was introduced by the Single European Act for environmental matters and enlarged to a general principle of community policy by the Maastricht Treaty, the 'community shall take action if and only in so far as the objectives of the proposed action cannot be sufficiently achieved by the Member States and can, therefore, by reason of the scale or effects of the proposed action, be better achieved by the community.'[1]

The issue which will therefore be addressed in this chapter fits, from a legal perspective, in the discussion concerning the interpretation of the subsidiarity principle. This subsidiarity principle indeed allows for a new and probably more critical approach concerning the proper role of Europe with respect to product liability. The question arises what reasons can be advanced for a full harmonization of product liability law. To answer this question, attention will be paid to the economic literature on the optimal level of regulation within federal systems.

It is, moreover, not only academically interesting to address the optimal level of regulation of product liability in Europe. The European Commission itself has also established that the product liability Directive in its current version is not able to reach the goal of harmonizing marketing conditions, which it is, according to the preamble, supposed to achieve. Therefore, on 28 July 1999 a green paper on liability for defective products was launched in which the Commission addressed several features of the product liability Directive which may be reconsidered. One of these issues, although this is only briefly addressed in the green paper, may be the question on the proper division of tasks between Europe and the Member States concerning the regulation of product liability (COM (1999) 396 final).

The chapter is set up as follows: after this introduction the economics of product liability will be summarized in Section 7.2. This seems necessary to be able to provide an adequate judgement of the product liability Directive and the proposals for reform. Then, the European product liability and product safety Directives will be briefly introduced in Section 7.3, to turn immediately to the corpus of the chapter, being the criteria for centralization of product liability and product safety (Section 7.4). In the light of these criteria the question will be asked whether the product liability Directive could effectively reach the goals set and can be considered to promote economic efficiency (Section 7.5). A public choice perspective is presented to explain some of the 'defects' of the product liability Directive (Section 7.6). Finally, a few recent developments will be discussed in Section 7.7 and a few concluding remarks are formulated in Section 7.8.

7.2   ECONOMICS OF PRODUCT LIABILITY: AN INTRODUCTION

It seems useful to start with a brief summary of the economic literature on product liability,[2] since this will provide us a framework to test the efficiency of the European Directive.

7.2.1   The Economic Theory of Product Liability

In the economic literature attention has mostly been paid to the question of how the law can give incentives to producers to induce them on the one hand to spend efficient care on the products they manufacture and on the other hand to produce a sufficient number of products. Indeed, if too many products were to be put on the market, the risk of a product accident could also be increased. The relevant question then is whether the law should set rules to induce parties to reach these efficient care and production levels. And if it were found that a legal intervention is necessary the next question arises whether these efficient levels could best be reached through a fault rule or through a strict liability rule.

Coasean bargaining
The starting point is the Coase theorem (1960). The first publications on economic analysis of product liability applied the Coase theorem to product liability (McKean, 1970a, 1970b; Buchanan, 1970; and especially Oi, 1973). They showed that in a zero transaction-cost setting the choice of the liability rule will have no effect on the care taken by the producer, nor on the quantity of products put on the market. The well-informed consumer will always base his purchase decision on the full price of the product, being the cost price, increased with the expected accident costs.[3] As long as the conditions for the Coase theorem are met, both an efficient output and efficient care will follow, irrespective of the legal rule applied (no liability, negligence or strict liability). It is important too that under these conditions the choice of the legal rule also has no distributional consequences (Hamada, 1976). Indeed in a Coasean setting choosing a strict liability rule, for example to 'protect' the consumer, seems meaningless, since the expected accident costs will then still be passed on to the consumer through the price system. Therefore, in these circumstances, legal intervention does not seem very useful. On the contrary: if consumer groups are not homogeneous, but the expected accident costs differ for every consumer[4] the introduction of a strict liability rule might have adverse effects, since safer products might disappear from the market.[5] The reason is that the producer does not known which are the consumers with high-expected accident costs. He will therefore set the quality (care) standard at the level of an average consumer and safer products will disappear from the market.[6] These problems caused by heterogeneous consumer groups have often been advanced as an argument against strict liability.

Strict liability for 'full internalization'
The papers using the Coase theorem to analyse product liability were subjected to criticism, since it was held that the theorem does not help since the conditions will almost never be fulfilled in a product liability setting. One argument often heard in this respect is that the consumer has no information with respect to the accident risk.[7] Although consumers can indeed be poorly informed with respect to some risks,[8] this is certainly not true for all risks. The

consumer might be well aware of the risks of, for example, a lawn mower. In addition, it should be mentioned that often information could be provided through legislative measures. If these were successful, the conditions for the Coase theorem could again be met. Only if a consumer underestimates the accident risk and the information deficiency cannot be cured through regulation or otherwise, should a liability rule induce the producer to spend enough care on the safety of his products. If consumers remain uninformed non-liability will certainly not lead to an efficient result since producers will have no incentive to invest in safety equipment if this benefit (reduction of expected accident costs) is not recognized by the consumer. It is generally held that a fault rule can induce the producer in such a case to take efficient care, but only a strict liability rule will also lead to an optimal output of products. In this respect strict liability is considered to be a good remedy for underestimation of the risk by consumers.[9]

The latter conclusion is also true when harm is caused to third parties, for example bystanders, who have no connection at all with the producer. A Coasean solution is of course excluded under these circumstances since the transaction costs will be prohibitive. There is also no 'contact' between a producer and third parties through the price mechanism (see Hamada, 1976; Veljanovski, 1981, p. 131). Again, a fault rule would induce the producer to take efficient care, but consumers would purchase too many products. Therefore, the market price would be too low, since it would not reflect the expected accident costs and, given this demand, a too large output of products will follow (see Polinsky, 1983, p. 103 and Shavell, 1987, pp. 49–50). This inefficiency can, again, only be remedied by the introduction of a strict liability rule. Since under such a rule the market price will reflect the expected accident costs, both efficient care will be taken by the producer and an efficient quantity will be produced (Shavell, 1980, p. 3).

Up to this point we have shown that economic theory does not jump to hasty general conclusions with respect to the desirability of a fault or a strict liability rule. Such an answer depends on whether the victim is a consumer or a third party and if it is a consumer a further distinction is made depending on whether or not the consumer underestimates the risk of a product accident. However, if consumers do underestimate the risk, or if the harm is caused to third parties, the literature clearly points to the advantages of strict liability from an efficiency viewpoint. These are mostly referred to as the full internalization of the harm through the strict liability rule. However, the economic theory does not stop here. Until now it was assumed that the behaviour of the victim had no influence on the accident risk, that both producers and consumers were risk-neutral and that the market was perfectly competitive. The literature has, however, shown that when these assumptions are relaxed the advantage of strict liability, expressed earlier, does not prevail any longer.

Victim's care

It has been stressed that in a bilateral accident situation where the victim also influences the accident risks, liability rules should also give victims an incentive to take appropriate care and not to engage too often in dangerous activities. If the victim has an important influence on the accident risk most authors hold that a fault rule will be preferred to a strict liability rule, even if the latter is combined with a contributory negligence defence. One of the reasons given is the unwillingness of courts to consider the contributory negligence of victims, which might easily affect their incentives. In addition, only a fault rule will lead to an efficient activity level by the victim. It is therefore held that if the victim has an important influence on the accident risk and it is thus more important to control his activity level than it is to control the injuries, a fault rule will be preferred.[10]

Market power

It has also been pointed out by Polinsky and Rogerson (1983) that a strict liability rule might be problematic in the case where the producer has market power and consumers underestimate the risk of a product accident. When producers have market power, market prices will be relatively high, which will lead to too little demand for the product. This process is increased in the case of strict liability. Then the market price will still be higher than the full price of the product (cost price + expected accident costs). Under a fault rule the market price will be lower since the expected accident costs are not calculated into it. The basic idea of Polinsky and Rogerson is that when consumers underestimate the risk and producers have market power a fault rule might be preferable. The reason is that under a fault rule the market price will be lower and since the consumers underestimate the risk they will not take the expected accident costs into account in their buying decision. Thus demand will increase. Therefore, they argue that with a fault rule one can make use of the underestimation of the accident risk by consumers to fight the natural tendency of the monopolist to limit the output. So the surprising conclusion is that when the producer has market power he should almost be 'rewarded' for it by introducing a fault rule. Thus it can be avoided that the monopolist reduces the output and that an inefficiently limited number of products is brought on the market.[11]

Attitudes toward risk and insurance

Finally it should also be mentioned that until now risk neutrality of all the market participants was assumed. If one introduces risk, one could examine whether producers or consumers are risk-averse and allocate the liability accordingly, given the insurance function of a strict liability rule for victims.[12] This is, however, not very useful, since it is often difficult for the regulator to examine the attitude toward risk of all parties involved *ex ante*. In addition, consumers must be averse to some risks but not to others. Moreover, producers also might be averse to the risks of, for example, serial damage. Therefore it is hard to draw conclusions on the attitude toward risk with respect to the desirability of a certain liability rule.

In addition one would only have to take the insurance (compensatory) function of liability rules into account for risks for which no commercial insurance coverage can be found on the market. In practice both producers and consumers can insure the product risk. In this respect there is, however, an important difference between various types of insurance, which follow from different liability rules. Under a strict liability rule producers will always have to pay compensation. When they are risk-averse, they will purchase third party liability insurance. Victims will always be compensated through the strict liability rule so, irrespective of their attitude toward risk, they would have no demand for insurance. Under a fault rule rational producers will have an incentive to take due care to avoid liability. Since producers will not be found liable, consumers will not be compensated through liability rules and risk-averse consumers might purchase first party insurance (see Polinsky, 1983, pp. 100–101).

There is, however, an important difference between both insurance schemes when it comes to the question whether the adverse selection problem can be cured. Under first party insurance the victim himself knows exactly whether he poses a high or a low risk and what type of insurance coverage he needs. Given the different preferences for different types of insurance coverage a narrowing into small-risk pools by the insurer is possible and the adverse selection problem can be avoided. This is not the case in third party insurance schemes. Due to asymmetrical information on the size of the risk between the insurer and the insured the premium will be set at an average level.[13] For the low-risk members of the group this premium will be relatively too high, which will lead the good risks to leave the risk pool. According to Priest this leads to a process whereby always the best risks will be leaving the pool, which leads to an overall unravelling of the risk pool. In a recent article he argues precisely that the current insurance crisis in the US has been caused by this incurable adverse selection problem.[14] His defence is that these problems are much more serious in third party insurance than in a first party insurance scheme and that the development toward an increasing use of third party insurance schemes has caused the insurance crisis in the US. If this were true one would of course have another strong argument against strict liability, since only under this rule will risk-averse injurers or producers take third party liability insurance.

In sum: the economic theory advances strong arguments in favour of a strict liability rule when consumers underestimate the risk of a product accident or when the harm is caused to third parties. However, if the victim has a substantial influence on the accident risk, or if the producer has market power and the consumers underestimate the accident risk, or if one takes into account the influence of insurance, strong arguments could be advanced in favour of a fault rule.

7.2.2   Criteria for (Product) Safety Regulation

Next we also need to address briefly the question why product liability alone may not be sufficient to guarantee an optimal product safety. These issues have been addressed in the well-known 'criteria for safety regulation' developed by Wittman (1977) and Shavell (1984a, 1984b; see also Skogh, 1982).

Information
A first criterion, which may play a role in favour of *ex ante* regulation of product safety is the information needed to evaluate the risk. It is very possible that a government agency may *ex ante* be better able to evaluate the risk that certain products may cause harm and may in addition better evaluate the optimal way to reduce this risk, than private parties would. This may more particularly be the case if the costs for examining the optimal safety devices would be high. *Ex ante* regulation would thus pass on information to the market on optimal safety devices (Shavell, 1984, pp. 359–60; see also Silva and Cavaliere, 2000, pp. 297–8).

Insolvency
A second, well-known criterion is insolvency. Liability rules (including product liability) obviously only deter if the manufacturer has money at stake to compensate his victim. Although many manufacturers may have large financial capacities, most of them are structured as corporations, which benefit from limited liability. Hence, as recent cases have shown, the risk that damage caused by product liability would be larger than the wealth of a manufacturer is real. In that case a problem of underdeterrence arises.[15]

It has, however, been pointed out in the literature that this problem of insolvency particularly causes underdeterrence in the case of strict liability and less so in the case of the use of a negligence rule. Indeed, under strict liability a problem of underdeterrence already arises as soon as the magnitude of the loss will be larger than the injurers' individual wealth. He will, in that case, consider the accident as one with a maximum magnitude of his individual wealth and therefore only take the care necessary to avoid that accident. That care may be lower than the optimal care. Negligence has the advantage that the injurer continues taking care as long as his costs of care are lower than his wealth, since taking care will free the manufacturer from liability.[16] This, therefore, once more balances the conclusion that strict liability may be the efficient rule for product liability. This is true on the condition that the insolvency problem can be cured, otherwise a risk of underdeterrence might arise.

Moreover, this insolvency problem may generally be an argument in favour of *ex ante* regulation by government whereby a safety standard is set *ex ante* and enforced with sanctions. If, however, insolvency is the reason to introduce regulation, these sanctions should obviously be preferably of a non-monetary nature (Shavell, 1985).

Deterrent effect of a tort suit

There may, however, be a third argument which is probably the most powerful in favour of safety regulation in case of product accident, being the risk that manufacturers may, for many reasons, escape a liability suit. The reasons can be manifold (Shavell, 1984a, p. 363). Victims may have difficulties proving that their loss was caused by a product defect; this may be due, *inter alia*, to problems of proving causation. The most important problem is probably latency, being the fact that a long time lapse may happen between the moment that the product was put on the market and the moment that the damage occurs. If, for example, harm only occurs 20 years after a product was brought on the market, the manufacturer may already be out of business and can hence not be reached by tort law any longer. These are all powerful arguments in favour of applying safety regulations for product risks.

Combination of product liability and product safety regulation

Moreover, the literature has equally indicated that although there are, hence, strong arguments in favour of *ex ante* regulation of product risk, this is no argument to rely solely on regulation for a number of reasons. Regulation can be outdated fast, regulation is not flexible enough, there is always the risk of inefficient regulatory standards as a result of interest group activities and regulation is totally dependant upon public enforcement by inspectors and public prosecutors, which may be weak. For these and many other reasons, many have argued that product safety should be guaranteed both by *ex ante* regulation and *ex post* liability rules.[17] However, one should be careful with this conclusion as well. Viscusi showed that in the American experience an overlap between regulation and product liability has caused inefficiencies (Viscusi, 1988). Of course it should be avoided that tort law leads to overdeterrence in the form of inefficient safety requirements (Silva and Cavaliere, 2000, 311–15).

So far we have therefore reached the conclusion that, from an economic perspective, a combined use of *ex ante* regulation and liability rules is justified to guarantee product safety. The question we will now have to turn to is whether it is also justified to regulate those issues at the European level. Before doing so we will first address how Europe has generally dealt with these issues.

7.3   EUROPEAN PRODUCT LIABILITY AND PRODUCT SAFETY

7.3.1   Product Liability

History and purpose of the Directive of 25 July 1985
A first draft was presented in 1974 but this was already modified in 1975 (see Reich, 1986). The first official Proposal for a Directive was presented by the Commission of the EEC on 9 September, 1976.[18] This Proposal was debated in the Economic and Social Council[19] and in the European Parliament,[20] which both suggested important changes to the initial proposal, for example, with respect to the problem of development risks. Following these discussions, the Commission published a revised proposal in 1979.[21] It was only more than five years later that the Council finally passed the Directive on 25 July, 1985.[22]

Reading the Considerations, which precede the Directive, it is apparent that the purpose of the Directive was the approximation of the laws of the Member States.[23] It was argued that this approximation was necessary, because the existing divergences between liability rules in the different Member States could distort competition. The various approaches to product liability in the Member States had led to different liability rules and safety standards. If product liability claims and investments in safety become an important factor in production costs, the different product liability rules might indeed result in different marketing conditions and could distort competition. For the same reasons, it is also held that differing levels of product liability might affect the free movement of goods within the common market.

The goal of approximating the laws of the Member States could be achieved through (the old) art. 100 of the EEC Treaty, which allowed harmonization through Directives of the EEC council in all cases where the functioning and establishment of the common market were directly concerned (see also Reich, 1986, p. 135). Since 'harmonization article' 100 was the legal basis for EEC jurisdiction in this matter, it is relevant to examine whether the Directive under discussion did indeed realize this harmonization objective. This point will be addressed below.

It is interesting to note that the considerations preceding the Directive refer not only to the possible distortion of competition and the endangering of the free movement of goods as justifying the need for harmonization, but also to the consumer protection argument. Indeed, the argument is advanced that the existing divergences in the product liability rules of the Member States might 'entail a differing degree of protection of the consumer property'. This harmonization of the level of consumer protection seems to have become an important goal of the Directive too. Consumer protection will not only be harmonized, as the first consideration suggests, but the level of consumer protection will also be increased. This becomes clear when reading the other considerations preceding the Directive, where the notion 'protection of the consumer' is mentioned as much as twelve times. So, this would indicate that the goal of the product liability Directive is not just to harmonize existing laws, but to harmonize them at a higher level of consumer protection. However, in this respect some authors suggest 'that the primary motive for the EEC intervention is to create uniform marketing standards through harmonized liability rules and not the promotion of consumer interests'. They argue that one of the reasons for EEC harmonization was a fear that the American 'product liability explosion' might start in Europe too. In that respect the Directive would only be intended to stifle excessive Member States' initiatives based upon the US model.[24]

Main principles of the product liability Directive
It is, within the scope of the chapter, obviously not possible to provide a detailed overview of the contents of the product liability Directive; therefore a brief overview of the main points will be provided.

The first article of the Directive gives the key rule for product liability, stating that the producer shall be liable for damage caused by a defect in his product. The following articles develop what is meant by the different notions which are used in article 1. The considerations preceding the Directive make clear that this concerns a 'liability without fault'. A product according to article 2 means all movables which have been industrially produced. The Directive was not applicable to 'agricultural products and game'. These are 'the products of the soil, of stock farming and officeries'.[25] The producer according to the Directive is not only the manufacturer of a finished product. This is also the case for the producer of any raw material or the manufacturer of a component part. Also those, who, by putting their name, trademark or other distinguishing feature on the product, present themselves as producer, are considered producers. The same is true for all importers of products into the community. Suppliers are, as a general rule, not liable under the Directive.

A product is considered to be defective under the Directive when it does not provide the safety which a person is entitled to expect. The considerations make clear that the defectiveness of the product should be determined by reference to the lack of safety which the public at large is entitled to expect. An element to be taken into account is the use to which it could reasonably be expected that the product would be put as well as 'the time when the product was put into circulation'. The burden of proof lies, according to article 4, on the victim, who has to prove the damage, the defect and the causal relationship between the defect and the damage.

Non-liability clauses are invalid according to article 12 of the Directive.

There are, however, certain exclusion grounds for the producer. For example article 7 (b) excludes liability if the producer can prove that, having regard to the circumstances, it is probable that the defect which caused the damage did not exist at the time when the product was put into circulation by him or that this defect came into being afterwards.

Article 10 of the Directive states that a limitation period of three years shall apply to proceedings for the recovery of damages. In addition article 11 provides that the rights of the victim pursuant to the Directive shall be extinguished upon an expiry of a period of 10 years.

Finally article 16 of the Directive introduces the option for the Member States to limit the producers' liability to an amount which may not be less than 70 million ECU if the damage resulted from death or personal injury and if it was caused by identical items with the same defect (so called serial damage).

The green paper on liability for defective products makes clear that the goal of the Directive was to provide a balanced approach providing, on the one hand, a protection to victims, but avoiding, on the other hand, a 'crushing liability', for example by requiring the victim to prove the defective nature of the product and by providing limitations in time.[26]

7.3.2   Product Safety

Goals and purpose
In addition to the product liability Directive the Commission has also issued a variety of Directives providing harmonized safety standards for specific items, such as machines, for example. Moreover, on 29 June 1992 a Council Directive 52/59 on general product safety was issued. This Directive clearly aimed at removing differences in safety standards, since the Commission considered that those differences might endanger the establishing of the internal market. The goals of this Directive are probably best understood by citing the considerations:

> Whereas it is important to adopt measures with the aim of progressively establishing the internal market over a period expiring on 31 December 1992; whereas the internal market is to compromise an area without internal frontiers in which the free movement of goods, persons, services and capital is insured;
>
> Whereas some Member States have adopted horizontal legislation on product safety, imposing in particular, a general obligation on economic operators to market only safe products;
>
> Whereas those legislations differ in the level of protection afforded to persons;
>
> Whereas such disparities and the absence of horizontal legislation in other Member States are liable to create barriers to trade and distortions of competition within the internal market.

This Directive therefore had as its goal to remove trade barriers, which could result from differing product safety standards, within the framework of the internal market programme.

According to Silva and Cavaliere (2000, p. 312) European regulation of product safety has always been concerned with two main aims: (1) To guarantee a minimum level of safety to all European consumers, and (2) to harmonize the different national legislation in order to prevent the erection of non-tariff barriers to free trade among European countries.

Main principles

The Directive contains, *inter alia*, in article 3 a general obligation on producers to place only safe products on the market. Producers are also expected to provide consumers with the relevant information to enable them to assess the risks inherent in a product throughout the normal or reasonably foreseeable period of its use.

However, article 4 of the Directive provides that:

> where there are no specific community provisions governing the safety of the products in question, a product shall be deemed safe when it conforms to the specific rules of national law of the Member State in whose territory the product is in circulation, such rules being drawn up in conformity with the treaty, and in particular article 30 and 36 there of and laying down the health and safety requirements which the product must satisfy in order to marketed.

In other words, this general product safety Directive functions as a stopgap for issues not covered by other Directives fixing harmonized safety standards. In the absence of specific community provisions the conformity of a product to the general safety requirement shall be assessed having regard to voluntary national standards giving effect to a European standard or, where they exist, to community technical specifications or, failing these, to standards drawn up in the Member State in which the product is in circulation, or to the code of good practice in respect of health and safety in the sector concerned.

The considerations preceding the Directive and article 13 of this general product safety Directive specify that this Directive does not affect victims' rights with respect to the product liability Directive. In other words it is not because a product is considered 'safe', because it corresponds with a code of good practice, that this would mean that the product can no longer be considered defective within the meaning of the product liability Directive.

The Directive moreover provides for specific obligations on the Member States to make regulations in such a way that products placed on the market are safe and it contains a duty to notify the Commission of the measures taken under the general product safety Directive.

7.4 CRITERIA FOR (DE)CENTRALIZATION

7.4.1 Starting point: 'bottom up federalism'

The question whether regulation should be promulgated at central (European or federal) level or at a more decentralized level (or, to put it in a more balanced way, what kind of regulations should be set at which level) has been addressed in the economics of federalism. The starting point for the analysis is usually the theory of Tiebout about the optimal provision of local public goods.[27] Tiebout argued that when people with the same preferences cluster together in communities, competition between local authorities will, under certain restrictive conditions, lead to allocative efficiency. If, for example, there are in one community citizens with a high preference for sporting facilities and in another one a majority of citizens with a preference for opera, the first community will probably construct sporting facilities, whereas the second will probably provide an opera house. If someone living in the second community would prefer sporting facilities instead of the opera house, he could then move to the first community, which apparently provides services that better suit his preferences. The idea is that well-informed citizens will move to the community that provides the local services that are best adapted to their personal preferences. Through this so-called 'voting with the feet' competition between local authorities will lead citizens to cluster together according to their preferences. In practice one can notice that different communities do indeed offer a variety of different services. The idea is that the citizen can influence this provision of local public goods either by influencing the decision making (vote) or by moving (exit).

This basic idea applies not only to community services, but also, for example, to fiscal decisions (see, for example, Inman and Rubinfeld, 1994; Kirchgässner and Pommerehne, 1993; Oates, 1972) and environmental choices (see Oates and Schwab, 1988). In addition, this idea of citizens moving to the community that provides services which best correspond with their preferences can also be applied with respect to legal rules. Thus, it has been argued by Van den Bergh (1994) that a competition between legislators will lead to legal systems competing against each other, to provide legislation that corresponds best to the preferences of citizens. Also Ogus (1999) argued that the various lawmakers in the nation-states would create competitive market for the supply of law. The idea therefore is that in an optimal world, citizens will cluster together in states that provide legal rules that correspond to their preferences. Well-informed citizens, who may be dissatisfied with the legislation provided, could move (voting with the feet) to the community that provides legislation that corresponds best to their preferences. This idea, assuming that those different legal systems offer different legal rules thus explains the variety and differences between the legal systems (Van den Bergh, 1998, p. 134). Moreover, it also shows that differences between the various legal rules of different countries should not necessarily be judged as negative, as is often the case in Europe today. The idea of competing legal systems can probably best be seen 'in action' in international private law where actors can choose the legal systems that best suit their needs in a choice of law regime.[28] Frey and Eichenberger have proposed an extreme form of this competition between legal orders by suggesting the emergence of Functional Overlapping competing Jurisdictions (FOCJ), whereby citizens could choose different governmental unities for different functions of government (Frey, 1996; Frey and Eichenberger, 1996; Casella and Frey, 1992). See in this respect also the contribution by Frey included in this volume.

Obviously, this system, assuming that a competition between legal orders leads to allocative efficiency in the provision of legal rules, works only if certain conditions are met. One condition is that citizens have adequate information on the contents of the legal rules provided by the various legislators, in order to be able to make an informed choice. In addition, exit is often costly, so people may stay even if the (legal) regime does not suit their needs optimally.[29] Moreover, a location decision is obviously made under the influence of a set of criteria, whereby the legal regime may not be decisive.[30] Usually the job location and residence are that important that in reality there is often little left for people to choose (Rose-Ackerman, 1992a, p. 169). Finally, as we will discuss below, this system of competition between legal orders works only if the decisions in one legal order have no external effects on others.

In economic literature, this Tiebout model is used to argue that, from an economic point of view, decentralization should be the starting point, since competition between legislators will lead to allocative efficiency. Van den Bergh uses this theory as well to provide criteria for centralization/decentralization within the European Union. Taking Tiebout as a starting point and assuming that competition between decentralized legislators will lead to an optimal provision of legal rules, the central question is: why centralize? Van den Bergh therefore criticizes a part of the current discussion in the European legal literature which seems to focus on the question why there should be decentralization (referred to by Van den Bergh as 'top down federalization'). According to economic theory, that is the wrong question. Starting from Tiebout's model, there is reason to believe in what Van den Bergh calls a 'bottom up federalization', assuming that in principle the local level is optimal, since the local level has the best information on local problems and on the preferences of citizens. Only when there is a good reason, should decision making be moved to a higher level.[31] Economic theory has indeed suggested that there may be a variety of reasons why the local level is not best suited to take decisions and where central decision making can lead to more efficient results.

These criteria for centralization will now be applied to product liability and product safety.

7.4.2 Transboundary Character of the Externality

The Tiebout argument in favour of competition between local communities obviously works only if the problem to be regulated is indeed merely local. Once it is established that the problem to be regulated has a transboundary character, there may be an economics of scale argument to shift powers to a higher legal order that has competence to deal with the externality over a larger territory. This corresponds with the basic insight that if the problem to regulate crosses the borders of competence of the regulatory authority, the decision-making power should be shifted to a higher regulatory level, preferably to an authority which has jurisdiction over a territory large enough to adequately deal with the problem (compare Ogus, 1998, p. 414; Kimber, 1995; Esty, 1996 and Rose-Ackerman, 1992a, pp. 164–5). 'Economic theory provides a straightforward but unrealistic answer to regional pollution problems: draw 'optimal' jurisdictional boundaries' (see Rose-Ackerman, 1995, p. 38).

This externality argument in favour of centralization traditionally plays an important role with respect to environmental problems (see Oates and Schwab, 1988 and Van den Bergh, 1998, p. 140). The question, however, arises how this 'transboundary externality' argument relates to product liability. One can certainly argue that the product liability area is a totally different one from the traditional tort as far as the potential of affecting international trade is concerned. The chance that 'normal' tort might have an interstate effect is, with a few exceptions (like the transboundary pollution case), relatively small, whereas, given mass production, products nowadays are seldom just meant for the national market. Indeed, as Schwartz argued in the American context, the imperatives of mass production require a manufacturer to sell the same product throughout the nation, so that the need for uniformity in product liability law seems huge (Schwartz, 1996, p. 924). For the same reason Ackerman (1996, p. 451) argues that product liability is in principle a good candidate for national law. These arguments, however, mainly amount to the point that uniformity in product liability law would come in 'handy' in the American context,[32] they do not explain why the mere fact that products cross national borders would constitute the risk that states would be able to shift external costs to others.

Indeed, the starting point for the analysis remains, as Van den Bergh rightly points out, that different communities in the Member States may have different preferences concerning both the level of product safety and product liability law. The fact that these differing preferences lead to differing legal solutions should in principle, as discussed above, be considered as a benefit instead of a problem (Van den Bergh, 1998, pp. 133–4). He therefore argues that a problem only arises if, for example, a producer in the Netherlands would produce products which comply with the Dutch (supposedly low) product liability and product safety standards and would largely export products to, say, Belgium and France, where (again supposedly) the required level of product safety would be much higher. In this hypothesis a 'transboundary externality' problem would only arise if the consumers in Belgium and France would not have the possibility to file a lawsuit against the Dutch manufacturer. This problem is, however, not very realistic since the victims will in this case be the French and Belgian citizens who presumably have a higher product liability standard which would then also be applied on the Dutch manufacturer. In other words, manufacturers of defective products are generally liable in damages for harm suffered in export markets (see Van den Bergh, 1998, p. 141).

Of course the fact that, in the example given, the manufacturer is located in the Netherlands and the products are marketed in Belgium and France, and the harm is suffered equally in those countries, may lead to a few practical problems for victims, but these do not necessarily immediately justify central regulation with the corresponding loss of differentiated regulation according to preferences. First of all, choice of law regimes may be used to guarantee, for example, that the French and the Belgians can have their (supposedly higher standard) product safety and product liability law applied. This, however, is criticized by Schwartz who points at the fact that in this example the court in say, France, will apply high standard French law on the Dutch manufacturer. The effect therefore is that the Dutch manufacturer will be confronted with the higher standard French law. From this Schwartz implies that a regime of state product liability law is hence inconvenient as a means for expressing state values. In the view of Schwartz (1996, pp. 931–2, 937–41) France would express its sovereignty by subordinating the sovereignty of the Netherlands through the application of French law. Still, it can hardly be seen how this argument can justify central regulation. The effect of the choice of law regime is precisely that the Dutch manufacturer will not be able to externalize harm by shifting this only to export markets. Of course this presumes that a system is in place which allows the Belgian and French victims to sue the Dutch manufacturer. But this is, in the European context, precisely given through the (recently revised) European Convention with respect to the jurisdiction and execution of judgements of 1968. Of course one should be aware that even with this convention it might still remain difficult for victims to recover losses in another state (see Kirstein and Neunzig, 1999). This practical problem can, however, not be remedied by harmonization. It is indeed not differences in legal rules that cause difficulties in the transboundary enforcement of claims, but different rules of civil procedure in the Member States.

In sum, the mere fact that different states would hold different preferences with respect to product liability and product safety and that therefore different regimes would exist, can, as such, hardly be considered as an argument for centralization as long as states are not capable of externalizing harm to victims in third countries. A problem might in that respect merely exist, so Van den Bergh has argued, if the rules of the import country do not allow a full internalization because the injurer may escape the payment of damages. Van den Bergh gives the example of a situation where a state would not allow recovery in tort in case of causal uncertainty, meaning that the manufacturer would not be held liable unless the victim can prove 'beyond reasonable doubt' that the particular manufacturer caused his loss. A problem could, according to Van den Bergh (1998, p. 142), also arise if a legal system would not allow recovery of non-pecuniary losses. In those cases there would be inefficiencies in national product liability law of the importing state which would indeed allow exporting manufacturers to externalize harm. This, however, assumes for example that the decision not to compensate non-pecuniary losses would be inefficient and would not be a reflection of national values and preferences of citizens.

7.4.3 Race for the Bottom

There may be an economic argument for a regulation of product safety problems, in that there is a risk that a 'race to the bottom' between countries would emerge to attract foreign investments. As a result of this, prisoners' dilemmas could arise, whereby countries would fail to enact or enforce efficient legislation. Centralization can be advanced as a remedy for these prisoners' dilemmas. This race for the bottom argument could, in theory, play a role in the case of product safety as well.[33] It would mean that local governments would compete with lenient product safety regulation to attract industry (compare Rose-Ackerman, 1992a, pp. 166–170). The result would be an overall reduction of product safety below efficient levels. This should correspond with the traditional game theoretical result that prisoners' dilemmas create inefficiences.

The basic idea behind this argument applied to product liability would be that product liability law may impose costs on industry. If governments highly fear these costs and would prefer to favour national industry, they could do so by lowering product standards. If lowering product standards would be a way to attract industry, distortions could occur which would justify centralized decision-making.

There are, however, some weaknesses in the application of this argument on the area of product safety. First of all product liability and product safety law may effectively create costs for the manufacturing industry but, as was explained in the economic analysis above (see Section 7.2) these costs can often be passed on to the purchasers of the product (Van den Bergh, 1998, pp. 137–9). Second, in as far as the liability of a producer in the sense of the product liability Directive (being the manufacturer) is concerned, it is difficult for states to engage in a race to the bottom for the simple reason that the harm may well occur in another state. Imagine, again, that France would like to attract industry with a lenient product liability regime. In doing so it can hardly attract manufacturing industries that largely depend upon the export market. Their exposure to product liability will indeed depend upon the legislation applicable in the state where the harm will occur. It is, therefore, especially as far as the liability of manufacturers is concerned, unlikely that states would engage in a race to the bottom to attract industry (see Ackerman, 1996, p. 458 and Van den Bergh, 1998, p. 139).

This shows that the theoretical basis for a race to the bottom risk in case of product liability is relatively weak (Van den Bergh, 1998, pp. 136–7). This argument would only justify centralization if it could be proven that without centralization a risk of destructive competition would indeed emerge.[34] There is no proof of such a destructive competition towards lower product safety standards and this risk is, moreover, not very realistic (Faure, 1998, pp. 46–7). Indeed, one can doubt that the law of tort, and more particularly product liability, plays a significant role in attracting or repulsing businesses to or from a given state. Other elements, such as labour conditions, the amount of direct government regulation and taxes may be far more important than the level of product liability in location decisions of business (Ackerman, 1996, p. 459). Moreover, if product liability were to have any effect as far as a race for the bottom is concerned, it is even more likely that states would wish to protect accident victims instead of corporate interest. Consumer advocates may call this a 'race for the top', although a system whereby foreign manufacturers are penalized with overprotective product liability law may well be considered inefficient and in that (reverse) sense a race towards the bottom (Ackerman, 1996, p. 458 and Schwartz, 1996, p. 932).

7.4.4   Harmonizing Marketing Conditions

In the European debate the question of centralization has never focused on the race to the bottom. In Europe a different, somewhat related, argument has been used to harmonize legislation of the Member States in a variety of areas. This has been the legal argument that the creation of harmonized conditions of competition is necessary to avoid trade distortions. Simply stated, the argument runs that complying with legislation imposes costs on industry. If legislation is different these costs would differ as well and conditions of competition within the common market would not be equal. This argument apparently assumes that total equality of conditions of competition is necessary for the functioning of the common market. This argument, also referred to as 'levelling the playing field for European industry' is obviously closely related to the desire to create a common European market. This 'harmonization of conditions of competition' argument is different from the economic race for the bottom argument and more linked to the European political idea of the creation of the common market. It is the traditional argument that uniform rules in Europe are necessary to guarantee free movement of goods within the EC (see Van den Bergh, 1998, p. 136). What can be said about this argument?

Probably a difference should be made in this respect between product safety standards on the one hand and product liability rules on the other hand. It could be argued that differences in product safety standards may indeed endanger interstate trade. Therefore rules with respect to, *inter alia*, a free flow of products and services may certainly contribute to the European goal of market integration. Where the preamble to the Directive of 29 June 1992 on general product safety states that disparities and the absence of horizontal legislation in other Member States are liable to create barriers to trade and distortions of competition within the internal market, this is probably true. However, the question arises whether these goals of market integration can only be achieved via this far-reaching instrument of total harmonization and more particularly the question arises whether this may justify a harmonization of rules of private law, such as product liability. Indeed, the political goal of market integration may justify the need for some rules aiming at the reduction of trade restrictions (think about the case law of the European court of justice with respect to the free movement of goods) and may justify a minimum harmonization of product standards in the framework of the single market initiative. In that respect the Directive on general product safety in fact only provides for a general obligation to place only safe products on the market, but safety standards may still be drawn up in the Member State in which the product is in circulation or may rely on codes of good practice, which need not necessarily be European.[35]

Ogus (1994, pp. 177–9) is relatively enthusiastic on these product safety directives, precisely because the harmonization is limited to 'essential safety requirements'. To meet these requirements the member stages can still use their national standards, whereby voluntary standards set by expert committees will allow for an easy mutual recognition. The approach chosen in the product safety directives, therefore, even promotes competition between different national and European standard systems, so Ogus holds.

The goal of 'levelling the playing field' is much more apparent in the product liability Directive. That Directive is clearly justified on the ground that differing liability rules in the Member States would hamper the conditions of competition. The considerations preceding the Directive read:

Whereas approximation of the laws of the Member States concerning the liability of the producer for damage caused by the defectiveness of his products is necessary because the existing divergences may distort competition and affect the movement of goods within the common market.

The weakness of this argument is that it assumes that differences in marketing conditions are always and necessarily a problem for the creation of a common market. Conditions of competition are obviously never equal, as the 'levelling the playing field' argument assumes. In the ideal case of totally equal marketing conditions, there would also be no trade. This political goal of market integration may moreover be questioned on economic grounds.[36] In addition one should realize that even if product liability law were totally harmonized in Europe, this would still not create a level playing field, since differences in, for example, energy sources, access to raw materials and atmospheric conditions will still lead to diverting marketing conditions (see Van den Bergh, 1999, p. 6).

There is, in addition, a strong counterargument, in that there are many examples showing that economic market integration is possible (without the distortions predicted by the race for the bottom argument) with differentiated legal orders. Public choice scholars have often advanced the Swiss federal model as an example where economic market integration goes hand in hand with differentiated legal systems (Frey, 1994). It is apparently possible to create a common market without a total harmonization of all legal rules and standards (see equally Revesz, 1997, pp. 1338–41).

Finally, 'the proof of the pudding is in the eating'. The question can therefore be asked whether the European product liability Directive, as it has been drafted, can indeed achieve a total harmonization of marketing conditions. This question will be addressed in the next section.

7.4.5   Transaction Costs

There may, however, be one final economic argument in favour of harmonization, based on transaction costs reduction.[37] This argument is often advanced by European legal scholars pleading for harmonization of private law in Europe, and is based on the argument that differences in legal systems are very complex and only serve Brussels law firms.[38] This argument cannot be examined in detail here.[39] It is obviously too simple to state that a harmonized legal system is always more efficient than differentiated legal rules because of the transaction costs savings inherent in harmonized rules.[40] This argument neglects the fact that there are substantial benefits from differentiation whereby legislation can be adapted to the preferences of individuals.[41] Moreover, given the differences between the legal systems (and legal cultures) in Europe the costs of harmonization may be huge – if not prohibitive – as well.[42] The crucial question therefore is whether the possible transaction costs savings of harmonization outweigh the benefits of differentiated legal rules. There is little empirical evidence to support the statement that transaction costs savings could justify a European harmonization of all kinds of legal rules. Moreover, the transaction cost savings are likely to be relatively small (see Van den Bergh, 1998, pp. 146–8). However, the transaction costs argument may play an important role to justify, again, a coordination of product safety standards to prevent states from hindering a free flow of products and services (see generally Vogel, 1995, pp. 52–5). Indeed, some cooperation between states seems necessary to avoid that if a product is mass produced and internationally distributed, interstate trade would be hampered as a result of varying national product safety standards (Schwartz, 1996, pp. 924–5). Indeed, also in international law it is well known that diverging health, safety and related regulatory standards between countries of origin and countries of destination, especially in cases where these standards are more stringent in countries of destination, provide a source of allegations by countries of origin that they are subject to discrimination in countries of destination. This might result in a violation of the GATT and regulatory harmonization will therefore occur to minimize product incompatibilities to allow producers to maximize access to export markets. Harmonization is therefore certainly useful to avoid pointless incompatibilities which do not reflect different preferences (Trebilcock and Howse, 1998, pp. 21, 30). These transaction costs arguments do therefore apply in the field of economic regulation and product safety. Indeed, the information required to formulate these rules may be useful for the whole of Europe and the formulation of uniform rules in these cases may save on information costs and can, hence, promote interstate trade. Therefore, once more, the Directive on general product safety, taken in the framework of the 1992 programme to establish the internal market, may well be considered as an instrument which saves on transaction costs (Van den Bergh, 1998, pp. 145–6).

The question, however, arises whether these transaction costs savings as a result of harmonized rules can also be expected for product liability. One could argue that a manufacturer who markets his products Europe-wide would, in the absence of harmonization, need specialized legal counsel in every state and their insurance underwriters would have to calculate the liability exposure separately in accordance with each state's product liability law (Ackerman, 1996, p. 453). This argument, however, as mentioned above, neglects the fact that there is a benefit in differentiated liability rules, which reflect varying preferences. Moreover, the costs of harmonization in the field of private law (which is so rooted in legal culture) may be huge and the alleged transaction costs savings may be less than expected. Indeed, even in the case of a harmonized legal rule, manufacturers still would need local counsels to try cases. Accordingly, scale economies under a harmonized rule would likely be insignificant (see Ackerman, 1996, p. 453, note 135). Here again 'the proof of the pudding is in the eating', so that the question arises whether the European product liability Directive has been able to create the legal certainty required, reducing transaction costs for manufacturers.[43]

One may conclude so far that there are a few arguments in favour of harmonized product safety standards, the most important one being the facilitating of interstate trade via uniformity and reduced transaction costs. There are, however, fewer arguments at first sight in favour of harmonized product liability rules.

7.4.6 Balance

The result of applying the criteria advanced by Van den Bergh (see his contribution to this volume) to products liability is that there would be arguments in favour of centralized European rule making if (1) there would be inefficiencies in national product liability law which would allow manufacturers to externalize damage caused by product defects, or (2) if it would be established that states could attract industry with lenient product safety standards. The latter is, however, unlikely, since states would to the contrary enact legislation to protect victims of product accidents within their own jurisdiction with high standard product liability legislation. There may be transaction costs savings of uniform product liability law if a Directive were able to create legal certainty and achieve a full harmonization, which needs to be examined below. The answer to that question is also relevant to verify the justification given by the European Commission for the European product liability Directive, being that it would harmonize marketing conditions in Europe. The question therefore arises whether the European product liability Directive has been able to achieve these goals.

7.5 EFFECTIVENESS OF THE PRODUCT LIABILITY DIRECTIVE OF 1985

7.5.1 Goals of the Directive

As we have stated above (see Section 7.3.1) the European products liability Directive had two goals: first, it aimed at creating equal marketing conditions to 'avoid distortions of competition'. Second, it wished to achieve a high level of consumer protection. Both goals can, within the focus of this paper, be rephrased in economic terms. The question whether the product liability Directive actually leads to harmonization is obviously useful to judge the desirability of a European action in the first place. If the Directive would have been able to create full harmonization of product liability, it might have created transactions costs savings to such an extent that they may have outweighed the advantages of differing product liability laws. The question whether the contents of the Directive leads to an increased consumer protection may simply be rephrased by asking whether the product liability regime chosen in the Directive promotes economic efficiency.

7.5.2 Harmonization

A first question which had to be asked is whether the justification given in the considerations preceding the Directive, being that the existing divergences before the product liability Directive may distort competition and affect the movement of goods within the common market, is actually correct. It is undoubtedly true to argue that before 1985 there were different product liability regimes in the Member States, but the question arises whether these differences were that important that they 'may distort competition and affect the movement of goods within the common market', as the product liability Directive argues. A Dutch author, Van Wassenaer van Catwijck (1986b), has indicated that although the product liability regimes did indeed differ, insurance premiums for the coverage of the product liability risk were not substantially different. If that is true, the differences in marketing conditions were probably not as large as the Commission holds. More important is obviously the question whether the Directive in the 1985 version could reach the harmonization goal at all. It is in fact very unlikely that this is the case.[44]

Indeed, according to article 13 all the different, already existing, product liability laws remain in effect, which means that already existing differences will remain unchanged. In addition at many points the Directive itself refers to national legislation, for example with respect to the rights of contribution or recourse (article 5 and 8,1), with respect to non-material damage (article 9), the suspension or interruption of the limitation period (article 10,2) and with respect to nuclear accidents (article 14). It should also be mentioned that in three cases the Directive expressly allows the Member States to derogate from the provisions of the Directive – namely liability for primary agricultural products, liability for development risks and the introduction of a financial limit on liability. Moreover, the Directive cannot of course bring any harmonization for all the product accidents to which it does not apply, because of limitations in the definitions of 'product', 'producer' and 'damage'. Many notions in the Directive are also unclear and can give rise to interpretation problems.[45] These problems might lead to different interpretations of the provisions of the Directive by the legislator and courts of the different Member States. These interpretation problems can be solved by the European Court of Justice in

Luxembourg. But it often takes a long time before an interpretation problem is brought before the Court and as long as there is no definitive solution, these interpretation problems of unclear notions in the Directive might again endanger the harmonization objective. Interpretational problems are all the more likely in practice since even the language differences of the various translations of the Directive can lead to different interpretations of the same provision.[46] It was just mentioned that the product liability Directive gave several options to the Member States, concerning the including of primary agricultural products, the liability for development risks and the possibility of introducing a financial limit on liability. This has obviously also caused differences, as we just indicated. These differences as far as the transposition of the Directive in domestic law is concerned are shown in annex 1 to the green paper on liability for defective products which is included in the annex to this chapter.

Since it is clear that this product liability Directive cannot reach an approximation of the Member States legislation, it has been suggested that this was only used as an argument to give the EC competence in this matter.[47]

There are other inconsistencies that are worth mentioning in an effectiveness evaluation of the Directive. Both the introduction of the 10 year extinguishing period and the optional introduction of a financial limit on liability have been defended by referring to the introduction of liability for development risks. In the final version the producer is in principle not liable for development risks, but nevertheless the extinguishing period as well as the optional financial limit remained, although the reason given has disappeared. In addition one notices that the Directive is said to introduce a 'liability without fault', but nevertheless the conduct of the producer will still be important, for example when the defectiveness of a product is assessed and with respect to the defect notion. So, in fact, the fault notion still plays a role in establishing whether there is liability under the Directive.

For all these reasons some authors qualify the Directive itself as a defective product.[48]

7.5.3 Efficiency and Consumer Protection

The Directive also claims to provide an increased consumer protection. The question arises whether the Directive is indeed aiming at the protection of consumers. Moreover, this question can also be rephrased by asking whether the Directive promotes economic efficiency, by comparing the regime of the Directive with the economic model explained above.

Consumer protection?

As far as the 'protection of the consumer' is concerned one can argue that in comparison with existing product liability schemes in some Member States, for example Germany and France, the Directive can not add a lot as far as consumer protection is concerned.[49]

Indeed, damage caused by primary agricultural products was excluded from the scope of the Directive. For material damage there is a lower threshold. There are short limitation and extinguishing periods. The Member States can even introduce a financial limit on liability. One could oppose these remarks on the basis that for some countries, which had no product liability system at all[50] the Directive substantially improves the situation of the victim of a defective product. One could say the same for countries which already had a product liability system since, according to article 13, the liability system of the Directive is only added to the already existing system so that the victim is always better off. This is, however, only true on a short-term basis. Most authors hold that the Member States are not allowed to introduce after 30 July, 1985 a product liability system which would give more rights to the victim than does the Directive (see Duintjer Tebbens, 1986, p. 373 and Van Wassenaer van Catwijck, 1986b, p. 81). This interpretation is also followed in the green paper. If this were true, then the Directive does limit the right of Member States and also limits the protection of the consumer in the future.[51] It is therefore unclear even whether the Directive does indeed provide consumer protection, certainly when one regards this on a long-term basis.[52]

A detail which should also be mentioned, is that the notion consumer protection, which is so often used in the considerations preceding the Directive, is in fact misleading. A 'consumer' is a purchaser, who buys a product. The Directive is, of course, not at all limited to a protection of the buyer of the product. Also third parties that suffer harm from a defective product can benefit from the protection of the Directive. Indeed, for many Member States the main improvement of the Directive is that also third parties now benefit from the strict liability of the producer. The damage suffered by someone who stood in a contractual relationship with the producer (the consumer), was often already subjected to strict liability of the producer. In addition, the damage caused to a victim 'as consumer' being the damage caused to the purchased product itself, is excluded by the Directive (Article 9 (b)). For these reasons it appears that the term consumer protection which is so often used with respect to the Directive, is not that well chosen. What is meant is the protection of the victim, whether this is a consumer or not.

Some economic effects of the EC Directive[53]

Apparently the drafters of the EC Directive judged that the best way to realize the protection of the consumer, of which they spoke so much, was to implement a generalized strict liability rule for harm caused by a product defect. The first thing that is striking when one compares this rule with the economic theory of product liability discussed above, is that the Directive advances one single rule to deal with all product accidents, whereas the economic theory is much more balanced and detailed. Depending upon whether or not the victim is a consumer, whether the latter has information on the product risk, what the influence of insurance is and so on, economic theory would only hold that a strict liability rule is efficient in some cases, but certainly not in all.

At the policy level it is, using all the relevant criteria, almost impossible to give advice to the legislature to use one single rule for all product accidents. There is even a question as to whether the legislator would have to define such a rule. An obvious alternative would be to let the judge decide what type of liability rule should govern the product accident. Thus case law could take into account all the relevant criteria and the application of the strict liability rule could be limited to certain product accidents. The Directive, which introduces one strict liability rule for all product accidents, disregards all the various factual situations, which make different liability rules efficient. Thus, by using one single rule inefficiencies will unavoidably be created since the strict liability rule will also be applied where this would be inefficient taking into account the abovementioned criteria. It is also doubtful whether the savings in administrative costs by using one legal rule outweigh the inefficiencies. The costs of applying the economic criteria for strict liability should not be that high either. Particularly if they can easily be recognized (for example whether the victim was a consumer or a third party) an individualized product liability system where strict liability will only be applied in some cases could be used by the judge at relatively low costs.

One of the criteria was also applied for a long time in legal practice. Indeed, in most legal systems, product accidents whereby the victim stood in a contractual relationship with the producer were treated differently from those where the victim is a complete stranger to the producer. One of the reasons for introducing the generalized strict liability in the Directive was that this different treatment was considered 'unjust'. However, this distinction is quite sound from an economic point of view. As was mentioned above, if the victim stands in a contractual relationship with the producer a Coasean solution is in principle possible if the consumer is well informed on the accident risk. Such a solution is, of course, always excluded in the event that the victim is a third party because of the prohibitive transaction costs. So there is a good economic reason for treating both situations differently.

Of course the EC Directive does not introduce a general strict liability rule for all damage caused by a product. The produce will only be liable when the damage was caused through a defect in the product. It looks as if this is more a fault liability since a product is often defective because the producer did not take sufficient care. However, liability is indeed strict since the producer will always incur liability when harm was caused by a defect in his product even if he can prove to have taken due care. The producer only escapes liability when the harm was not caused by a defect of the product. Given the broad defect notion in the Directive a product is almost already considered defective by the mere fact of having caused the harm.[54] Therefore, there is not, from an economic point of view, a substantial difference between a strict liability for all damage caused by a product and strict liability for damage caused by a defect in the product as in the Directive.[55] It was mentioned above that the general strict liability rule for all activities, which is used in the Directive, might create inefficiencies since it will also be applied in cases where a fault rule would be preferable from an efficiency viewpoint. It should not be forgotten, however, that the purpose of the Directive was the harmonization of product liability law in Europe. If this should succeed it could create benefits which could easily outweigh the disadvantages of the generalized strict liability rule discussed above. Indeed, if a single product liability rule were to be created in all Member States this could contribute to the creation of equal marketing conditions and thus to the realization of the internal market. This could bring substantial savings (compare Van den Bergh, unpublished manuscript), which could easily outweigh the inefficiency of the use of a single rule. This, however, will not be the case in practice since it was shown in the previous subsection that the Directive can never bring a harmonization of product liability law in Europe. So the inefficiencies remain without any compensating benefit for the realization of the internal market.

Distributional effects

One could go one step further and argue that the Directive does not only create several inefficiencies, but that it is also problematic from a distributive point of view. Many lawyers favour the introduction of strict liability since it would protect the consumer. It is even argued that strict liability would be necessary to restore the broken balance between producers and consumers. The Coase theorem teaches that also from a distributive point of view there will be no difference between a fault rule and a strict liability rule. Fully informed consumers will only take into account the full price of the product (cost price + expected accident costs) and will base their purchase decision upon this full price. Even if the legislator would like to protect the consumer by introducing a strict liability rule, the producer will still add the expected accident costs to the cost price. The consumer will again pay the full price since the expected accident costs are passed on to him, which is reflected in a higher market price. Since producers and consumers are bound through the price mechanism, every shift of liability to the producer will be passed on to the consumer. In this setting a legal intervention to redistribute wealth to the consumer by introducing a strict liability rule seems therefore useless (see Hamada, 1976).

When consumer groups are heterogeneous, the introduction of strict liability will even have adverse distributional effects. Indeed, the most important part of damages is lost income. The expected damages are therefore of course higher for high-income consumers than for low-income consumers. The producer will, however, take into account an average expected damage and will add this to his cost price to get one single market price for all consumers. The effect is that when low-income consumers still buy the product, they 'pay' for the expected damages of the high-income consumers. Therefore strict liability in a product liability setting creates a redistribution from poor to rich consumers (see Adams, 1987, pp. 6–7). For the same reason Priest argued that the product liability explosion the US hurts especially the low-income groups (Priest, 1987).

This effect will be stronger still when the strict liability rule does not only apply on harm suffered by consumers, but is extended to damages caused to third parties, as the EC Directive does. In that case the market price will again be higher since the producer will also have to pay for damage caused to third parties. The increased expected damages will again be passed on to the consumer who pays a higher market price for the damage a product he bought can cause to third parties. The consumer has no possibility to pass on this increased price and therefore he, in effect, pays for the protection of third parties.

So the expansion of strict liability to damage caused to third parties redistributes wealth from consumers (of the product) to third parties. Consumers will indeed have to pay for the protection of third parties. This again increases the adverse redistributive effect of poor consumers paying higher prices for the expected damages of third parties. Since lost income is an important part of the damage, again the high-income groups do indeed benefit from the redistribution.

This shows that the generalized strict liability which has been introduced by the EC Directive will not only create inefficiencies, but is also based on wrong ideas concerning the protection of consumers.

Curing externalities?
So far, in our analysis of the European product liability Directive, we argued that the Directive can hardly lead to a harmonization of marketing conditions or to a lowering of transaction costs (given all uncertainties and information problems). Another point, made by Van den Bergh, is that the product liability Directive can also not be considered to cure the risk of externalizing damage caused by defective products since the Directive does not address the issue where such a risk of externalization may occur. First of all Van den Bergh refers to the fact that such an externalization may occur in case non-pecuniary losses are insufficiently compensated under national law, which may lead to underdeterrence (see Section 7.4.2). Another problem may arise if full scientific proof of a causal link with a certain product defect is required and, for

example, proportionate liability is not accepted. The Directive does not cure these problems, since it does not touch upon the issue of causation, nor upon the compensation of non-pecuniary loss, which is explicitly left to the national Member States (Van den Bergh, 1998, p. 145). Moreover, the Directive allows for a financial limit on compensation, which is generally considered inefficient, especially in the case of strict liability (see Faure and Hartlief, 1998). Therefore the Directive in fact increases the risk of cross border externalities, so Van den Bergh (1998, p. 145) argues. Finally there is a problem in that the Directive, as we indicated above, does not apply to retailers. Above it was indicated that a state cannot attract industry with lenient product liability legislation for manufacturers, but it could attract retailers by doing so (see Ackerman, 1996, p. 458). The EC Directive does not cure that risk since it does in principle not apply to retailers (see further Van den Bergh, 1998, p. 139).

7.5.4 Test

After this analysis of the effectiveness of the European product liability Directive, it seems that the way the product liability Directive is structured makes the case for European harmonization in fact even weaker. If we compare the analysis of the effectiveness of the Directive presented in this section with the criteria for centralization discussed in the previous section we can conclude as follows:

1. The EC product liability Directive is not able to cure the risk of interstate externalities caused by product damage, if there were already such a risk.
2. There is no empirical evidence of a risk that states could attract manufacturers with lenient product liability legislation (the Directive only applying to manufacturers). On the contrary, there might be a risk of a 'race to the top', protecting national victims of product related accidents.
3. The product liability Directive can, given its high reliance on national law, never lead to a 'levelling of the playing field' or a 'harmonization of marketing conditions'.
4. The product liability Directive, which in fact adds an additional layer of complexity to the labyrinth of conflicting standards of liability, does not lead to uniformity or a lowering of transaction costs (compare Ackerman, 1996, p. 454).

Obviously many of these weaknesses are well known to the European Commission itself. Precisely for that reason the product liability Directive provided for a review every five years 'in fact to proceed towards greater harmonization with a view to establishing a regulatory framework which is as comprehensive, coherent, balanced and effective as possible for protecting victims and insuring legal certainty for producers'.[56]

7.6   PUBLIC CHOICE CONSIDERATIONS

A question which can obviously not be avoided is whether some of the inefficiencies found with respect to the product liability Directive can be explained on the basis of public choice theory, which pays a lot of attention to the role of interest groups in legislation.[57] Many scholars have written about the lack of transparency at the European level and the strong lobbying activities in Europe. Several aspects of the European product liability Directive can undoubtedly be considered the result of lobbying.

Interest group considerations might explain why a product liability Directive came into being at all. Since it cannot achieve a 'harmonization of marketing conditions' the Directive might have another reason than the formally stated goal. One important reason might have been the fear of producers in Europe for an American type product liability crisis. As we indicated above (Section 7.3.1) one motive for the Directive was to avoid that some Member States would go too far in their wish to protect 'consumers'. The Directive aims at a balanced approach, so it is stressed many times in the green paper. For that reason the manufacturers are also 'protected' with, for example, some defences, thresholds, relatively short statutes of limitations and the option to impose a financial cap on liability. Since the Directive is clearly mandatory for the areas it covers (meaning that Member States are not allowed to go further in protecting victims in the areas which the Directive covers), the Directive could at least avoid the problem that some Member States might take too far-reaching product liability regimes. But the Directive may also be considered 'defective' in reaching that goal since the areas which could precisely have an increase in liability exposure, for example, the non-pecuniary losses, are not dealt with by the Directive.

Public choice explanations might also have influenced specific features of the Directive. This is obviously the case for the exclusion of primary agricultural products from the scope of the Directive in its original version. Some authors hold that indeed the increased protection of strict liability is only necessary against the increasing risks of modern industrial production. Strict liability for agricultural products would unnecessarily increase the insurance burden (Duintjer Tebbens, 1986, p. 370). This explanation, however, is not convincing. Even if agricultural products are produced industrially, they were still excluded from the scope of the Directive. This means that a consumer will not be able to claim damages against a breeder of veal who has employed artificial hormones or against a grain producer who used dangerous pesticides

(Reich, 1986, p. 143). It is not at all clear why strict liability would not be necessary for those cases. The real reason for the exclusion of primary agricultural products was in fact that European farmers engaged in successful lobbying and convinced the politicians that the Directive's strict liability should not be applicable to them (Reich, 1986, p. 143 and Taschner, p. 259).

Another example constitutes the proposal which was made during the discussion preceding the EC product liability Directive to set up a compensation fund as alternative to product liability. This, however, stood no chance as a result of lobbying by the insurance industry who feared losing business (Van Empel and Ritsema, 1987, p. 53). Therefore Van den Bergh argues that the European product liability Directive is to a large extent to be considered as the result of rent-seeking by industry instead of an instrument to increase economic welfare (Van den Bergh, 1998, p. 151).

The same can be said, moreover, for the general justification for many European Directives, being the 'harmonization of conditions of competition'. This argument is often used by industry in Member States where strict national regulation already applies. In those cases European harmonization has the main effect that artificial barriers to entry are erected. This might also have played a role in the context of the European product liability Directive and it merits careful analysis whether this has not also played a role with respect to the general product safety Directive. One must not forget that in some Member States, especially in the North, such as Germany, the Netherlands and Belgium, a relatively high and elaborate level of product safety existed. If this were the case, industry in those Member States would have an interest to lobby for stringent safety standards at the European level, for the simple reason that they already have to comply with the safety standards nationally. By making their stringent national standards the European norm they can impose these stringent norms also upon their southern competitors. Indeed, as Ogus (1994, p. 198) holds: producers will favour stringent specifications standards if they result in protection against domestic and foreign competitors.

One should, therefore, always be careful with the harmonization of conditions of competition argument, as it is represented in European rhetoric, since it may be in the interest of particular interest groups that conditions of competition are harmonized.

Moreover, one should also be careful with respect to the European product safety Directive in so far as this refers to technical specification standards or codes of good practice, in that standards may, once more, function effectively as barriers to entry. This is a point that certainly merits further empirical investigation.

Finally, in the context of a public choice analysis, one should obviously also point at the interests of the European bureaucracy itself. Until 1985 Europe had done relatively little as far as the harmonization of private law is concerned (for obvious reasons of differing legal cultures). It might have been that a European product liability Directive, although it did not fulfil the economic criteria for centralization, might have served the interests of the Brussels bureaucracy to show that Europe could bring about a piece of legislation in an area which is considered important by many lawyers, touches upon manufacturers' interests and is moreover very sensitive in the public opinion. Hence, the fact that the Commission wanted a European product liability Directive may to some extent also simply have been due to the prestige that this Directive would, as one of the first in the area of private law, provide the European Commission.

7.7   RECENT DEVELOPMENTS

7.7.1   Including Primary Agricultural Products

There was increasing criticism on the exclusion of primary agricultural products after the BSE crisis. One obvious effect of the exclusion of primary agricultural products from the scope of liability under the Directive is that the liability will in fact be passed on to the industrial processor or producer. If, for example, babyfood has been derived from veal which has been treated with hormones, this will not lay a strict liability on the farmer, but on the producer of the finished product (Reich, 1986, p. 143). Of course the cattle breeder might be liable under a fault rule, according to his national tort law (Taschner, 1986, p. 259).

For these reasons the product liability Directive was amended by Directive 1999/34/EC of 10 May 1999 (Official Journal L141, 4 June 1999). The goal of this Directive is to amend the product liability Directive to include defective agricultural products as well. Again, the functioning of the internal market is given as the most important justification:

> It is necessary and appropriate in order to achieve the fundamental objectives of increased protection for all consumers and the proper functioning of the internal market to include agricultural products within the scope of Directive 85/374/EEC (see Recital 9).

The idea is that including primary agricultural products within the scope of the product liability Directive would help to restore consumer confidence in the safety of agricultural products. This Directive, including the agricultural products, simply changed the definition of 'product' in the product liability Directive of 1985 and enters into force on the day of its publication in the Official Journal, which was 4 June 1999.

One could argue that with this new Directive, forcing the Member States to apply the product liability regime mandatorily also on agricultural products (whereas before this was optional), one of the criticisms of the Directive (protecting the farmers as a result of lobbying) has disappeared. However, this quick action by the Commission probably indicates more that the sensitivity to European public opinion and the decreasing influence of the agricultural lobby are probably more important reasons for action by the European Commission than the concerns to promote economic welfare.

7.7.2   Green Paper on Liability for Defective Products

Objectives of the green paper
The product liability Directive of 1985 had called for a five year review to analyse the working of the Directive.[58] This five year review has resulted in a green paper of the Commission which was launched on 28 July 1999 which is addressed to the larger European business and consumer community with two aims:

1. It allows to seek information which will serve to assess its application in the field in view of the experience of those concerned (in particular industry and consumers) and to establish definitely whether it is achieving its objectives;
2. It serves to 'gauge' reaction to a possible revision as regards the most sensitive points of this legislation.[59]

The Commission wishes to promote reflection and debate and therefore invites replies provided on facts. Obviously the Commission has indicated guidelines for discussion concerning all of the important topics in the product liability area, such as the existence of financial limits, the 10 year deadline, the burden of proof, the assessment of the insurability of risks, the suppliers' liability and the type of goods and damage covered. Although the green paper clearly states that it does not prejudge the Commission's position on these areas, the fact that a lot of topics which were previously highly criticized are now put on the agenda for possible reform is interesting in the light of the analysis provided in this chapter.

Inefficiencies revisited?
First, a number of features of the product liability Directive which could be criticized from an economic prospective are now openly put on the agenda for possible review (which will obviously not necessarily mean that such a review will take place). Interesting in that respect are *inter alia*:

- The fact that the financial limit on liability is put on the agenda for possible reform. There has been debate to increase the option for a ceiling to EUR 140 million, but the question is equally asked whether the existence of financial limits is strictly justified.[60]
- The Commission is also asking the question whether there would be a need to require producers to have insurance cover for risks linked to production. Currently the product liability Directive does not require producers to have any kind of financial cover. Economic analysis indicated that strict liability with insolvency may create inefficiencies, so that this question certainly merits attention.
- The question is also addressed whether the product liability under the Directive should be extended to suppliers. So far, the product liability Directive, with a few extensions, only applied to manufacturers. In that respect the criticism was formulated in the literature that if retailers are excluded from the product liability regime, the Directive can also not be considered as an appropriate means to cure a 'race for the bottom risk' (see above, Section 7.4.3).

It is interesting that some of the issues which were criticized from an economic perspective are now open to possible review. From a normative perspective it can of course be hoped that the European Commission takes the lessons from economic analysis into account.

More transparency?
Second, there seems to be a trend towards more transparency in the (European) decision-making process, at least on paper. One of the criticisms which could be made on the way that the product liability Directive of 1985 came into being was that apparently many interests have played a role, but that it is not easy to find out what the precise results of the lobbying activities were. The Commission now invites comments on the green paper in the widest possible spirit of transparency:

> It was the Commission's intention that the assessment process should be governed by transparency and that producers, consumers, insurers, practitioners and any other sectors concerned should be able to make known their experience and views on implementation and the subsequent development of producers' liability. In this spirit of transparency, the replies will not be confidential and can be made public unless the participants in the consultation process explicitly request otherwise.[61]

Transparency is also an issue as far as the contents of the Directive is concerned. The Commission regrets that today there is no provision in the Directive for any means of making its implementation more transparent. There is, for example, no obligation on producers to keep records of claims against them. The Commission therefore asks whether it would be useful to increase the transparency of the way in which operators apply the rules, especially by identifying the cases involving defective products that are still on the market.[62]

This increasing attention to the transparency issue seems, of course, nice on paper and corresponds with a general concern in Brussels to react to the criticisms concerning the lack of transparency. If the review procedure concerning the Directive were indeed to be truly transparent, this would obviously make lobbying efforts for industry far more costly and might indeed increase the chances that the Directive would be reviewed in a way which corresponds more with public interest.

However, the green paper clearly is still very much concerned with the evolution of product liability law in the US. Differences between European product liability law and US product liability are extensively discussed in the green paper, among others the issue of punitive damages. The Commission concludes:

> Seen in this light, the European producer is better off, as the European Directive establishes a uniform and coherent framework of liability, without the most criticized elements of the American system (the role of juries, punitive damages, etc.).[63]

The central goal for a possible revision of the product liability Directive should, therefore, in the words of the Commission, be 'maintaining the balance'. The Commission holds that apparently the European system of product liability constitutes a conciliatory approach, balancing interests of both producers and consumers and the Commission sets as a guideline that this internal balance of the European product liability Directive should be maintained.[64]

Therefore one cannot escape the impression that already this green paper on liability for defective products has largely been issued because of the still growing concern concerning the expanding American product liability regime and the corresponding need to protect European business. This concern to maintain the position of European business in 'the global context' appears clearly from the questions in this respect, which the Commission puts as follows:

> Do you think that the Directive weakens the position of European businesses vis à vis their foreign competitors because of the conditions governing liability for defective products?
> What are the main reasons for this, and how can it be avoided?
> What is the impact of European businesses of exporting products to markets with stricter legislation (or legal practice) such as the United States (in terms of costs, production methods, insurance, level of litigation etc.)?[65]

Subsidiarity?

Third, an interesting question obviously arises as to how the Commission considers the task of Europe now that it has (differently from in 1985) to take into account the subsidiarity principle. Does it accept the consequence of 'less Europe' for product liability? The Commission has, on the one hand, as we have just indicated, a lot of attention for the effects of European product liability on the global position of European business, but on the other hand also for the effects of the Directive on intra-community trade. The Commission repeats that the internal market was the goal for the coming into being of the product liability Directive: 'The existence of harmonized legal conditions is intended to make trade easier, since the producer is in the same legal position no matter where his products are distributed'.[66] The Commission, however, agrees that the system of harmonization which is provided in the Directive is 'both incomplete and complementary to any other national producer liability scheme', as we have equally indicated above. However, the Commission argues that the Directive of 1985 should only be seen as an initial step towards establishing a genuine producer liability policy at community level and that the process of reviewing the Directive is in fact to proceed towards greater harmonization. The Commission acknowledges that the objective of total harmonization can only be reached by upholding the present position that no Member State can adopt stricter rules under the Directive. Without spending a lot of words on this, the Commission nevertheless asks the question whether it would be useful to allow each Member State to adopt stricter liability rules, therefore introducing a 'minimum' clause in the Directive.[67]

Although formulated most cautiously, the Commission obviously acknowledges that the Directive in its current form can never reach the goal of total harmonization and therefore at least opens the discussion whether Member States should be allowed to adopt stricter rules. The question whether, in the light of subsidiarity, even more powers to the Member States in this area would be justified is, however, not discussed by the Commission.

7.7.3   White Paper on Environmental Liability

In 2000, the Commission also launched a white paper on environmental liability.[68] It is interesting to take a brief look at this white paper on environmental liability to see how the Commission deals with the subsidiarity issue in yet another area of private law. The Commission's approach seems to be far more careful in this area than with respect to product liability where 'total harmonization' is apparently the policy goal. The Commission proposes a strict liability for dangerous activities which are regulated by EC environment-related law for traditional damage (health and property) contaminated sites and damage to biodiversity. For non-dangerous activities there will be a fault-based liability for damage to biodiversity. Here, the Commission apparently does not propose a European-wide similar environmental liability regime, but links the EC liability regime with existing EC environmental legislation. The idea is that by using liability law, the implementation of the EC environmental legislation can be promoted.[69] Obviously, the argument that a community regime for environmental liability should be drafted 'to create a level playing field' in the internal market is again mentioned, but at the same time the Commission states that 'the existence of any problem of competition in the internal market caused by differences in Member States' environmental liability approaches is still unclear'. The Commission specifically focuses its environmental liability regime on damage to biodiversity since most existing Member States' environmental liability regimes do not cover this type of damage.[70] The approach seems therefore to be rather limited in that it focuses merely on those areas where Member States have apparently not enacted legislation and limits itself to liability resulting from activities regulated under EC environment-related law.

Moreover, the subsidiarity issue is expressly addressed, stating that the Commission in fact only intervenes to guarantee that the goal of article 174 (1) of the EC treaty (which requires the community policy on the environment to contribute to preserving, protecting and improving the quality of the environment, and to protecting human health) can be achieved.[71] Interestingly enough the Commission also discusses the possibility of installing a European regime for transboundary damage only. In the literature it has been suggested that if interstate externalities are a reason for centralization, the European Directive should not necessarily cover both local and community-wide pollution.[72] This idea of a 'transboundary only' regime was rejected, since this could lead to inequalities in treatment of victims in Member States depending on whether they were victims of transboundary or local pollution.[73] Nevertheless this white paper on environmental liability shows that the Commission now (the white paper was issued on 9 February 2000) seems to be aware of the arguments advanced in economic literature in favour of (de)centralization and at least discusses them.

7.7.4   Report from the Commission

As a result of the Green Paper, the European Commission received about a hundred comments from national and European consumer organizations, industry associations and public administrations of Member States. On the basis of all those reactions, the Commission drafted a second report. Indeed, according to article 21 of the Directive, the Commission is supposed to report on the application of the products liability Directive to the council. A first report on the application of the Directive of 13.12.1995 (Com (95) 617) simply concluded that there was too little information available on the application of the Directive, so that the Commission did not consider it appropriate to submit any proposals for amendments. On the basis of the aforementioned Green Paper, the Commission published a second report on 31.01.2001 (Com (2000) 893 final).

One of the striking conclusions of this report is that the products liability Directive is seldom applied in practice. The number of product liability cases seems to be low in general; the number of cases which is handled on the basis of the Directive seems to be even lower.

In this report, the Commission also discusses the question as to whether all the issues which were announced for revision in the Green Paper should be reformed or not. The conclusions in that respect are astonishing. After the Commission has discussed all the reactions and suggestions for revision (report, p. 13–27) it only concludes that, at this moment, too little information is available for any reform. Since the Commission judges that too little information is available to draw firm conclusions, it holds that it would be premature to envisage any changes to the current liability system under Directive 85/374.

However, several follow up measures are suggested in the short and medium term. One of these issues is that a reflection should start with 'whether greater harmonization between the different liability systems currently existing would be advisable and, if this was the case, what means would be feasible' (report, p. 30). It is striking that, once more, the Commission only examines whether more harmonization might be advisable, but does not address the more relevant questions; whether the lack of practical importance of the Directive should perhaps lead to less harmonization.

7.8   CONCLUDING REMARKS

In this chapter I looked at the question whether product liability and product safety in Europe should be regulated in a decentralized or centralized manner. After a discussion of the economics of product liability and a description of the main features of the product liability and product safety Directives, the economic literature was examined to look at the question whether product safety and product liability should be centralized or decentralized. Europe has traditionally justified harmonization in all kinds of areas, also for product liability, by referring to the traditional argument that conditions of competition should be harmonized to create a level playing field. This argument seems, however, far too general to fit into the economic criteria for centralization. These provide for more balanced answers with respect to the types of subject matter which should be regulated at the centralized or at the decentralized level. These economic criteria were confronted mainly with the way the product liability Directive of 1985 is shaped. The conclusion was that this product liability Directive shows, on the one hand, many inefficiencies and defects and seems also unable to reach its goal of 'harmonization of marketing conditions'. This objective as such has also been criticized on economic grounds since it does not necessarily correspond with economic efficiency.

The main economic argument in favour of centralization, a reduction of transaction costs, may work for product safety, but is far less convincing for instruments of private law, such as product liability. But also as product safety is concerned one should not accept a harmonization of product standards without any critical analysis. If product safety harmonization merely aims at removing useless incompatibilities, such a harmonization seems a useful tool to facilitate international trade. However, the danger always exists that in fact high safety standards are introduced at the European level as mandatory safety regulations to create barriers to entry. Also the various European safety regulation Directives therefore certainly merit further research.

Given the fact that the product liability Directive in its current form cannot reach the objectives it has set and shows various defects and inefficiencies, it may to some extent be explained as the result of lobbying by interest groups. Industrial interest groups probably desired a European product liability Directive which balanced the interests of producers and consumers in order to avoid an 'American' product liability crisis. Moreover, even the Commission argued (in the green paper on liability for defective products and the subsequent Report) that the product liability Directive was only a first step towards harmonization. The own interests of the European bureaucracy of the Commission probably also explains the willingness of the Commission to issue a Directive in the area of liability law, although it should have been clear for the Commission as well that this Directive could never meet the goal of harmonization of marketing conditions.

Product liability in Europe has come to a crucial point now, since the Commission has invited all interested parties via a green paper to comment on the future of the product liability Directive. On paper the Commission calls for more transparency, which may reduce the influence of interest groups. In addition there seems to be, although limited, scope for taking the subsidiarity principles seriously, with respect to product liability. The Commission advanced the option of merely having a basic European product liability regime and giving powers to the Member States to adopt stricter rules (which is not allowed under the product liability Directive today). It would be desirable that at the occasion of this debate on the revisions of the Directive the Commission not only looks at the possibility of minor revisions of the Directive, but reexamines critically the basic question why there needs to be a regulation of product liability at the European level in the first place. Economic literature can, as we have tried to show, provide useful and balanced insights to structure a fundamental debate concerning that question.

NOTES

1. Art. 3 B (2) EC treaty. This formulation has not been changed by the Treaty of Amsterdam, but it has been renumbered to article 5.
2. For a similar overview of the economic literature see Silva and Cavaliere (2000), pp. 294–8.
3. For simple examples see Shavell (1987) and Polinsky (1983, pp. 95–7). See also Silva and Cavaliere (2000, p. 295).
4. A common example is that the potential loss caused by the burning of one's hand through a defective toaster will be much higher for a high quality piano player than for the average economist.
5. This point has been made by Oi (1973) and has been developed by Adams (1987).
6. The reason is, of course, asymmetrical information; see Akerlof (1970).
7. This was especially stressed by Goldberg (1974) in a critique on the work by Oi. For a reaction see Oi (1974).
8. For example the carcinogenic effects of asbestoses.
9. See Adams (1987, p. 12); Polinsky (1983, p. 99); Shavell (1980, p. 4); formal proof of this statement is provided by Shavell on pp. 14–17. See also Silva and Cavaliere (2000, p. 295). A simple example is given by Polinsky on pp. 989.
10. Shavell (1980, pp. 7 and 20; 1987, pp. 48–51). This will often be dependent upon the nature of the activity and the potential harm.
11. Similar points have been made by Hamada (1976, p. 233) and by Epple and Raviv (1978, p. 86). See also Silva and Cavaliere (2000, p. 295).
12. For an analysis along these lines see Shavell (1982, pp. 120–32).
13. See the basic article by Akerlof (1970).
14. Priest (1987). The point had also been made by Epstein (1985).
15. See more generally, on this judgement proof problem, Shavell (1986).
16. This point has been made by Landes and Posner (1984), and by Silva and Cavaliere (2000, p. 296).
17. This point cannot be elaborated further here. See more generally on the combined use of tort law and regulation Rose-Ackerman (1991; 1992a, pp. 118–31; 1992b).
18. Official Journal, C 241/9 of 14 October, 1976.
19. Official Journal, C 114/15 of 7 May, 1979.
20. Official Journal, C 127/61 of 21 May, 1979.
21. Official Journal, C 271/3 of 26 October, 1979.
22. Official Journal, L 210/29 of 7 August, 1985.
23. For the goals of the Directive see also Van Wassenaer van Catwijck (1986a, pp. 793–4).
24. Reich (1996, p. 136). A detailed analysis of the American product liability crisis is provided by Silva and Cavaliere (2000, pp. 299–305).
25. This has, however, recently been changed. This will be discussed in the section dealing with recent developments.
26. See the section in the green paper on 'maintaining the balance' (pp. 18–19), where the Commission especially underlines its fear that Europe should not follow the American example of an expanding product liability.
27. Tiebout (1956). For a discussion of this theory, see Rose-Ackerman, Susan (1992a, pp. 169–70).
28. Although the choice for a particular level regime may not always be related to the quality of the legal system but, for example, to the quality of the court or arbitration system. The latter explains according to Ogus (1999, p. 408), the popularity of English law in choice of law clauses in contracts.
29. As Ogus (1998, p. 407) states, there should be no barriers to the freedom of establishment and to the movement of capital.

30. That is one of the reasons why Frey and Eichenberger argue in favour of FOCJ: the choice for one legal or institutional regime should not be exclusive; there may be 'overlapping' jurisdictions depending upon the different functions (Frey, 1996, pp. 315–27; Frey and Eichenberger, 1996, pp. 335–49) .
31. A major American supported of this 'presumption in favour of decentralization' is Revesz (1997).
32. And might therefore fit into the transaction cost argument, to be discussed below.
33. For a discussion see Van den Bergh (1998, pp. 136–9).
34. In the words of Rose-Ackerman (1992a, p. 173): 'If state and local laws seem designed to protect local business rather than reflect genuine differences in tastes across jurisdiction, the federal government should take a hard look to determine the possible interference with inter-state commerce'.
35. See article 4 (2) of the Directive 92/59 of 29 June 1992 on general product safety.
36. See for a critical analysis Van den Bergh (1999).
37. For a somewhat related but different argument relating to economic and diseconomics of scale in administration, see Rose-Ackerman (1992a, pp. 165–6).
38. This is one of the arguments made by the Danish scholar Lando (1993) in favour of harmo-nized private law.
39. It is further developed and criticized by Van den Bergh (1998).
40. Compare Rose-Ackerman (1992a, p. 172) who argues that uniform federal regulation may reduce search costs and tends to produce a more stable and predictable jurisprudence.
41. See, for the environmental case, Mendelsohn (1986).
42. That point has especially been made by Legrand (1997, p. 111).
43. Van den Bergh (1998, pp. 146–7) rightly points at lots of interpretation problems in the European product liability Directive (which we will discuss below) which backs up the conclusion that the transaction costs savings may be small, simply because a full harmo-nization of rules of private law is apparently difficult to achieve.
44. Almost all authors agree on that point. See Duintjer Tebbens (1986, pp. 373–4; Storm, 1985, p. 245; Van Wassenaer van Catwijck, 1986b, p. 81).
45. One can, for example, think about the defect notion in article 6, which might lead to differ-ent interpretations.
46. See, for instance, the different meaning of the 'lower threshold' of article 9 in the French and the Dutch version. Another example is that in the English text the producer's liability is called a 'liability without fault' whereas in the Dutch version it is just mentioned as 'liabil-ity'. For other examples see Faure and Vanbuggenhout (1987–1988).
47. Schmidt-Salzer (1986), p. 1104. Article 100 of the EEC treaty indeed gave legislative competence to the community in order to harmonize the different legislations of the Member States. It has, however, heavily debated whether this article 100 was an appropriate basis to ground the legislative power of the EC with respect to product liability (see Krämer, 1986).
48. This is the title of the article by Storm (1985).
49. For a comparison between the European products liability Directive and German/French law see Van Wassenaer van Catwijck (1986b, pp. 80–81).
50. Which basically means that the victim had a tort based action in which he had to prove a fault of the producer.
51. This is of course more painful for Member States which had no product liability law on 30 July, 1985 than for Member States which already had an elaborated product liability system on that date.
52. Also Cornelis (1987–1988) notices that in comparison with previously existing Belgian Product Liability Law, the victim is worse off under the applicability of the Directive.
53. For an economic analysis of the product liability Directive see also Burrows (1994) and Silva and Cavaliere (2000).
54. One could argue that as soon as a product causes serious injuries it does not provide the safety which a person is entitled to expect and is therefore defective according to article 6 of the Directive.
55. For an economic analysis of liability for defective products see Shavell (1987, pp. 58–60). For an analysis of the notion of defect in the Directive see Finsinger and Simon (1989).

56. Green paper on liability for defective products, p. 11.
57. See for a discussion of the harmonization efforts from a public choice perspective, Van den Bergh (1998, pp. 148–51).
58. See article 21 of the product liability Directive which stat es 'Every five years the Commission shall present a report to the Council on the application of this Directive, and, if necessary, shall submit appropriate proposals to it'.
59. See green paper on liability for defective products, p. 2.
60. Green paper on liability for defective products, p. 26.
61. Green paper on liability for defective products, p. 8.
62. Green paper on liability for defective products pp. 28–9.
63. Green paper on liability for defective products, p. 13.
64. Green paper on liability for defective products, pp. 18–20.
65. Green paper on liability for defective products, p. 14.
66. Green paper on liability for defective products, p. 10.
67. See green paper on liability for defective products, pp. 11–12.
68. Com (2000) 66 final of 9 February 2000.
69. White paper on environmental liability, p. 12.
70. White paper on environmental liability, pp. 12–13.
71. White paper on environmental liability, p. 27.
72. Van den Bergh (1999, p. 10) suggested that a distinction should be made between regional and interstate pollution.
73. White paper on environmental liability, pp. 25–6.

ANNEX 7.1

Table 7.A1 Directive on liability for defective products: transposition in domestic law

Member State	Adoption	Entry into force	Liability for defective agricultural products (art. 15.1.a)*	Liability for development risks (art. 15.1.b)	Financial ceiling (art. 16)
Belgium	Law of 25.2.91	1.4.91	No	No	No
Denmark	Law No. 371 of 7.6.89	10.6.89	No	No	No
Germany	Law of 15.12.89	1.1.90	No	No	Yes
Greece	Law 2251/1994 (replacing decree-law of 1988)		Yes	No	No
Spain	Law No. 22/1994 of 6.4.94	8.7.94	No	No (apart from food and medicinal products)	Yes
France	Law No. 389–98 of 19.5.98	23.5.98	Yes	No (apart from products derived from the human body)	No
Ireland	Law No. 28 of 1991	16.12.91	No	No	No
Italy	Decree-Law No. 224 of 24.5.88	24.5.88	No	No	No
Luxembourg	Law of 21.4.89, amended by Law of 6.12.89	2.5.91	Yes	Yes	No
Netherlands	Law of 13.9.90	1.11.90	No	No	No
Austria	Law No. 99 of 21.1.88, amended by Law No. 95 of 11.2.93, Law No. 917 of 29.12.93 and Law No. 510 of 12.7.94	1.7.88	No (apart from GMOs)	No	No
Portugal	Decree-law No. 383 of 6.11.89	21.11.89	No	No	Yes
Finland	Law No. 694 of 17.08.90, amended by Law No. 99 of 8.1.93 and Law No. 879 of 22.10.93	1.9.91	Yes	Yes	No
Sweden	Law No. 18 of 23.1.92, amended by Law No. 1137 of 3.12.92 and Law No. 647 of 10.6.93	1.1.93	Yes	No	No
United Kingdom	Law of 15.5.87	1.3.88	No	No	No

Note: *Following the adoption of Directive 99/34/EC, the member states are obliged to extend Directive 85/374/EEC to primary agricultural products.

Source: Green paper on liability for defective products, pp. 35–6.

REFERENCES

Ackerman, R.M. (1996), 'Tort law and federalism: whatever happened to devolution?', *Yale Law and Policy Review*, (Symposium Issue), 429–63.

Adams, M. (1987), 'Wohltat oder Plage – eine ökonomische Analyse', *Betriebsberater*, Beilage 20/1987 zu Heft 31/1987, 5–10.

Akerlof, G. (1970), 'The market for "lemons": quality uncertainty and the market mechanism', *Quarterly Journal of Economics*, 488.

Buchanan, J. (1970), 'In defense of caveat emptor', *University of Chicago Law Review*, 64–73.

Burrows, P. (1994), 'Products liability and the control of product risk in the European Community', *Oxford Review of Economic Policy*, **10**, 68–83.

Casella, A. and B. Frey (1992), 'Federalism and clubs. Towards an economic theory of overlapping political jurisdiction', *European Economic Review*, **36**, 639.

Coase, R.H. (1960), 'The problem of social cost', *Journal of Law and Economics*, **3** 1–44.

Cornelis, L. (1987–1988), 'Aansprakelijkheid voor gevaarlijke producten', *Rechtskundig Weekblad*, **51**, 1139–59.

Duintjer Tebbens, H. (1986), 'De Europese richtlijn produktaansprakelijkheid', *Nederlands Juristenblad*, 369–74.

Epple, D. and A. Raviv (1978), 'Product safety, liability rules, market structure, and imperfect information', *American Economic Review*, 86.

Epstein, R. (1985), 'Product liability as an insurance market', *Journal of Legal Studies*, 650–52.

Esty, D. (1996), 'Revitalizing environmental federalism', *Michigan Law Review*, **95**, 625.

Faure, M. (1998), *Aktuelle Regulierungspraxis bei Heilwesenschäden in Europa mit Ausblick auf die EG-Rechtscharmonisierung*, Detmold: Ecclesia.

Faure, M. and W. Vanbuggenhout (1987–1988) 'Produktaansprakelijkheid. De Europese richtlijn: harmonisatie en consumentenbescherming?', *Rechtskundig Weekblad*, **51**, 1–14 and 33–49.

Faure, M. and T. Hartlief (1998), 'Remedies for expanding liability', *Oxford Journal of Legal Studies*, **18**, 681–706.

Faure, M. and T. Hartlief (1996), 'Towards an expanding enterprise liability in Europe? How to analyse the scope of liability of industrial operators and their insurers', *Maastricht Journal of European and Comparative Law*, **5**, 235–70.

Finsinger, J. and J. Simon (1989), 'An Economic assessment of the EC Product Liability Directive and the Product Liability Law of the Federal Republic of Germany', in Michael Faure and Roger Van den Bergh (eds), *Essays in Law and Economics*, Antwerp: Maklu, pp. 185–214.

Frey, B. (1994), 'Direct democracy: politico-economic lessons from Switzerland', *American Economic Review*, **84**, 338–42.

Frey, B. (1996), 'FOCJ: competitive governments for Europe', *International review of Law and Economics*, **16**, 315–27.

Frey, B. and R. Eichenberger (1996), 'To harmonize or to compete? That's not the question', *Journal of Public Economics*, **60**, 335–49.

Goldberg, V. (1974), 'The economics of product safety and imperfect information', *Bell Journal of Economics*, **5**, 683–8.

Hamada, K. (1976), 'Liability rules and income distribution in product liability', *American Economic Review*, **66**, 228–34.

Inman, R. and D. Rubinfeld (1994), 'The EMU and fiscal policy in the new European Community: an issue for economic federalism', *International Review of Law and Economics*, **14**, 147–61.

Kimber, C. (1995), 'A comparison of environmental federalism in the United States and the European Union', *Maryland Law Review*, **54**, 321.

Kirchgässner, G. and W. Pommerehne (1993), 'Tax harmonization and tax competition in the European Community: lessons from Switzerland; paper presented at the Cost Meeting in Luzern, November 1993.

Kirstein, R. and A.R. Neunzig (1999), 'Internationale Zuständigkeit von Gerichten und die Anerkennung ausländischer Urteile' in K.E. Schenk, D. Schmidtchen, E. Streit and V. Vauberg (eds), *Jahrbuch für neue politische ökonomie, globalisierung und Rechtsordnung*, Mohr: Siebeck, p. 345–68.

Krämer, L. (1986), 'EEC Consumer Law', in *Droit et Consommation*, Brussels, pp. 274–5.

Landes, W. and R. Posner (1984), 'Tort law as a regulatory regime for catastrophic personal injuries', *Journal of Legal Studies*, **13**, 421–2.

Lando, O. (1993), 'Die Regeln des Europäischen Vertragsrecht', in Peter-Christian Müller-Graff (ed.), *Gemeinsames Privatrecht in der Europäischen Gemeinschaft*, 473–4.

Legrand, P. (1997), 'The impossibility of legal transplants', *Maastricht Journal of European and Comparative Law*, **4**, 111–24.

McKean, R. (1970a), 'Products liability: trends and implications', *University of Chicago Law Review*, 3–63.

McKean, R. (1970b), 'Products liability: implications of some changing property rights', *Quarterly Journal of Economics*, 611–26.

Mendelsohn, R. (1986), 'Regulating heterogeneous emissions', *Journal of Environmental Economics and Management*, **13**, 301.

Oates, W. (1972), *Fiscal Federalism*.

Oates, W. and R. Schwab (1988), 'Economic competition among jurisdiction: efficiency enhancing or distortion inducing?', *Journal of Public Economics*, **35**, 333–54.

Ogus, A. (1994), *Regulation, Legal Form and Economic Theory*, Oxford: Clarendon Press.

Ogus, A. (1999), 'Competition between national legal systems. A contribution of economic analysis to comparative law', *The International and Comparative Law Quarterly*, **48**, 405–18.

Oi, W. (1973), 'The economics of product safety', *Bell Journal of Economics*, **3**, 3–28.

Oi, W. (1974), 'The economics of product safety: a rejoinder', *Bell Journal of Economics*, 689–95.

Polinsky, A.M. (1983), *An Introduction to Law and Economics*, Boston: Little, Brown.

Polinsky, M. and W. Rogerson (1983), 'Products liability, consumer misperceptions, and market power', *Bell Journal of Economics*, 581–9.

Priest, G. (1987), 'The current insurance crisis and modern tort law', *The Yale Law Journal*, **96**, 1521–90.

Reich, N. (1986), 'Product safety and product liability', *Journal of Consumer Policy*, 137ff.

Revesz, R. (1997), 'Federalism and environmental regulation: lessons for the European Union and the international community', *Virginia Law Review*, **83**, 1331–46.

Rose-Ackerman, S. (1991), 'Regulation and the law of torts', *American Economic Review, Papers and Proceedings*, 54–8.

Rose-Ackerman, S. (1992a), *Rethinking the Progressive Agenda. The Reform of the American Regulatory State*, New York: Free Press.

Rose-Ackerman, S. (1992b), 'Environmental Liability Law', in T.H. Tietenberg (ed.), *Innovation in Environmental Policy, Economic and Legal Aspects of Recent Developments in Environmental Enforcement and Liability*, Brookfield: Elgon, pp. 223–43.

Rose-Ackerman, S. (1995), *Controlling Environmental Policy. The limits of public law in Germany and the United States*, New Haven: Yale University Press.

Schmidt-Salzer (1986), 'Die E.G. Richtlinie Produkt-Haftung', Betriebs-Berater, pp. 1103–11.

Schwartz, G.T. (1996), 'Considering the proper federal role in American tort law', *Arizona Law Review*, **38**, 917–51.

Shavell, S. (1980), 'Strict liability versus negligence', *Journal of Legal Studies*, 1–25.

Shavell, S. (1982), 'On liability and insurance', *Journal of Economics*, 120–32.

Shavell, S. (1984a), 'Liability for harm versus regulation of safety', *Journal of Legal Studies*, 357–74.

Shavell, S. (1984b), 'A model of the optimal use of liability and safety regulation', *The Rand Journal of Economics*, 271–80.

Shavell, S. (1985), 'Criminal law and the optimal use of non-monetary sanctions as a deterrent', *Columbia Law Review*, 1232–62.

Shavell, S. (1986), 'The judgement proof problem', *International Review of Law and Economics*, 43–58.

Shavell, S. (1987), *An Economic Analysis of Accident Law*, Cambridge, MA: Harvard University Press.

Silva, F. and A. Cavaliere (2000), 'The Economic Impact of Product Liability: Lessons from the US and the EU Experience', in G. Galli and J. Pelkmans (eds), *Regulatory Reform and Competitiveness in Europe, I., Horizontal Issues*, Cheltenham: Edward Elgar, pp. 292–323.

Skogh, G. (1982), 'Public insurance and accident prevention', *International Review of Law and Economics*, 67–80.

Storm, P. (1985), 'Een gebrekkig product', *TVVS*, 241–6.

Taschner, H. (1986), 'La future responsabilité du fait des produits défecteux dans la communauté européenne, *Revue du Marché Commun,* 257.

Tiebout, C. (1956), 'A pure theory of local expenditures', *Journal of Political Economy*, **64**, 416–24.

Trebilcock, M. and R. Howse (1998), 'Trade liberation and regulatory diversity. Reconciling competitive markets with competitive politics', *European Journal of Law and Economics*, **6**, 5–37.

Van den Bergh, R. (1994), 'The subsidiarity principle in European community law', *Maastricht Journal of European and Comparative Law*, **4**, 337–66.

Van den Bergh, R. (1998), 'Subsidiarity as an economic demarcation principle and the emergence of European private law', *Maastricht Journal of European and Comparative Law*, **2**, 129–52.

Van den Bergh, R. (1999), 'Economics in a legal straight-jacket: the difficult reception of economic analysis in European law', paper presented at the workshop Empirical Research and Legal Realism. Setting the agenda, Haifa, 6–9 June 1999.

Van den Bergh, R., 'Competition law and competition in Europe after 1992. Will free riders become the heroes of the internal market?', unpublished manuscript.

Van Empel, M. and Ritsema, H. (1987), *Aansprakelijkheid voor producten*, Deventer, Kluwer.

Van Wassenaer van Catwijck, A.J.O. (1986a), 'Products liability in Europe', *The American Journal of Comparative Law*, 793–4.

Van Wassenaer van Catwijck, A.J.O. (1986b), *Produktaansprakelijkheid*, in *Serie Praktijkhandleidingen*, Zwolle: Tjeenk Willink.

Veljanovski, C.G. (1981), 'The Economic Theory of Tort Liability – Toward a Corrective Justice Approach', in Paul Burrows and Cento Veljanovski (eds), *The Economic Approach to Law*, London: Butterworth.

Viscusi, W.K. (1988), 'Product liability and regulation: establishing the appropriate institutional division of labour', *American Economic Review*, 300–304.

Vogel, D. (1995), *Trading Up, Consumer and Environmental Regulation in a Global Economy*, Cambridge: Harvard University Press.

Wittman, D. (1977), 'Prior regulation versus post liability: the choice between input and output monitoring', *Journal of Legal Studies*, 193–211.

8. Vocational qualifications and the European labour market: the challenges and the prospects

Jean-Baptiste Calendini and Christophe Storaï

Granting the citizens of the member states of the European Union the personal right of free circulation and free settlement is a characteristic feature of the process of construction of the European Community such as it was instituted by the Treaty of Rome signed on 25 May 1957. Therefore, recognition of degrees and qualifications is an essential aspect that guarantees the use of that basic right. Even though significant progress has been made in this sphere, there are still a number of dissuasive and often invisible barriers which contribute towards the fragmentation of the European area (Pertek, 1998). In connection with that idea, it would seem judicious to contemplate a more general problem focused on the potential emergence of a vast European labour market as a result of the establishment of the Single Market for goods, services, capital and currency. In addition to the questions one might ask concerning occupational mobility inside Europe, another more fundamental question relating to the institutions and the organization of the employment market in Europe arises: is it possible and desirable to think of a *convergence*, if not a *harmonization*, of the employment markets in the member countries of the European Union?

The purpose of this chapter is to prepare the ground for an answer to that question[1] while identifying the multidimensional constraints of that potential process. For instance, during the 1980s, the governments of the member states have adopted policies aimed at deregulating the labour laws. Whereas the common and clearly defined purpose of such arrangements was to spur increased flexibility on the labour market, the forms and extents of such deregulation, on the other hand, lacked uniformity (Deakin and Mückenberger, 1993). Hence, the establishment of the European Market poses an essential problem on both the political and institutional planes: is the achievement of a genuine harmonization of social and labour laws among all the countries of the European Union conceivable considering the differing national traditions in the area of labour legislation and of the tensions ensuing from the comparison of Community laws and the legal systems specific to the sovereign states?

To clarify this debate, we will proceed in two stages: in the first stage, we will devote our efforts to shedding light on the constraints, dimensions and challenges relevant to the conformity of qualifications and to the erection of a European area for occupational mobility in the 1990s. In the second stage, we will concentrate on making explicit the complex theoretical link relating the notions of labour market and vocational qualification.

8.1 THE DIMENSIONS, CONSTRAINTS AND CHALLENGES INVOLVED IN THE PROCESS OF CONVERGENCE OF VOCATIONAL QUALIFICATIONS IN EUROPE IN THE 1990S

Since the EC, which later became the European Union, is perceived as a genuine economic and social entity and as an area of exchange and economic cooperation, the mobility of individuals is not considered simply as a fundamental right but, more positively, as an essential vector of economic development of the Community. To pave the way for such conceptual evolution, the European Commission set down, as far back as 1988, directives aimed at giving impetus to the process of multilateral recognition of degrees by the member countries. It is well known that such cooperation between the EC members in the area of equivalent rating of degrees has created a constructive vision for establishing a set of European qualification standards.[2]

8.1.1 The Constraints and Dimensions Inherent to a System of Conformity of Vocational Qualifications

For all that, mutual recognition of qualifications by the member states of the European Union faces some hurdles. Such hurdles are not perforce of a methodological or technical nature. They are basically related to society-specific differences (Merle and Bertrand, 1993).[3] How then could a common conceptual process of the notion of qualification be constructed if the meaning of that notion is perceived differently in each country?

The emergence of a *European market of qualifications* is all the more problematic since the objectives pursued in laying down joint plans of action to codify and authenticate skills are restrained by the poor prospects of a harmonization of the educational structures and institutional systems governing the award of qualifications still under the responsibility of the member states.[4] However, the effort of codification and development of Community qualification standards has a totally different dimension insofar as most countries are faced with radical changes in their educational and vocational training systems. In fact, it is the methods of acquisition and authentication of skills which are called into question in the debates between the countries: how to proceed with the authentication of the skills acquired by practice? What importance should be given to theoretical apprenticeships? What kinds of complementarity could there be between first-degree course and ongoing training?

It is doubtless that the debate concerning qualifications extends considerably over recognition of qualifications since the process of employment structuring and the principles of operation of the educational structures are inevitably put in the hot seat.[5] Nevertheless, establishing a system of *conformity* of qualifications is made difficult by the fact that there are a variety of conflicting types of employment organization, training structures, job classifications and methods of collective bargaining. The chances are, however, that a minimal consensus would be attained on a common definition of qualification that would be too restrictive and would unfailingly bear little significance to the European situation or to any national reality.

To avoid such a pitfall, it may be suggested that vocational profiles should be defined which make it possible to step over the labour cut-outs that often vary from one country to another. The goal is to increase the readability of qualification procedures

> by elaborating a common description of labour activities and vocational skills which corresponds more to a *function* than to a profession. The idea is to develop a basic system of reference for a function or a specific set of tasks knowing that national contexts, methods of carrying out activities and use of skills may vary more or less significantly. (Merle and Bertrand, 1993, p. 46)

Even though the notion of vocational profiles is an instrument of increasing transparency and mutual understanding of qualification systems, it still creates some technical problems relating, namely, to how detailed should the description in the profiles be and also to linking systems of reference to employment classifications by kind applied in the member countries.[6] This viewpoint may seem to depart from the task of establishing a definition of European qualifications; however, it puts forward a judicious initiative to give a better account of how diverse the reality of employment is through an attempt to foster a pragmatic dialogue with the aim of establishing common frameworks of reference for the various States.

8.1.2   The Challenges of Conformity and Comparability of Vocational qualifications

The difficulties encountered in making educational structures and institutional systems governing qualifications in most European countries converge, must not overshadow the fact that the member states are faced with essential challenges of a similar nature. These challenges consist in creating mechanisms for a smoother transition between first-degree courses and ongoing training while taking into account cross-sectional skills in defining the systems of reference of occupational activity and in adopting advanced methods of authentication of academic, professional and other acquired experiences. This situation unveils numerous challenges inherent in the process of defining the objectives of cooperation between the member states and the political tendencies as far as the comparability of vocational skills conformity is concerned.

Overall, two models of codification and delivery of qualifications seem to dominate the European debate in the early 1990s. The first model aims at setting down *quality standards* for vocational skills to be used as a common reference in awarding qualifications to individuals. The point is to adopt *European qualification standards*, so to speak. The second model attempts to define common bases for all the member states, for testifying the skills acquired by individuals. Such bases hinge on the notions of a *portfolio of skills* or of a *European qualification passport*. Besides the problems involved in translating them effectively into practice, countries expressed a number of reservations on both models. Some countries, like the UK, view the first approach with a favourable eye because it is supposed to be an instrument of ongoing dialogue and a more effective means to make national systems converge towards European standards. Others, like France, consider that the second model would make it unnecessary to establish systems of conformity (with all the pitfalls involved therein). Also, the notion of portfolio is perceived as an instrument of recognition of the individual qualifications.[7]

Such divergences in assessment, however, correspond fundamentally to a more radical analytical opposition as regards the establishment of qualification systems. In Great Britain, for instance, the National Vocational Qualifications (NVQs) system, set down in 1986 (compare Merle and Bertrand, 1993, pp. 53–6), rests on reference systems of skills laid down by professional organizations. For each profession, the said systems give an accurate description of work situations and the skills required to master them. The means of acquisition of such skills are totally open: vocational practice may, potentially alone, lead to obtaining the qualification while academic criteria for skill acquisition are by no means favoured. Conversely, in France, the vocational training and qualification system relies on both the elaboration of national degrees for which carrying out a specific degree course is required, and on a very uneven consideration, which varies from one sector of activity to another, of such degrees in the classification systems within sectors and corporations.[8]

Thus, two trends can be delineated as far as conformity and codification of qualifications are concerned. The first trend is akin to a *certifying logic* according to which vocational reference systems are based on the analysis of skills as they are mobilized in real work situations, regardless of the methods of acquisition of such skills, while the second trend corresponds to a *degree-awarding logic* according to which authentication of skills eventually sanctions the accomplishment of a degree course and aims at guaranteeing mastery by degree-holders of a range of knowledge and capabilities that are readily available within a larger professional scope. This reasoning is generally dominated by considerations pertaining to level (rank of degrees within a scale).

However, the consistency and relevance of both ways of reasoning can only be appraised within the institutional contexts where they are rooted. The historical development of the educational system and the functional structure of the labour market exert a fundamental impact on the more systematic adoption of each of these two trends (Eyraud, Marsden and Sylvestre, 1990).[9] Hence, at the drawn of the Single European Market, debates concerning the prevalence of one model over another are inevitably distorted by national society-specific traits, although both of them evidence a genuine will to work together in order to define common conceptual bases. In the face of the flimsiness of tangible conclusions resulting from debates concerning standardization and conformity of qualifications, the EC authorities have made an autonomous intellectual endeavour that has resulted in the elaboration of a *European normative model* of authentication and certification of vocational skills.

8.1.3   The Vision of the European Commission: The System of Skills Accreditation

Faced with the structural changes in its societies, which draw the outlines of an economy based on knowledge and skills, the European Commission published a white paper on *Teaching and Learning: Towards the Learning Society* in 1995. In this paper, the European Commission develops an argument in favour of a very flexible system, which adopts and improves the certifying logic mentioned earlier. Establishing a system of 'accreditation of skills' is given priority. It is based on a principle very similar to the NVQs. In broad terms, skill is defined therein as a personal capacity to carry out a number of tasks or operations, which will be translated into quality norms and standards. It differs from the English model in so far as it does not mention any job or craft specifically, in other words, the mastery of a set of skills without there being a direct link with any professional context in particular. For this model, the method of authentication preferred is testing.

While the first indications in the white paper clarify, by way of illustration, some fields of knowledge in which tests of authentication may be required (test of proficiency in a foreign language, test in accounting techniques, and so on), methodological advances have been achieved since which sharpen knowledge and skills while differentiating them. Hence a distinction is drawn between what falls within *fundamental knowledge* (mathematics, management techniques, computer science, and so on), what is considered part of technical or *vocational skills* (marketing, management techniques, mechanics, and so on) and what has to do with *key skills* (logistics, decision-making capabilities or forecasting and risk management, and so on) which are akin to the *savoir-être* specific to French terminology. Some attempts have resulted in setting-up tools such as 'computer-use licence' which has proved to be a great success in Scandinavian countries.

This model is interesting because it highlights some of the weaknesses of the systems in application. First, it strives to take into account more effectively *cross-sectional* or *transferable* skills in the light of the more urgent requirements of the *learning society* in terms of inter-occupational mobility. Obviously, viewed from this angle, vocational degrees can hardly specify those skills 'if only because the existing vocational training system often requires taking again the same degree course in order to have one's acquired skills authenticated' (Merle, 1997, p. 42). Furthermore, European accreditations are advantageous (not purely symbolically) because they enable each individual to evaluate their knowledge and any remaining discrepancies with the existing standards. This mode of reference shows, however, significant technical deficiencies. Of course, the scope of authentication covered by certification is clearly limited to some classes of situation.

Secondly, the test method recommended in the white paper cannot stand a careful scrutiny of its viability. In this regard, it seems astonishing that such a proposal was formulated while tests have, for a long time, been a target of severe criticism in the United States, namely on account of their inability to identify the capabilities which foreshadow a good performance level in a work situation. It was precisely on the basis of that contesting argument that the debate on skills in a business environment has arisen.

> Viewed from this angle, due observation of work situations together with the occupational environment play a decisive role. It is rather in this direction that most corporations which embark on a skill-based process seem to evolve, thus restoring all its weight to the contextual dimension of knowledge and know-how. (ibid., p. 43).

Hence, the proposals put forward concerning the white paper obviously show a number of dark aspects, ambiguities and methodological failings which handicap the overall reach of operational tools. It should be noted, however, that the majority of such tools are experimental even though the end-purpose seems to be definitively set. It consists, no more no less, in ensuring transparency and skill transfer most efficiently in order to achieve a better management of *the human capital stock*[10] on the European scale.

This brief reminder of how the debate evolved in Europe over the last decade throws light on a possible shift in the stand of the EC countries.[11] While the stands taken in the early 1990s were imbued with a deep respect for national cultures, which certainly derives from a willingness to abide by the principle of subsidiarity in such a sensitive field, the tendencies defined on the basis of the white paper are far more voluntarist. They express a deep concern about a radical reform of national systems of authentication and certification of qualifications that are supposed to respond only to a part of the challenge that faces the European economies with the advent of a society based on knowledge.

8.2 THE LABOUR MARKET AND VOCATIONAL QUALIFICATION: AN INTRICATE THEORETICAL LINK

8.2.1 The Theoretical Bases of the White Paper

The European conception, as it emerges from the white paper, is clearly inspired from a market representation of relations and adjustments which guarantee, within any economic system, the compatibility in quality between employment offers and demands. It expresses an extremely orthodox vision of the functioning of the labour market. Basically, this outline is limited to individuals and skills while the function of the accreditation process is restricted to facilitating market exchange. The processes that contribute to shaping the professional competence and status of workers are hence given little weight. Skills are not recognized on the grounds of past experience and of the progress rules governing qualification within a trade or a specific type of work organization. They are relevant only in view of their immediate usefulness regardless of the circumstances in which they are built and developed.

There are a number of consequences to adopting such a vision. First of all, labour relations take place in a timeless environment. Recognition of skills, which is granted on the basis of their use value, still depends on the state of market competition and on the pace and impact of technological changes. The risk for qualifications to become obsolescent is managed only according to the market and not within the framework of long-term contracts binding employer and employee. Secondly, the collective components of the economy are severely diminished. In this regard, dilution of groupwork and blurring of professional identities, as a result of the emergence of new work organizations, are the harbinger of an increasing individualization of work relations which consecrates the relevance of a far more competitive functioning of the labour market in the face of the challenges involved in 'lifelong learning'.

This analysis rests on the following essential presupposition: that there is a

qualification referent, a measure that makes it possible to translate the quali-
tative characteristics of a person into goods. It is exactly because qualification
may be cut down to a standard object that the market appears as the most
appropriate mode of regulation for an efficient distribution of its use within an
economy. Such a reductionist stand comes up against two hurdles: on the one
hand, quantifying a vocational capability is an extremely difficult exercise; on
the other hand, defining a qualification is impossible unless it is entrusted to a
labour organization or to some social organization.

8.2.2   Qualification: An Institutional Construct

All the endeavours undertaken to take out the notion of qualification from the
scope of social interaction have, in fact, been theoretically signed away, as it
were. Such is the case of the neoclassical approach that rests on the concept of
human capital to establish a measure of useful capacities on the basis of which
the market carries out exchanges in the labour market. In this regard, evaluation originates in prices, namely through a scale of wages, which supposedly
reflects the differences in qualification. However, this viewpoint turns out to
be disputable: on the plane of theory, research has established that it is impossible to define a qualification *per se*; that is, to objectivize its content by clear-
ing up the means that help to crystallize it into capital. The same reproach can
be levelled at theses inspired by the Marxist theory, especially because of their
attempt to highlight reasonings of underqualification–overqualification of
labour which take for granted the definition of a qualification indicator.[12]

There is a strong foreboding that if the notion of qualification cannot be
explicated within the formal frameworks in which the neoclassical and the
Marxist theories confine it; it is exactly because it slips any pure value theory.
The intellectual dead-ends that this programme of research has run into call for
a deep change in how the subject matter is presented and for considering it,
henceforth, as the expression of a synthesis-based judgement that takes
account of bias, which operates within a specific area with regard to the capabilities that a worker uses within the context of his occupation. The merit of
such definition is that it establishes qualification within a theoretical framework that assigns to institutions a crucial part in regulating labour markets.

The proposal formulated herein does not prejudge adherence to any theory
in particular. Rather, it serves as an analytical background on the basis of
which a number of endeavours attempt presently to establish the theoretical
foundations of an institutional reading of the labour market and, on a wider
scale, of the functioning of economies.

The emphasis laid on contextualizing the notion of qualification leads into
a set of theoretical enrichments which leaves aside market regulation of vocational aptitudes and labour relations. Embracing the microeconomic viewpoint

makes it possible, for example, to see qualification as the matter of an organized relationship between employer and wage earner. The reasoning of cooperation or that of conflict–cooperation is viewed, in many models, as the most
highly recommended to encourage the building of vocational capabilities.
Hence is restored the temporal dimension of labour relations. Furthermore,
present endeavours relating to the impact of human resources on corporate
performance show that an efficient skill management cannot be limited to
taking account of individual skills alone. Efficiency relies more on collective
skills, which greatly depend on the quality of organizational coordination.

Reassertion of the group dimension within labour organizations seems
eventually to reflect the simple fact that theorization of productive environments goes far beyond market semantics. Nevertheless, an exclusively micro-
economic viewpoint would allow only a limited description of the factors that
create productive capacities and acknowledge their legitimacy. Therefore,
going beyond the confines of one corporation becomes necessary and leads to
adopting a more macroscopic approach.

8.2.3 National Systems of Certification and Authentication of Qualifications: From Society-Specific Consistencies to Dynamics of Change

The fact that the European countries display significant differences in their
qualification systems is now a proven and well-documented reality. The
pioneer research carried out by Maurice, Sellier and Sylvestre (1982) launched
a vast programme of research that attempts to understand and explain the
divergences. France, Germany and the UK each present a clearly different
situation in this field. This is mainly due to the specific trajectory that each of
them has followed in the twentieth century and which combine very diversely
the variables of the principle of qualification building. The educational
systems, the methods of organization and functioning of the labour market, the
forms and spheres of labour relations are all the engine of a structural dynamics which, gradually and more or less unevenly, would result in a society-
specific qualification system.

In the UK, the basic features of the qualification system are linked to a form
of organization of the labour market which is characteristic of the vocational
market. Such a form gives a preponderant place to vocational training through
apprenticeship, to codification of training sessions during employment according to the proper procedures of the trade, to inspecting and negotiating the job
in detail with the aim of defending the trade. Therefore, the component that
structures qualification is the trade itself.

In Germany, the principles that determine the professional competence
and status of the participants are degree-centred. Degrees are, in fact, an

exceptionally stable collective landmark. They are the basis of coordination and mobilization of collective participants. Corporations earmark significant investments to this system for at least two reasons: on the one hand, they are stakeholders in the vocational training process: a degree is acquired through work and training programmes; on the other hand, they give great credit to degrees upon hiring. Such reasoning underlines the possible emergence of very well structured vocational markets where the systems of reference (knowledge, know-how, *savoir-être*) are considered a part of work organization inside corporations.

In France, while qualification is considered the domain of corporations that is traditionally based on the notion of internal markets, the link is still weak between the educational and training system and employment. This fact compounds the difficulties in matching the aspirations of the young generation with corporate needs.

The characteristics of qualification certification and authentication systems are thus correlated to the mode of functioning of the labour market. The general lesson to be drawn is that any attempt at reforming a system without giving due consideration to the overall structure where it fits runs a strong risk of failure. The chances are against France adopting a system like NVQs or even another European system of skill accreditation: this kind of instrument is not likely to enjoy any recognition. Therefore, it would be sensible to think that the harmonization of qualification systems is an unattainable goal, devoid of any social meaning.

Notwithstanding, stressing the society-specific consistency of models does not mean that such models must be given a characteristic of functional stability, which makes them impervious to changes in their environment. At present, each system is faced with developments that have a more or less strong impact on its consistency. Analysing the case of France yields some interesting teachings in this regard.

Since the early 1980s, the trend of destabilization of the internal labour markets and of their system of rules (including the rule of seniority) has been strong and has inevitably affected in retrospect the cohesion of the organization as a whole. Disruptions are heightened by the new considerations relating to the capacity of workers to take initiatives and to act autonomously in opposition to qualification for job positions. The idea of qualifying organizations is gaining ground and the concept of competition is replacing the concept of qualification. Such changes are not only semantic, they reveal a more radical change in the existing paradigm.

There is indisputably an urgency to overhaul the French system to face up to the impact of such developments. Some pressures are being exerted to proceed with system deregulation to bring it closer to the European conception. Nevertheless, the first signs prove that the French model has been adapted with an unexpected amount of flexibility. Whether it is a matter of establishing new plans of action concerning the authentication of acquired experience (reform of vocational degrees, adoption of vocational qualification contracts) with the purpose of promoting again the value of practical knowledge and experience within the system of knowledge, or a matter of the endeavours undertaken in order to create cross-sectional degrees, everything proves that the French system is now capable of absorbing any 'shocks' with which it is confronted. The threat of the long-debated structural crisis is now vanishing.

As an outcome of this experience, each system, despite the recurring weaknesses or failings, has its own institutional resources that enable self-reform. The case of Germany illustrates this hypothesis just as well because, when faced with the same challenges, this country did not abandon its dual system but sought simply to increase its sensitivity to present-day challenges. This diagnosis leads us to understand that there are path institutional interdependencies, which put more or less strong restraints on the evolution of society-specific systems. Europe would undoubtedly make an error of assessment in leaving them out of account while favouring the hypothesis of one vast and free labour market.

CONCLUSION

Qualification systems, which are strongly integrated and deeply rooted in the economic history of each country, are presently undergoing significant evolution. This is specifically due to the thoughts and initiatives taken by the educational system as regards the authentication of acquired vocational experience which favour not only regulations less focused on sanctioning degree courses but also attempts at rethinking the role of vocational training and apprenticeship in real work situations in defining vocational qualification. For all that, the deep changes facing corporations turn out comparatively to share some similarities: requirement of polyvalence and adaptability of operators' skills, development of quality policies, seeking greater flexibility in production.

We should note objectively the persistence of strong national particularities in the sphere of labour management institutions (classification systems within corporations, forms of collective bargaining) as well as in the sphere of educational structures (the respective share of academic contents and vocational skills) and vocational training systems (transition between the first degree course and ongoing training) (Aventur, Camp and Möbus, 1999).[13] Having said this, the idea of giving up the creation of a common framework of reference to define qualifications must not be topical.

On the contrary, the pragmatic processes seem particulary opportune for encouraging the convergence of systems of codification and authentication of qualifications. As specified by Merle and Bertrand (1993, pp. 51–2):

> Seen from this angle, two tendencies look particularly promising: – to encourage exchanges at the level of activity sectors while relying on the opportunities that gradually stem from dialogue between European labour and management at this level. Also, making systems of codification and authentication converge would remain illusive as long as it is formulated in general terms. The prospects of success would be higher if the actors of an activity sector discuss the specific circumstances in each country, considering its particular context, in which the problems relating to the effects of technical and organizational changes on vocational training and qualification systems are raised. . . . – To elaborate a more prospective approach to qualifications. The majority of sectors must not only make the existing manpower adapt but also anticipate future needs in order to improve awareness of technical changes and of the development of products and methods of production and services management.

Before the idea of creation of a real European market of qualifications, which is still very hypothetical, is translated into practice, it seems more judicious to adopt a more progressive process with the aim of reaching a consensual conception of the idea of 'qualification' itself. This method of analysis suggests that many precepts are necessary. First of all, following the phrase *'lifelong training'* which implies a permanent process of development and renewal of knowledge, qualification must be viewed as *a lifelong, ongoing process*, which is less the result of an academic type of apprenticeship but, rather, the outcome of formal knowledge acquired through a vocational training system, of the improvement of individual aptitudes through professional and personal experience and of the development of know-how in a real work situation. Secondly, qualification, viewed as the sum of individual acquired experiences, must be assessed only in the light of *the present needs of the productive system* and of the development of the labour systems. Finally, the conception of qualifications, the elaboration of vocational training courses and of degrees corresponding thereto must be the outcome of *a collegial decision-making process in which both the State and the collective actors of the activity sectors take part.*

The few foregoing principles have two advantages: on the one hand, they make it possible to overstep the forging of a technical definition of the notion of qualification, which may generate conceptual divergences between the member states; on the other hand, such precepts may be used as a common framework of reference for the elaboration of national policies in the area of vocational training and qualification. However, the idea of bringing to convergence, if not harmonizing, vocational qualification systems and the European labour markets presupposes a strong and credible European integration.

In fact, European integration is now a process that each country has to come to terms with. It means that a supranational entity, whose legitimacy is not yet well established, would be brought to bear on the national institutional realities. The implementation of integration exerts severe constraints on the spheres of competition regulations or economic and financial policies. On the other hand, the more the challenges involved are crucial, the more delicate it becomes to carry it out into practice. European debates concerning the labour market reveal the extreme caution of the stands taken and, in broader terms, the willingness to leave in abeyance the major political tendencies pertaining to that matter. However, such caution must be qualified because there undoubtedly prevails inside the European Commission a liberal vision of how the labour market should function. The recommendations issued by the Commission over the last decade have constantly revealed a concern to steer the functioning of the labour markets towards a flexible model that is akin to the theoretical representation of the neoclassical analysis. The proposals it sets forth, in the field of authentication and certification of vocational skills, draw considerably upon that tradition and corroborate, if need be, the possible emergence of a market conception of economic efficiency.

Consequently, must we consider that the convergence of society-specific models towards a European market of vocational skills is irreversible? Or, on the contrary, would it be more pertinent to contemplate common political tendencies as regards the conception and management of vocational skills while ensuring that the national society-specific experiences, adopted to rise up to collective challenges, preserve their particularities?

NOTES

1. Which is particularly important for the participants involved because of the requirements of an emerging Single Market (states, corporations, trade unions and workers).
2. In the mid 1990s, the debates concerning degree courses and the modes of awarding qualifications abounded in Europe. In this regard, the French example relevant to engineer qualifications with a training-through-research branch and other branches of the *ingénieur des techniques* type, was an evidence of that reality.
3. It is such a cultural and historical diversity among countries that increases the complexity of setting legal frameworks for the labour market across Europe (Supiot, 1999).
4. 'Each member state claims educational exception to their benefit considering their own educational and vocational training system as a model while they acknowledge that the evolution of the system may be inspired by the experience of others or by the results of cooperation among the members of the EC' (Bousquet, 1998, p. 25). It should be noted that educational and labour management institutions are deeply rooted in the production/labour management relations that were built along history.
5. Compare Merle and Bertrand (op. cit. p. 44). The authors make it clear that the possible emergence of sectional phenomena, the selectivity of some branches of study together with the position enjoyed by academic teaching and practical vocational training are likely to develop.
6. For instance, France has many classifications by purpose: the directory of employment and trades intended to contribute to placing job-seekers, system of classification of collective conventions, statistical nomenclatures.

7. The same portfolio of skills may be adopted for a number of professions of equal level.
8. Authentication of acquired experience, as stipulated in the Law issued on 20 July 1992, enables any person proving that they had at least five years experience in a professional activity to be exempted from part of the examinations entitling them to a degree (Kirsch and Savoyant, 1999, p. 2). However, passing the examinations most often implies that the appropriate courses have been taken. In the selection process prior to hiring, namely of young people, the level attained in schooling is given great weight.
9. Negotiation efforts with the aim of adopting forms of mutual recognition of vocational qualifications underlie the idea that a skilled worker may hold a qualified employment in any member country of the European Union. Attainment of this objective remains strongly linked to the distinctive features of the European labour markets. Differentiation between these markets may be carried out at various levels (in terms of methods of qualification, concerning degrees of investment made by the wage-earner and the employer in vocational training and so on). However, the structural distinction between *professional markets* and *domestic labour markets* clarifies one of the major obstacles to harmonizing qualification systems in Europe.
10. This expression is quoted from the white paper where it is widely used.
11. In fact, it seems that the signing of the Maastricht Treaty in 1992 has spurred the Commission to show greater normativeness in its recommendations concerning reform on the labour markets.
12. In this regard, qualification is assessed by looking into the degree of work complexity to the structure of work distribution which is dependent on technology used or on capitalist relations.
13. By relying, in our comparative study, on two types of in-service training practices (which are used either at the initiative of the employer or the individual) as keys to understanding the situation in the fifteen countries that make up Europe, the authors can clearly make out two realities: on the one hand, there is a plethora of diverse situations depending on how organized in-service training is on the relations that it has built with the educational system and the labour market; and on the other hand, it appears an unequal use of individual initiative in Europe as a result of the part played by training as a cultural tradition of lifelong learning and the importance of public incentives or as a result of collective bargaining.

REFERENCES

Aventur, F., C. Campo and M. Möbus (1999), 'Les facteurs de développement de la formation continue dans l'Europe des quinze', *Cereq Bref*, 150, février.

Bousquet, A. (1998), *Education et formation dans l'Union européenne*, Paris: La documentation française.

Deakin, S. and U. Mückenberger (1993), 'La déréglementation et les marchés du travail européens', *Formation-Emploi*, 43, juillet–septembre.

Eyraud, F., D. Marsden and J.J. Sylvestre (1990), 'Marché professionnel et marché interne du travail en Grande-Bretagne et en France', *Revue Internationale du Travail*, **29**, avril.

Kirsch, E. and A. Savoyant (1999), 'Evaluer les acquis de l'expérience. Entre normes de certification et singularité des parcours professionnels', *Cereq Bref*, 159, décembre.

Maurice, M., F. Sellier and J.J. Silvestre (1982), *Politique d'Education et Organisation Industrielle en France et en Allemagne, Essai d'Analyse Sociétale*, Paris: PUF.

Merle, V. (1997), 'L'évolution des systèmes de validation et de certification. Quels modéles possibles et quels enjeux pour la France?' *Formation Professionnelle*, 12, septembre–décembre.

Merle, V. and O. Bertrand (1993), 'Comparabilité et reconnaissance des qualifications en Europe. Instruments et enjeux', *Formation-Emploi*, 43, juillet–septembre.

Pertek, J. (1998), 'Une Dynamique de la Reconnaissance des Diplômes à des Fins Professionnelles et à des Fins Académiques: réalisations et nouvelles réflexions', in J. Pertek (ed.), *La Reconnaissance des Qualifications dans un Espace Européen des Formations et des Professions*, Brussels: Bruylant.

Supiot, A. (1999), 'Transformations du travail et devenir du droit du travail: une perspective européenne', *Revue Internationale du Travail*, **138**(1).

9. Decentralized interregional cooperation in Europe

Sylvie Graziani and Michel Rombaldi

The development of global economy has encouraged the emergence of new directions for *l'école de la régulation'*. This has led to changes in the content and nature of public governance.

Within this new context, interregional cooperation becomes an essential element of decentralized public governance renewal. This form of cooperation is particularly well suited for the Mediterranean.

9.1 A NEW METHOD OF GOVERNANCE

9.1.1 The Consequences of Global Economy

Globalization brings with it a breaking down of the national coherence of productive systems. Up until now, the governance carried out by the nations owed its coherence to the existence of frontiers. Today, it can be said that, due to its almost complete disappearance of these frontiers, these have become lost within a transnational governance (Theret, 1992).

Soon it will no longer be possible for us to identify national economies (Reich, 1993), which will slowly make way for new entities: the region-states (Ohmae, 1996).

Globalization and the emergence of new economic powers encourages this spatial reorganization of the economy. Aglietta (1995) does not believe in a homogeneous tripartite distribution (North America, Asia, Europe), but is fairly convinced that we are heading towards a regulation fragmented into a number of zones that are more or less imbricated. Conversely, others (Gerbier, 1995) feel that different methods of governance can coexist while being based on a global tripartite functioning. This new method of governance would appear to be emerging in areas such as the European Union, the North American Free Trade Agreement (NAFTA) and the Association of South East Asian Nations (ASEAN), which are each developing in an autonomous manner.

We may thus observe several types of organization for productive systems, of which no one type in particular is able to impose its organization framework on the others (Boyer and Durand, 1993). We would appear to be heading towards territorial governance, in other words a multipolar economy.

We are not only witnessing a change in the spatial content of governance but also a modification in its very nature. Along with the European Union (EU) seems to be emerging a new and 'larger organization programme' of public policy (Dehove, 1997). Thus is born a new form of governance that is founded on the competencies existing at different levels of the institutional authorities. The coherence of this novel institutional architecture relies on programming procedures as well as on joint funding whose implementation is based on principles of subsidiarity,[1] of additionality[2] and of multilateral joint responsibility.[3]

It is true that at present, to borrow the concept of Mazier (1997), Europe is an incomplete institution that is not quite able to either coordinate national policies or to infuse a veritable comprehensive policy. There is a clear discordance between the European monetary policy, in particular since the setting up of the European Monetary Union (EMU), and the national budget policies. In fact, we are currently experiencing a transitional period of European construction and the final outcome will depend on the political decision that will be taken (Federal Europe or Europe of States). It is probable that European integration, if it is to be followed through to its conclusion, will necessarily bring with it a reduction in the autonomy of national economic policies (Maillet, 1992) as well as a strengthening of regional and transborder policies.

9.1.2   A New Institutional Structure

This territorial reconfiguration brings with it problems in the spatial scope of the governance methods but also in the transfer of competencies, which was previously controlled at the national policies level.

In the previous fordism type of regulation, the national government almost totally controlled governance as it both represented the guarantor of social cohesion and facilitated the drawing up of institutionalized compromises (Aglietta, 1976).

The crisis of the fordist type of organization is also that of the national government acting as the main operator of the method of governance. Today we are witnessing a two-tier transfer of competencies; towards the top in the direction of transborder and international authorities such as the EU or the IMF, and downwards in the direction of the territorial communities (decentralization law of 1982 in France).

The national government thus sees itself slowly stripped of its ruling powers, including monetary, agricultural and industrial policy, which are transferred to higher levels, and to training or regional planning policies that come under decentralized territorial control.

To reach a greater coherence in public intervention requires a central vision of the governance process which can only be realized at the highest institutional level, which here would be at the European level. We consider that there exists a hierarchy among all of these different levels and that the regions, particularly those in France, are not completely autonomous (Pecqueur, 1989). They are present within an institutional structure linked to different forms of organization ranging from Europe to the regions.

At the same time, however, the success of public policy depends on how well it is accepted and on the methods of implementation at the different lower levels, such as that of the national government and the territorial communities. This apparent contradiction can only be lifted by a joint decentralized programming that incorporates these different levels within the framework of contractual procedures such as is done with the nation/region planning contract or European programmes.

We can also observe that, among these three levels, there appeared more informal governance levels, the definition of which are less precise but that could play an important role in the future. These concern mostly the interregional cooperation programmes dealing with spatial aspects, such as those dealing with the Latin and Atlantic area.

9.1.3 The New Public Intervention

The decline of the Welfare State does not announce the end of public policies as had previously been thought, but rather indicates that the limits of a national governance have been reached, a form of governance that no longer corresponds to the requirements of globalization. It foreshadows the arrival of a new form of public governance better adapted to these changes.

The new type of governance is arising from the closely linked coordinate and hierarchical institutional structures. The optimal efficiency of such a construction will strongly depend on the relationships existing among the various institutions (Boyer, 1986). These relationships are characterized by vertical and horizontal cooperation. Within this configuration, the regional level could even be given a certain degree of autonomy, while still remaining linked to the central policies developed by the international institutions (Saillard, 1995).

The problem of linking these different levels of the new institutional structure remains to be broached. Although, from a methodological point of view, this problem would appear to favour a form of governance based on joint programming and financial principles, the nature of the controlling authorities remains to be determined. Two scenarios can be envisaged based on the current political discussions on the future of the European Union:

- a supranational governance of the federalist type with a governance authority possessing a monopoly on governance (important role of the Commission) and an irreversible decline in the nations,
- an inter-state governance from which the nations would conserve the greater part of their prerogatives based on a simple harmonization of national policies (in this case it is the European Council that would become the deciding authority).

The positioning of the conceptual and decisional framework of the joint programming is very important (see Figure 9.1). For the case of a transborder governance, this positioning is at the top of the pyramid, that is to say that it is connected to the European decisional authorities through the 'cohesion policy' and it is linked in a contractual partnership-like manner with the two other lower levels. Within this configuration the states play a secondary role.

For the second scenario, the joint programming depends mainly on the State, and is closely linked to the decentralized planning. Europe and the region both participate financially in these programmes. Within this framework, it is of course the states that remain the main decision-making authorities. Insofar as the interregional cooperation efforts are concerned, they come more under the first scenario as they give a rather wide latitude of autonomy to the territorial authorities involved. In fact, this horizontal-type cooperation will complement the vertical programming mechanisms.

9.2   INTERREGIONAL COOPERATION AS A MEANS OF ORGANIZING PUBLIC POLICIES

9.2.1   A New Method of Cooperative Governance

The forms of organization developed by human communities are inseparable from the evolution of productive systems. Each method of governance corresponds to public or private forms of institutional organization, among which interregional cooperation appears currently to be preferred.

We know that, to be effective, the market requires an institutional follow-through that currently takes on the form of closely linked coordinated or hierarchical institutional forms.

As they represent a codification of one or several fundamental social relationships (Boyer, 1986), it is in the interest of these institutional forms to cooperate, as is true for firms (Richardson, 1972) or even individuals (Axelrod, 1992). As indicated by Boyer (1986, preface), 'our historical experience suggests that few institutions can be optimized without considering their relationships with other institutions'.[4]

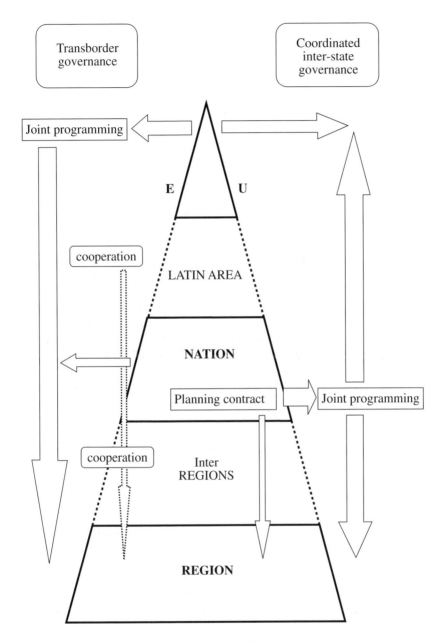

Figure 9.1   Interregional cooperation in transborder and interstate governance

The forms of cooperative public governance existing within decentralized structures can, at the present time, be considered one of the institutional forms able to make up for the waning form represented by the state. These new forms should lead to the creation of institutionalized compromises which could be developed within the framework of interregional cooperation.

In the same way that the new method of governance requires coordination mechanisms among individuals, which must go above and beyond a simple aggregation of individual strategies (Boyer and Durand, 1993), an institutional cooperation among the various levels of governance is of primordial importance. This must by far exceed a simple cooperation and thus lead to a veritable coordination of public policies in an attempt to insure a decrease in regional disparity.

In this context, multilateral cooperative regulation plays a decisive role. It should, contrary to the generally accepted idea that only the macrounits are capable of making macrodecisions (Levy-Valensi, 1993), be able to impose reference standards applicable by all. This institutionalization of the intermediate forms implies a coordination of the decentralized public policies.

The successful outcome of the territories, defined as an 'organizational complex' (Dupuy and Bernard, 1995), will depend to a great extent on these institutional agreements that affect the efficiency of the regulation method. In much the same way, the efficiency of the interregional cooperation strategies will depend on the arrangements made concerning problems shared by several regions.

The advantage of such a cooperation is particularly evident for small-sized local governments that lack the necessary funds, due to an insufficient critical mass, to stimulate regional development. Under these conditions, cooperation becomes necessary in order to optimize the resources brought into play. It is based on the complementarity of the territorial productive structures that this cooperation must be developed (Teboul, 1997).

Although local regulation consists of a group of collectively accepted agreements bringing with them a particular behaviour (Gilly and Pecqueur, 1995), cooperative regulation should produce the same effects but on a much larger scale. Interregional cooperation is thus in line with an approach encouraging joint representation, whose aim it is to make up for the limited efficiency of the market. The relationships of cooperation occur often under non-market conditions, which 'implies the development of institutions through collective apprenticeships' (Bellet, Colletis and Lung, 1993 p. 421).

Cooperation should allow an organizational synergy capable of being beneficial to each of the institutions. It is able to add value to joint projects since the costs associated with a lack of cooperation are higher than those incurred through cooperation. Interregional institutional cooperation, by encouraging the pooling of methods and procedures of public governance, leads to an increased efficiency of the public policies on regional development. The aim of this form of cooperation is, above all else, to allow both a better allocation of resources and a greater efficiency. It is based on concepts of mutual interest (Marchipon, 1995) and joint benefits (Humbert, 1995).

Interregional cooperation can be defined as being any agreement between two or several decentralized governing bodies whose aim it is to reach a set of previously fixed objectives. It fills the requirements specified in Table 9.1.

Interregional cooperation is made easier when there is spatial proximity:

- A spatiotemporal proximity, which is born of a region's geography but also of its history.
- An organizational proximity, which is more the result of how the agents organize themselves based on the institutions that they represent.
- An institutional proximity which is born of similarities among the forms of public governance.

The vast decentralizing movement has contributed to the increased participation of the territorial communities. As a result, this interregional cooperation is increasingly linked to the decentralization and development plans for the region.

Table 9.1   Requirements for interregional cooperation

General objectives	Specific objectives
* To improve institutional results	– Implement joint projects
	– Coordinate public policy
	– Organizational synergy
	– Economy of scale
	– Exchange of experience and know-how
	– Institutionalized compromise
	– Collective apprenticeship
* To strengthen social cohesion	– Reduce regional disparity
	– Harmonize the European territory
	– Regional planning
	– Strengthen solidarity
* To encourage regional integration in the Mediterranean	– Develop exchanges
	– Integrate mediterranean friendship countries
	– Encourage economic transition
	– Develop a Mediterranean network

9.2.2   Cooperation within the Framework of European Development

Cooperation in Europe is based on the idea of general interest. In its report entitled 'Europe 2000 Cooperation towards the development of the European region' (1994), the Commission particularly insisted on the need to establish cooperation for the development of Europe in order to avoid an accentuated disparity in regional development. Interregional cooperation thus becomes a means of harmonizing the European territory.

In this same report, the European Commission stresses the importance of transborder cooperation as Europe represents approximately 10 000 km of borders, of which 60 per cent are intra-community borders.

We can identify the following transborder cooperation efforts:

– Internal cooperation whose aim it is to reinforce the complementary nature among the regions of the Community.
– External cooperation that involves agreements among the non-member regions of the Union.

However, although a certain proximity, in the largest sense of the word, facilitates this cooperation, the problem concerning the relationships among partners possessing different economic levels remains to be broached. This is a crucial problem insofar as a balanced cooperation between the Northern and Southern Mediterranean regions is concerned.

To solve this problem, the European Union has implemented cooperation programmes that should lead to the development of a veritable network, thus allowing an exchange of ideas, methods and know-how. In fact, the objectives are even more ambitious as, in the long term, this may allow the emergence of regional economic development methods that could generate a veritable partnership.

Another aim of this cooperation is to strengthen pre-adhesion strategy in the Mediterranean. Regional cooperation between Mediterranean countries will require sustained community aid. To this end, a certain number of decisions have been taken over the past few years.

The European Council of Essen (the 9th and 10th of December 1994) stated that 'the community should also consider as a priority the development of cooperation links between bordering regions on either shore of the Mediterranean, in particular those operating in synergy with the pre-existing transborder and decentralized interregional cooperation of the community'.

The Mediterranean Euro conference of November 1995 stipulated in its declaration 'that regional cooperation developed voluntarily, in particular with an aim to develop exchanges among the actual partners, represented a key factor in the setting up of a free-trade zone'.

During the meeting of the territorial development ministers of the European Union that took place in Nordwijk, Holland, on the 9th and 10th of June 1997, whose aim it was to discuss a development plan for the European community, it was emphasized that all development efforts should encourage cooperation among the various levels in charge of territorial development (European, national and regional).

Today, the interregional cooperation programmes have become indissociable from the European construction efforts.

9.3 THE MEDITERRANEAN: A REGION FAVOURABLE TO COOPERATION

The first question concerning this institutionalized cooperation involves its scope of action. The zone to be adopted is not at all a technical problem but rather depends on stakes, the borders of which remain to be permanently set based on geographic and ethnic factors.

The Mediterranean basin appears to be a particularly favourable region for this type of cooperation.

9.3.1 Cooperation as a Means of Expressing a New Mediterranean Solidarity

The Mediterranean has a long and rich history. It was first a 'world economy' (Braudel, 1996), and then it later became a very heterogeneous and fragmented region, with a marked contrast between the North and the South. Far from being a drawback, this could in fact encourage cooperation. For this to be the case, it will be necessary to move on from a simple dialogue between the parties to the setting up of a veritable Euro-Mediterranean solidarity. Europe represents a natural area for the integration of Mediterranean countries to world economy (Chevallier, 1995).

Interregional cooperation strengthens European solidarity and thus participates in the creation of a more homogeneous territory, particularly within the Mediterranean, and it is in accordance with the desire to reinforce the idea of shared prosperity.

This cooperation must be conceived, at least in the long term, to encompass the entire Mediterranean region, in other words including the PSEM (Landaburu, 1993). The future of the Mediterranean is indeed at a crossroads between cooperation and disorganization, to coin the phrase of Gizard (1993).

For the cooperation to be efficient, it should be organized on the basis of 'dynamic centres'[4] that are linked to both intermediate and peripheral zones.

This partnership should be based on association agreements reflecting three major lines of priority cooperation: the stimulation of a transitional economy, the encouragement of an improved socioeconomic balance and the support of regional integration.

It is for this reason that the European Council of Corfu stressed, in June 1994, the need to strengthen Mediterranean policy within the European Union and thus encourage the Mediterranean basin to become a zone of cooperation guaranteeing peace, security, stability and well-being.

In October 1994, while evoking the social, political and economic interdependence between the EU and the eastern and southern countries of the Mediterranean, the Commission proposed the setting up of a European Mediterranean partnership able to lead to the creation of a free-trade zone in 2010.

9.3.2 Interregional Cooperation could Lead to a Mediterranean Network

Cooperation within the Mediterranean can be considered to be a progressive step-by-step evolution. First, it could begin within the area represented by the Latin area, which is the most homogeneous zone within the Mediterranean basin. This vision of cooperation concentrated mainly on the Latin area may appear restrictive as it leaves out the southern and eastern parts of the Mediterranean. It is important to understand, however, that this can only be a first step destined to strengthen solidarity in this zone. It is also a realistic conception of present day cooperation possibilities, as 'the Mediterranean is made up of peoples that are not able to unite by the year 2002' (Girard, 1993 p. 40).

Indeed, according to Daguzan (1993) 'the volatile nature of the Mediterranean region has particularly been demonstrated by the lack of an organization able to insure its stability and control', and this southern stability is essential to the security of Europe. This stability requires that the European Union takes into consideration the existing disparities in development, the ecoenvironmental problems and the flow of immigrants. Thanks to cooperative efforts, a veritable convergence policy could be set up in the Mediterranean.

Long-run prospects behove us to seek a 'multiple coastline' approach (Brunetta, 1988) for Mediterranean cooperation in order to reduce the North South imbalance and the risk of instability thereof. The aim to bear in mind is that of regional development within Mediterranean Europe.

Going from a national scale to a Mediterranean scale can only be achieved within the framework of bilateral or multilateral interregional cooperation. This could, for example, take on the form of a joint management of shared resources.

Subsequently, it will be necessary to go from a mere dialogue to the setting up of a veritable Mediterranean solidarity. Present day decisions do not sufficiently take into account the Mediterranean identity. Although Aymard and Bergeron (1992, p. 12) suggest that 'the world economy, for a long time autonomous, of the Mediterranean represented very early a spatial framework for the division of labour, the specialization of production and activities, and the exchange of commercial products over both short and long distances', Regnault (1993) states that, today, 'the Mediterranean does not represent an autonomous region of international division of labour, either in its entirety or its sub-systems'.

We will thus need to rid ourselves of this idea of an isolated inland centre that possesses a lower degree of development, but with very active marine peripheral activities, the dynamism of which were not based on the links among these activities but rather on those with the outside world.

Cooperation implies complementarity and thus regional specialization on the basis of a Mediterranean spatial division of labour.

As is suggested by the study of Mediterranean economics (CEFI, 1992 p. 21), 'there thus exists a complementarity of both resources and capabilities in the Mediterranean that predicts profitable exchanges for the entire region. These exchanges will specialize the regions and countries on the basis of a Mediterranean logic'. This specialization will be founded on a strong premise: to optimize resource allocation.

Interregional cooperation in the Mediterranean should also allow a strengthening of regional integration (Bensidoum, Chevallier, 1996) in view of creating a free-trade area. The regions could conceivably return to an economic coherence based not only on transactions but also on interregional cooperation. The Mediterranean would thus rediscover its true vocation, in other words become an area of trade (BURGEL et al., 1990), but also acquire 'a creative quality' (Fabre, 1994).

This cooperation will facilitate the exchange of ideas and sound economic development practices as well as encourage the joining of certain countries within the framework of a pre-adhesion process. It is thus the main integration factor for all the Mediterranean regions within the future European group.

NOTES

1. Subsidiarity means that only that which cannot be done at the lower levels should be performed at the higher levels.
2. The principle of additionality states that European funding should complement that of the member states and not replace it.
3. The same as is seen for the MEU constitution.
4. 'Each time, the expression implies a certain degree of economic coherence in the area examined and, particularly, that this area possess a dynamic centre around which can be seen

successive rings, namely median zones, and peripheral zones, the latter being even more disadvantaged than the former, but all being linked by trade', (Braudel, 1996 p. 320).

REFERENCES

Aglietta, M. (1976), *Régulation et Crise du Capitalisme*, Paris: Calman-Levy.
Aglietta, M. (1995), 'Le Système Monétaire International', in *Théorie de la Régulation. L'État des Savoirs*, Paris: La Découverte.
Axelrod, R. (1992), *Donnant-Donnant? Théorie du Comportement Coopératif*, Paris: Ed. O. Jacob.
Aymard, L. and L. Bergeron (1992), 'Préface', in *La Croissance Régionale dans l'Europe Méditerranéenne*, Paris: Ed. EHESS.
Bellet, M., G. Colletis and Y. Lung (1993), 'Introduction au numéro spécial: Économie de Proximité', *RERU*, 3.
Bensidoum, I. and A. Chevallier (1996), *Europe Méditerranée: le Pari de l'Ouverture*, Paris: Economica.
Boyer, R. (1986), *La Théorie de la Régulation: une Analyse Critique*. Paris: La Découverte.
Boyer, R. and J.P. Durand (1993), *L'Après Fordisme*, Paris: Syros.
Braudel, F. (1996), *Autour de la Méditerranée*, Paris: Ed. de Fallois.
Brunetta, R. (1988), *La Méditerranée: une Approche 'Multirivages', La Question Méditerranéenne*, Paris: Seuil.
Burgel, G. et al. (1990), 'La CEE méditerranéenne', *SEDES*.
CEFI (1992), *La Méditerranée économique*.
Chevalier, A. (1995), 'Les Échanges Commerciaux Euro-méditerranéens', in *Euro 6 Méditerranée. Une région à Construire*, R. Bistolfi, Paris: Publisud.
Daguzan, J.F. (1993), *La Méditerranée Inquiète*, Datar: Ed. de l'Aube.
Dehove, M. (1997), 'L'Union Européenne Inaugure-t-elle un Nouveau Grand Régime d'Organisation des Pouvoirs Publics et de la Société Internationale?', in *L'Année de la Régulation*, Paris: La Découverte.
Dupuy, C. and P. Bernard (1995), 'Conventions et Territoires', *RERU*, 4.
European Commission (1994), *Europe 2000. Coopération pour l'aménagement du territoire européen*.
Fabre, T. (1994), *La Méditerranée Créatrice*, Paris: Ed. de l'Aube.
Gerbier, B. (1995), 'Globalisation ou Régionalisation', *Economies et Sociétés*, HS, 33.
Gilly, J.P. and B. Pecqueur (1995), *Théorie de la Régulation. L'État des Savoirs*, Paris: La Découverte.
Gizard, X. (1993), *La Méditerranée Inquiète*, Paris: Ed. de l'Aube.
Humbert, M. (1995), 'Élargissement des Fondements Théoriques Standards des Politiques Industrielles', *Revue d'Économie Industrielle*, 71.
Landaburu, E. (1993), 'La Communauté Européenne et son Territoire', *L'Événement Européen*, février.
Levy-Valensi, S. (1993), 'La flexibilité du Travail: Nouvelle Norme de Régulation ou Simple Avatar de la Crise', *Économies et Sociétés*, Série R., 11.
Maillet, P. (1992), *La Politique Économique de l'Europe d'après 1993*, Paris: PUF.
Marchipon, J.M. (1995), 'La Stratégie Industrielle de l'Union Européenne: A la Recherche d'un Concept de Politique de Compétitivité Globale', *Revue d'Économie Industrielle*, 71.

Mazier, J. (1997), 'l'Europe: Enlisement ou Transition vers un Nouveau Régime de Croisssance', in *L'Année de la Régulation*, Paris: La Découverte.

Ohmae, K. (1996), *De l'Etat Nation aux Etats Régions*, Paris: Dunod.

Pecqueur, B. (1989), *Le Développement Local*, Paris: Syros.

Regnault, H. (1993), 'La Méditerranée dans la Division Internationale du Travail', in *La Méditerranée Inquiète*, Paris: Ed. de l'Aube.

Reich, R. (1993), *L'Économie Mondialisée*, Paris: Dunod.

Richardson, G.B. (1972), 'The Organisation of Industry', *The Economic Journal*, 82.

Saillard, Y. (1995), *Théorie de la Régulation. L'État des Savoirs*, Paris: La Découverte.

Teboul R. (1997), *L'Intégration Économique du Bassin Méditerranéen*, Paris: L'Harmattan.

Theret, B. (1992), *Régimes Économiques de l'Ordre Politique*, Paris: PUF.

PART THREE

Competitive Democracy and the Future
of Europe

10. A Europe of variety, not harmonization

Bruno S. Frey[1]

The integration of Europe is a fascinating and wonderful idea. One of the major ideas is to overcome the perennial *strife* between the European nations (whose worst outcomes were the two World Wars in the twentieth century). Moreover, the integration should help to solve the ongoing civil wars of long duration and bitterness that still plague this continent: in former Yugoslavia, Ireland, the Basque country and Corsica.

But Europe has not only a history of belligerence. It can be proud of its achievements in the arts, sciences, and the way of living. The basis of it all is *variety*: a Scot is unlike a Sicilian, a Breton unlike a Bavarian, and an Andalusian unlike a Prussian.

The idea developed here is based on *four* basic ingredients. The future Europe has to be:

- *peaceful*,
- *democratic*,
- *diverse*, and
- *productive*.

Our proposal of democratic decentralized jurisdictions differs drastically from the European Union existing today. In particular, (1) it emphasizes the role of citizens in the political process, and (2) decentralizes the political process to the functionally most appropriate level. The proposal thus seeks to redress the two well-known and often lamented shortcomings of the European Union: its *democracy deficit* and its *decentralization deficit*.

Our proposal also differs markedly from the various reform plans currently discussed to mitigate the two 'deficits'. Some seek to strengthen the European Parliament. But this measure does not necessarily engage the citizens of the EU more strongly in the political process nor does it really give them much more influence. Rather, it may even increase the distance between the citizens and the decision-making body (Strasbourg or Brussels are even more remote from the citizens of Europe than are the national capitals from their respective national citizens). Moreover, the concentration of over 600 professional politicians in the European parliament tends to invite the formation of yet another 'classe politique', now at the European level (similar to the Eurocrats among public employees).

The current plan to mitigate the 'decentralization deficit' is not more promising. The principle of subsidiarity is ineffective as long as the regions of Europe financially depend on Brussels and on the central governments of their nations. Political decentralization requires the power to tax for the lower levels of government. Only then are they induced and able to balance the benefits and cost of public expenditures. Only then is there fiscal responsibility, and only then are the politicians motivated to use the scarce resources to the benefits of the citizens in the lower governmental units.

The vision proposed here is quite radical, and perhaps difficult to accept, but it is not outlandish:

1. The proposal of democratic decentralized jurisdictions is based on concepts central to economics, and in particular to the economic theory of federalism (Bird, 1993; Breton, 1996), for example 'fiscal equivalence', 'voting by foot' or 'clubs'. However, they are combined in new ways, yielding a different type of federalism;
2. The proposal can be put into reality. Indeed, there are pertinent examples in history as well as today. Very importantly, the proposal can be introduced in *marginal* steps.
3. The proposal does not require the dismantling of the national states forming the European Union. Though the nationalism going with the concept of a nation has brought enormous harm to Europe in the twentieth century, it is still a strong force, and there is not much sense in directly attacking it. But what is proposed is that there should be other jurisdictions besides it, and that the nation's right of existence has to be demonstrated by its effectiveness to efficiently care for the preferences of the population.

The proposal should not be understood as a wholesale critique of the European Union. Rather, European integration has been very successful in opening markets within its confines. The four freedoms of liberal trade with respect to goods and services, and capital and labour have been achieved to a considerable degree. Though protectionist tendencies are still existing and make themselves felt almost daily, the European Union can be proud of having achieved a free market covering almost the whole of Western Europe.

The European Union is, however, not only a story of success but also one of failure. A wrong concept of Europe has increasingly taken over, and the unification process has taken a wrong turn. While these tendencies have accumulated over time, they have become dominant recently. This mistaken concept of Europe consists in *identifying integration with homogenization and harmonization*. There are hundreds of laws and directives in the European Union working in this direction. But the essence of Europe is its *variety*. The strength of Europe is its wide range of different ideas, cultures and policies. Diversity, and not unity, has been the crucial element of Europe's rise in history and continues to be so. A homogenized Europe loses its raison d'être, and will lose its economic and political role.

Integration should serve to foster this variability. It should set the rules under which the strength of the manifold components of Europe can develop. Opening up economic markets for free trade is exactly such a beneficial role: it allows suppliers to specialize in the production of differentiated goods and services following the law of comparative advantage. However, no such open and competitive *market for politics* has been established. On the contrary: the competition between governments was successfully restricted by the various European treaties and institutions. No steps have been undertaken to actively institutionalize competition between governmental units at all levels. Welfare can be improved substantially by promoting competition between newly emerging jurisdictions that are organized along functions instead of territories.

The *fifth freedom* here suggested allows for such *functional, overlapping competing jurisdictions*. They will be called by their acronym FOCJ (one such jurisdiction will be called FOCUS). FOCJ form a federal system of governments that is not dictated from above, but emerges from below as a response to citizens' preferences. This fifth freedom requires a *constitutional decision* (Frey, 1983; Mueller, 1996) which ensures that the emergence of FOCJ is not blocked by existing jurisdictions such as direct competitors or higher level governments. The European Constitution must give the lowest political units (communes) a certain degree of independence so that they can engage in forming FOCJ. The citizens must be given the right to establish FOCJ by popular referenda, and political entrepreneurs must be supported and controlled by the institution of popular initiatives. The FOCJ themselves must have the right to levy taxes to finance the public services they provide.

Section 10.1 specifies the concept of FOCJ and puts it into theoretical perspective. Section 10.2 evaluates FOCJ and discusses how the problems related with this type of jurisdictions may be overcome. Section 10.3 points out historical precursors, and Section 10.4 presents today's examples of FOCJ. In Section 10.5 the concept of competitive federalism is contrasted to other proposals. Section 10.6 offers concluding remarks.

10.1   OUR PROPOSAL FOR A EUROPE OF VARIETY

The federal units here proposed have four essential characteristics: they are

- *Functional (F)*, that is, the new political units extend over areas defined by the tasks to be fulfilled;
- *Overlapping (O)*, that is, in line with the many different tasks (functions) there are corresponding governmental units extending over different geographical areas;
- *Competing (C)*, that is, individuals and/or communities may choose to which governmental unit they want to belong, and they have political rights to express their preferences directly via initiatives and referenda;
- *Jurisdictions (J)*, that is, the units established are governmental, they have enforcement power and can, in particular, levy taxes.

FOCJ are based on theoretical propositions advanced in the economic theory of federalism. They nevertheless form a governmental system completely different to the one suggested in that literature. While the economic theory of federalism analyses the behaviour of *given* political units at the different levels of government, FOCJ *emerge* in response to the '*geography of problems*'.[2]

The four elements of FOCJ are now related to economic theory as well as to existing federal institutions, pointing out both similarities and differences to existing concepts.

10.1.1   Functions

A particular public service, which benefits a certain geographical area, should be financed by the people living in that area, that is there should be no spillovers. The different governmental units can cater for regional differences in the populations' preferences or, more precisely, to its demands. To minimize cost, these units have to exploit economies of scale in production. As the latter may strongly differ between functions (for example, between schools, police, hospitals, power plants and defence), there is an additional reason for unifunctional (or few-functional) governmental units of different sizes. This is the central idea of '*fiscal equivalence*' as proposed by Olson (1969) and Oates (1972). This endogeneity of the size of governmental units constitutes an essential part of FOCJ. However, fiscal equivalence theory has been little concerned with decision making within functional units. The supply process is either left unspecified or it is assumed that the mobility of persons (and of firms, a fact rarely mentioned) automatically induces these units to cater for individual preferences.

10.1.2 Overlaps

FOCJ may overlap in two respects: (i) FOCJ catering to different functions may overlap; (ii) two or more FOCJ catering even for the same function may geographically intersect (for example, a multitude of school FOCJ may exist in the same geographical area). An individual or a political community normally belongs to various FOCJ at the same time. FOCJ need not be physically contiguous, and they need not have a monopoly over a certain area of land. Thus, this concept completely differs from archaic nationalism with its fighting over pieces of land. It also breaks with the notion of federalist theory that units at the same level may not overlap. On the other hand, it is in this respect similar to Buchanan's (1965) *'clubs'* which may intersect.

10.1.3 Competition

The heads of FOCJ are induced to conform closely to their members' preferences by two mechanisms: while the individuals' and communities' possibilities to *exit* mimics market competition (Hirschman, 1970), their right to *vote* establishes political competition (see Mueller, 1989). It should be noted that migration is only one means of exit; often, membership in a particular FOCUS can be discontinued without changing one's location. Exit is not restricted to individuals or firms; as said before, political communities as a whole, or parts of them, may also exercise this option. Moreover, exit may be total or only partial. In the latter case, an individual or community only participates in a restricted set of FOCUS activities.

Secession has been suggested as an important ingredient for a future European constitution (Buchanan, 1991; European Constitutional Group, 1993). The right to secede stands in stark contrast to the prevailing concepts of nation states and federations where this is strictly forbidden and often prevented by force. Current European treaties do not provide for the secession of a nation from the European Union, and *a fortiori* for part of a nation.

For FOCJ to establish competition between governments, exit should be as unrestrained as possible. In contrast, entry need not necessarily be free. As for individuals in Buchanan-type clubs, jurisdictions and individuals may be asked a price if they want to join a particular FOCUS and benefit from its public goods. The existing members of the particular FOCUS have to democratically decide whether a new member pays an adequate entry price and thus is welcome.

Competition also needs to be furthered by political institutions, as the exit option does not suffice to induce governments to act efficiently. The citizens should directly elect the persons managing the FOCJ, and should be given the right to initiate popular referenda on specific issues. These democratic institutions are known to raise efficiency in the sense of caring well for individual preferences (for elections, see Downs, 1957; Mueller, 1989; for referenda Frey, 1994).

10.1.4 Jurisdictions

A FOCUS is a democratic governmental unit with authority over its citizens, including the power to tax. According to the two types of overlap, two forms of membership can be distinguished. (i) The lowest political unit (normally the community is a member), and all corresponding citizens automatically become citizens of the FOCJ to which their community belongs. In that case, an individual can only exit via mobility. (ii) Individuals may choose freely whether they want to belong to a particular FOCUS, but while they are its citizen, they are subject to its authority. Such FOCJ may be non-voluntary in the sense that one must belong to a FOCUS providing for a certain function, for example, to a school-FOCUS, and must pay the corresponding taxes (an analogy here is health insurance which in many countries is obligatory but where individuals are allowed to choose an insurance company). The citizens of such a school-FOCUS may then decide that everyone must pay taxes in order to finance a particular school, irrespective of whether one has children. With respect to FOCJ providing functions with significant redistributive effects, a minimal regulation by the central government may be in order so that, for example, citizens without children do not join 'school-FOCJ' which in effect do not offer any schooling and have correspondingly low (or zero) taxes. In this respect, Buchanan-type clubs differ from FOCJ because they are always voluntary, while membership in a FOCUS can be obligatory.

10.2   ADVANTAGES AND CLAIMED DISADVANTAGES OF FOCJ

10.2.1   Strengths

FOCJ compare favourably with traditional forms of federalism. One aspect concerns the governments' incentives and possibilities to satisfy heterogeneous preferences of individuals. Due to the concentration on one functional area, the citizens of a particular FOCUS have better information on its activity, and are in a better position to compare its performance to other governments. As many benefits and costs extend over a quite limited geographic area, FOCJ are often likely to be small. The exit option opened by the existence of overlapping jurisdictions is also an important means to make one's preferences known to governmental suppliers.

On the other hand, FOCJ are able to provide public services at low cost because they are formed in order to minimize interjurisdictional spillovers and to exploit economies of scale. When the benefits of a specific activity indivisibly extend over large areas, and there are decreasing costs, the corresponding optimal FOCUS may cover many communities, several nations, or even Europe as a whole. An example may be defence against outward aggression where the appropriate FOCUS may extend over the whole of Europe (even beyond the European Union).

The threat of dissatisfied citizens or communities to exit the FOCUS, and the benefit of new citizens and communities joining, gives an incentive to take individual preferences into account and to provide the public services efficiently. Quite another advantage of FOCJ is that they open up the politicians' cartel ('classe politique') to functionally competent outsiders. While all-purpose jurisdictions attract persons with broad and non-specialized knowledge to become politicians, in FOCJ, persons with a well-grounded knowledge in a particular functional area (say education or refuse collection) are successful.

A federal web composed of FOCJ certainly affects the role of the nation states. They will certainly lose functions they presently do not fulfil according to the population's preferences, or which they produce at higher cost than FOCJ designed to exploit cost advantages. On the other hand, the scheme does not purport to do away with nations but allows for multinational as well as small-scale alternatives where they are desired by the citizens. Nation states subsist in so far as they provide functions efficiently according to the voters' preferences.

10.2.2   Claimed Problems

Up to this point the advantages of FOCJ have been emphasized. However, there are also possible problems that will now be discussed.

Citizens are overburdened
In a federal system of FOCJ, each individual is a citizen of various jurisdictions. As a consequence, individuals may be overburdened by voting in elections and referenda taking place in each FOCUS. However, citizens in a direct-democratic FOCUS find it much easier to politically participate as they have only to assess one or a few concrete issues at a time.

Consumers are overburdened
An individual is confronted with a multitude of suppliers of public services, which is argued to make life difficult. This is the logical consequence of having more options to choose from, and is similar to supply in the private

sector. If citizens find it nevertheless to be a problem, a governmental or a private advisory service can be established which offers information and support for the consumers' decisions.

Coordination is needed

While coordination is obviously often needed, coordination between governments is not necessarily beneficial. It sometimes serves to build cartels among the members of the 'classe politique' who then evade or even exploit the population's wishes (see CEPR, 1993; Vaubel, 1994; Frey, 1994). As far as welfare increasing coordination is concerned, its need is reduced because the FOCJ emerge in order to minimize externalities. If major spillovers between FOCJ exist, new FOCJ will be founded taking care of these externalities.

Income must be redistributed

It is claimed that all forms of federalism – including FOCJ – undermine redistribution. Moreover, FOCJ are said to emerge on the basis of income. As far as redistribution is based on the citizens' solidarity or on insurance principles, this fear is unwarranted. Only as far as redistribution is a pure public good and thus must be enforced to prevent free-riding, a problem may arise. However, recent empirical research (Gold, 1991; Kirchgässner and Pommerehne, 1996) suggests that substantial redistribution is feasible in federal systems.

10.3   EXAMPLES IN HISTORY

Decentralized, overlapping political units have been an important feature of European history. The competition between governments in the Holy Roman Empire of German Nations, especially in today's Italy and Germany, has been intensive. Many of these governments were small. Many scholars attribute the rise of Europe to this diversity and competition of governmental units, which fostered technical, economic and artistic innovation (see, for example, Hayek, 1960; Jones, 1981; Rosenberg and Birdzell, 1986; Weede, 1993). The unification of Italy and Germany in the nineteenth century, which has often been praised as a major advance, partially ended the stimulating competition between governments and led to deadly struggles between nation states. Some smaller states escaped unification; Liechtenstein, Luxembourg, Monaco, San Marino and Switzerland stayed politically independent, and at the same time grew rich.

The above-mentioned governmental units were not FOCJ in the sense outlined in this contribution but they shared the characteristic of competing for labour and capital (including artistic capital) among each other. However, history also reveals examples of jurisdictions even closer to FOCJ.

The problems connected with Poland's strong ethnic and religious diversity (Catholics, Protestants and Jews) were at least partly overcome by jurisdictions organized along these features, and not along geography (see Rhode, 1960). The highly successful Hanse prospered from the twelfth to the sixteenth century, and comprised *inter alia* Lübeck, Bremen, Köln (today German), Stettin and Danzig (today Polish), Kaliningrad (today Russian), Riga, Reval and Dorpat (today parts of the Baltic republics) and Groningen and Deventer (today Dutch); furthermore, London (England), Bruges and Antwerp (today Belgian and Novgorod (today Russian) were *Handelskontore* or associated members. It was clearly a functional governmental unit providing for trade rules and facilities and was not geographically contiguous.

10.4   EXAMPLES TODAY

In two countries functional, overlapping and competing jurisdictions exist to some degree. They do not in all cases meet all the requirements of FOCJ specified above but they nevertheless show that democratic functional jurisdictions are viable.

10.4.1   US Special Districts

Single-purpose governments play a significant role in the American federalist system. Their number has increased more quickly than other types of jurisdictions (Zax, 1988). There are both autonomous and democratically organized as well as dependent special districts (for example, for fire prevention, recreation and parks). Empirical research suggests that the former type is significantly more efficient (Mehay, 1984). Existing jurisdictions tend to oppose the formation of special districts. In order not to threaten the monopoly power of existing municipalities, statutes in 18 states prohibit new municipalities within a specified distance from existing municipalities; in various states there is a minimum population size required and various other administrative restrictions have been introduced (see, for example, Nelson, 1990). Empirical studies reveal that these barriers tend to reduce the relative efficiency of the local administration (Di Lorenzo, 1981; Deno and Mehay, 1985), and tend to push toward local government (Martin and Wagner, 1978).

10.4.2   Swiss Communes

Many Swiss cantons have a structure of overlapping and competing functional jurisdictions that share many features of FOCJ. For example, in the canton Zurich (with a population of 1.2m, a size of 1700 km^2 and tax revenue of CHF

2800m) there are 171 political communes (with a tax revenue of CHF 3900m) which in themselves are composed of three to six independently managed, democratically organized communes devoted to specific functions and raising their own taxes. Examples of such types of functional communes can not only be found in the canton of Zurich but also in the cantons of Glarus and Thurgau (for the latter, see Casella and Frey, 1992). Cantonal bureaucracy and politicians have made various efforts to suppress this diversity of functional communes. However, most of these attempts were thwarted because the population is most satisfied with the public supply provided. The example from Switzerland – which is generally considered to be a well organized and administered country – shows that a multiplicity of functional jurisdictions under democratic control is not a theorist's wishful thinking but has worked well in reality.

10.5   COMPETING PROPOSALS

FOCJ differ in many crucial respects from other proposals for a future European constitution. One of the most prominent is Buchanan (1991) who stresses individual nations' right to secede but, somewhat surprisingly, does not build on Buchanan-type clubs. The European Constitutional Group (1993) focuses on the example of the American constitution, and presents constructivist proposals with respect to the houses of parliament and the respective voting weights of the various countries. Overlapping jurisdictions and referenda are not allowed for, and the exit option is strongly restricted. Other economics scholars (for example, Blöchliger and Frey, 1992; Schneider, 1992) suggest a strengthening of federalism in the traditional sense (that is, with multi-purpose federal units) but do not envisage overlapping jurisdictions. The report by the Centre for Economic Policy Research (1993, 1995) criticizes 'subsidiarity' (as used in the Maastricht Treaty) as an empty concept arguing that good theoretical reasons must be provided for central government intervention. But the report does not deal with the institutions necessary to guarantee that policy follows such theoretical advice. The idea of overlapping, not geographically-based, jurisdictions is raised (1993, pp. 54–5) but is not institutionally or practically worked out, nor is the need for a democratic organization and the power to tax acknowledged.

The proposal by European level politicians (Herman report of the European Parliament, 1994) deals mainly with the organization of the parliamentary system (the houses of parliament and the national vote weights) and to a substantial extent accepts the existing treatises as the founding blocks of the European constitution. The crucial idea of competition between governments is neglected; the report prefers to speak of the necessary 'cooperation' between governments – which in actual fact often serves to undermine the threat of competition.

FOCJ are also quite different from the regions envisaged in existing European treaties and institutions (see, for example, Adonis and Jones, 1991). A major difference is that FOCJ emerge from below while the 'European regions' tend to be established from above. Moreover, their existence strongly depends on the subsidies flowing from the European Union and the nation states (Sharpe, 1993). In contrast, the concept of FOCJ corresponds to Hayek's (1960) non-constructivist process view. It cannot *a priori* be determined from outside and from above which FOCJ will be efficient in the future. This must be left to the competitive democratic process taking place at the level of individuals and communities. The central European constitution must only make sure that no other government units, in particular the nations, obstruct the emergence of FOCJ. In contrast to Hayek, however, the scheme allows for a (closely restricted) set of central regulations, as mentioned above. Moreover, Hayek measures efficiency by survival in the evolutionary process while efficiency is here defined in terms of the fulfilment of citizens' demands.

'Subsidiarity' as proclaimed in the Maastricht Treaty is generally recognized to be more a vague goal than a concept with content (see, for example, Centre for Economic Policy Research, 1993, pp. 19–23). Even if subsidiarity were taken seriously, it would not lead to a real federal structure because many (actual or prospective) members of the European Union are essentially unitary states without federal subunits of significant competence (examples are the Netherlands, France or Sweden). The 'regions' existing in the European Union (examples are Galicia and Cataluña in Spain, or South Tyrol and Sicily in Italy) are far from being units with significant autonomous functional and fiscal competencies.

The Council of Ministers is a European decision-making institution based on federal principles (but nations only are represented) and organized according to functional principles (or at least according to the corresponding administrative units). However, this Council is only indirectly democratic (the ministers are members of governments which are democratically legitimized by the representative system) and the deliberations are not public. Exit from the European Union is not formally regulated, and exceptions to specific aspects of agreements reached (as in the Maastricht Treaty concerning the European Monetary Union and the Protocol on Social Policy, or in the Schengen Treaty concerning the free movement of persons) are granted reluctantly. Indeed, they are seen as damaging the 'spirit of Europe'. Whether differential degrees of European integration are framed as models of 'variable geometry', 'multi-track', 'multi-speed', 'two-tier', 'hard core', 'concentric circles', or as 'Europe à la carte', it always evokes fierce opposition. In a system of FOCJ, in contrast, functional units not covering everyone are taken as a welcome expression of heterogeneous demands among European citizens.

10.6   CONCLUSIONS

In view of the major advantages of FOCJ the economist's standard question arises: if this type of federalism is so good, why is it not more successful?

The organization of states today does not follow the model of FOCJ for two major reasons. An obvious, but crucial, one is that individuals and communities are prohibited from establishing such jurisdictions, and in many countries of the European Union, communities are not even allowed to formally collaborate with each other without the consent of the central government (see Sharpe, 1993, esp. p. 123ff.).

Secondly, a system of FOCJ cannot be observed because it violates the interests of politicians and public officials at the higher levels of government. The emergence of FOCJ reduces the public suppliers' power and increases citizens' influence by the newly introduced mechanisms of competition by exit and entry and by direct democratic elements. Both are regularly opposed by the *classe politique*. As politicians' discretionary room and therefore the rents appropriable are the larger, the higher the federal level, they favour a shift of competences in this direction, and oppose local decision making, especially by FOCJ, wherever possible.

In the countries of the European Union (and elsewhere) a federal system of FOCJ will not arise if these barriers are not overcome. A necessary condition is the new constitutional rules allowing the formation of FOCJ and giving citizens and governments the right to appeal to the Constitutional Court in case they are blocked.

FOCJ are a flexible concept. They can be introduced in small steps. An obvious first application is the functional units straddling communes situated on two or more member states of the European Union. Such FOCJ would make a substantial contribution to the coming together of Europe at a level directly benefiting the citizens. Such jurisdictions would contribute more to the emergence of a 'European spirit' than grand pronouncements by heads of states or pompous conferences and meetings.

Another obvious scope for applying FOCJ is the integration of the countries of the ex-Soviet empire into Europe. At present, the European Union insists that these nations fully accept the *acquis communautaire* though their economic and institutional development differs drastically from those of the present member states. Even staunch supporters of the present European system have to accept that it is impossible to integrate these countries into the EU without changing its constitution. This would present an excellent opportunity to open up the EU constitution to overcome the 'democracy' and 'decentralization deficit'.

NOTES

1. Blümlisalpstrasse 10, CH-8006 Zurich/Switzerland, Tel: +41-1-257 3731/30, Fax: +41-1-364 0366; E-Mail: bsfrey@iew.unizh.ch. The ideas developed here are the result of joint research with Professor Reiner Eichenberger of the University of Fribourg; see Frey and Eichenberger (1995, 1996, 1999).
2. Similar ideas can already be found in Montesquieu (1749). Burnheim (1985) mentions similar elements. In the economics literature related concepts have been proposed by Tullock, (1994), who calls it 'sociological federalism' (and Wehner (1992)). Casella and Frey (1992) discuss the concept and refer to relevant literature.

REFERENCES

Adonis, Andrew and Stuart Jones (1991), 'Subsidiarity and the European Community's constitutional future', *Staatswissenschaft und Staatspraxis*, **2**(2), 179–96.
Bird, Richard M. (1993), 'Threading the fiscal labyrinth: some issues in fiscal decentralization', *National Tax Journal*, **46**, 201–21.
Blöchlinger, Hansjörg and René L. Frey (1992), 'Der schweizerische Föderalismus: Ein Modell für den institutionellen Aufbau der Europäischen Union', *Aussenwirtschaft*, **47**, 515–48.
Breton, Albert (1996), *Competitive Governments. An Economic Theory of Politics and Public Choice Finance*, New York: Cambridge University Press.
Buchanan, James M. (1965), 'An economic theory of clubs', *Economica*, **32** (February, 1–14.
Buchanan, James M. (1991), 'An American perspective on Europe's constitutional opportunity', *Cato Journal*, **10**(3), 619–29.
Burnheim, John (1985), *Is Democracy Possible?: The Alternative to Electoral Politics*, Cambridge: Polity Press.
Casella, Alessandra and Bruno S. Frey (1992), 'Federalism and clubs: towards an economic theory of overlapping political jurisdictions', *European Economic Review*, **36** 639–46.
Centre for Economic Policy Research (CEPR) (1993), *Making Sense of Subsidiarity: How Much Centralization for Europe?*, London: CEPR.
Centre for Economic Policy Research (CEPR) (1995), *Flexible Integration. Towards a More Effective and Democratic Europe*, London: CEPR.
Deno, Kevin T. and Stephen L. Mehay (1985), 'Institutional constraints on local jurisdiction', *Public Finance Quarterly*, **13**, 450–63.
DiLorenzo, Thomas J. (1981), 'Special districts and local public services', *Public Finance Quarterly*, **9**, 353–67.
Downs, Anthony (1957), *An Economic Theory of Democracy*, New York: Harper and Row.
European Constitutional Group (1993), *A European Constitutional Settlement*, (Draft) London.
Frey, Bruno S. (1983), *Democratic Economic Policy*, Oxford: Blackwell.

Frey, Bruno S. (1994), 'Direct democracy: politico-economic lessons from Swiss experience', *American Economic Review*, **84**(2), 338–48.

Frey, Bruno S. and Reiner Eichenberger (1995), 'Competition among Jurisdictions. The Idea of FOCJ', in Lüder Gerken (ed.), *Competition among Institutions*, London: Macmillan, pp. 209–29.

Frey, Bruno S. and Reiner Eichenberger (1996), 'FOCJ: competitive governments for Europe', *International Review of Public Economics*, **16**, 315–27.

Frey, Bruno S. and Reiner Eichenberger (1999), *The New Democratic Federalism for Europe: Functional Overlapping and Competing Jurisdictions*, Cheltenham, UK and Lyme, US: Edward Elgar.

Gold, Steven D. (1991), 'Interstate Competition and State Personal Income-Tax Policy in the 1980s', in Daphne A. Kenyon and John Kincaid (eds), *Competition among States and Local Governments*, Washington, DC: Urban Institute Press, pp. 205–17.

Hayek, Friedrich A. von (1960), *The Constitution of Liberty*, London: Routledge.

Herman, Fernand (Reporter) (1994), 'Zweiter Bericht des Institutionellen Ausschusses über die Verfassung der Europäischen Union', Sitzungsdokumente A3-0064/94, Europäisches Dokument.

Hirschman, Albert O. (1970), *Exit, Voice and Loyalty*, Cambridge, MA: Harvard University Press.

Jones, Eric L. (1981), *The European Miracle*, Cambridge, UK: Cambridge University Press.

Kirchgässner, Gebhard and Werner W. Pommerehne (1996), 'Tax harmonization and tax competition in the European Community: lessons from Switzerland', *Journal of Public Economics*, **60**, 351–71.

Martin, Dolores and Richard Wagner (1978), 'The institutional framework for municipal incorporation', *Journal of Law and Economics*, **21**, 409–25.

Mehay, Stephen L. (1984), 'The effect of governmental structure on special district expenditures', *Public Choice*, **44**(2), 339–48.

Montesquieu, Charles Louis (1749), *De l'Esprit des Lois*, Paris: Garnier.

Mueller, Dennis C. (1989), *Public Choice II*, Cambridge: Cambridge University Press.

Mueller, Dennis C. (1996), *Constitutional Democracy*, New York: Oxford University Press.

Nelson, Michael A. (1990), 'Decentralization of the subnational public sector: an empirical analysis of the determinants of local government structure in metropolitan areas in the US', *Southern Economic Journal*, **57**, 443–57.

Oates, Wallace E. (1972), *Fiscal Federalism*, New York: Harcourt Brace Jovanovich.

Olson, Mancur (1969), 'The principle of "fiscal equivalence": the division of responsibilities among different levels of government', *American Economic Review*, **59**(2), 479–87.

Rhode, Gotthold (1960), 'Staaten-Union und Adelsstaat: zur Entwicklung von Staatsdenken und Staatsgestaltung in Osteuropa, vor allem in Polen/Litauen, im 16. Jahrhundert', *Zeitschrift für Ostforschung*, **9**, 185–215.

Rosenberg, Nathan and L.E. Birdzell (1986), *How the West Grew Rich. The Economic Transformation of the Industrial World*, London: I.B. Tauris.

Schneider, Friedrich (1992), 'The federal and fiscal structures of representative and direct democracies as models for a European Federal Union: some ideas using the public choice approach', *Journal des Economistes et des Etudes Humaines*, **3**, 403–37.

Sharpe, L.J. (ed.) (1993), *The Rise of Modern Government in Europe*, London: Sage.

Tullock, Gordon (1994), *The New Federalist*, Vancouver: Fraser Institute.

Vaubel, Roland (1994), 'The political economy of centralization and the European Community', *Public Choice*, **81**, 151–90.

Weede, Erich (1993), 'The impact of interstate conflict on revolutionary change and individual freedom', *Kyklos*, **46**, 473–95.

Wehner, Burkhard (1992), *Nationalstaat, Solidarstaat und Effizienzstaat*, Darmstadt: Wissenschaffliche Buchgesellschaft.

Zax, Jeffrey S. (1988), 'The effects of jurisdiction types and numbers on local public finance', in Harvey S. Rosen (ed.), *Fiscal Federalism: Quantitative Studies*, Chicago: The University of Chicago, pp. 79–106.

11. Enlargement of the European Union and the Approximation of Law: lessons from an economic theory of optimal legal areas

Dieter Schmidtchen, Alexander Neunzig and Hans-Jörg Schmidt-Trenz

11.1 INTRODUCTION

Enlargement of the European Union means extending the area in which Union Law rules. As the Commission in its 'Agenda 2000. For a stronger and wider Union' declares, new members have to 'take on the rights and obligations of membership on the basis of the acquis as it exists at the time of accession; they will be expected to apply, implement and enforce the acquis upon accession; in particular the measures necessary for the extension of the single market should be applied immediately' (Bulletin of the European Union, Supplement 5/97, p. 52). Currently, several applicant countries, among them Czech Republic, Estonia, Hungary, Poland, Slovenia, try to meet this challenge with the assistance of the European Commission.

If the European Union were only an economic entity, then the determination of the optimal size would seem to be an easy task: it should be as large as possible (see also Gros and Steinherr 1995, p. 503). But for the European Union as a legal area things might look different: presumably, its optimum size is neither one member state, nor is it all states in the world with their heterogeneous preferences, different income levels, and specific cultural and legal histories. But where exactly should the Union border be drawn?

This chapter addresses the enlargement issue from the point of view of the economic theory of optimal legal areas. For the purpose of this chapter an optimal legal area is defined as the group of economic agents for whom submitting to a protective agency enforcing a specific legal order maximizes net benefits (benefits net of costs). In the spirit of the social contract theory as developed by the Virginia School (see Buchanan, 1975, 1990) and the theory of clubs (see Buchanan, 1965; Allen, Amacher and Tollison, 1974; and Sandler and Tschirhart, 1980), states and state-like entities such as the European Union are viewed as law enforcement agencies, that is, protective clubs, with finite membership.

Each state works like a firm, organized in four divisions: government, legislation, police and courts. What matters from an institutional point of view is the production and enforcement of law. In Kronman's terms: the firm produces possessive and transactional security (Kronman, 1985). While for domestic, internal, transactions one monopolist, the protective state, has the responsibility for making and enforcing law, international, external, transactions establish contact with a multitude of legal systems and with the monopoly of power claimed by each state within its boundary. Given a multipolar system of protective states organized around the principle of the territoriality of law, each protective state can only ensure the possessive and transactional security of its clients within its territory; it cannot ensure their possessive and transactional security beyond state borders. From this point of view – which characterizes the New Institutional Economics of International Transactions – enlargement is a kind of merger of protective states involving the harmonization of law.

The new analytical framework provided by the economic theory of optimal legal areas allows the study of legal issues of the enlargement of the European Union. Rather than taking the enlargement decision as given, the optimal size of the Union is derived by taking account of the following economic parameters: the international allocation of human capital, the productivity of human capital, traditional trade barriers, administrative protectionism, differences in the regulatory setting and the legal orders, the enforcement costs of both internal and external transactions.

This chapter is theoretical and does not provide empirical evidence. However, all the parameters and variables used in the analysis can be operationalized. Thus, the approach adopted in this chapter allows for a derivation of empirically testable hypotheses. A further remark seems in order: the chapter addresses the enlargement issue from a purely economic point of view; so-called political as well as military considerations are neglected. However, it should be pointed out that these factors can be analysed using a generalized version of the model used here.

The rest of the chapter is organized as follows: Section 11.2 contains a rough outline of the theory of optimal legal areas. Section 11.3 presents several enlargement scenarios and derives a rule for the computation of the optimal degree of enlargement. Section 11.4 deals with the economics of the adoption of the acquis by the applicant countries. Section 11.5 concludes the chapter.

11.2   AN ECONOMIC THEORY OF OPTIMAL LEGAL AREAS

The social contract theory as developed by Buchanan (1975) and others uses the traditional rational choice model in order to explain how the 'Hobbesian problem of social order' can be solved by a voluntary, that is, unanimous, agreement upon a system of 'property rights' and the simultaneous installation of an enforcement institution, the 'protective state'. That agreement (or contract) is elaborated on the basis of an equilibrium situation without contract, the so-called natural equilibrium, prevailing in the 'state of nature'. The prospects for voluntary cooperation thus opened (on the grounds of antic-ipated increases of utility due to compliance with the contract at a post-consti-tutional level), determine the contents of the contract, as Buchanan (1975) has shown.

The governance of social interactions on the basis of a rule of law princi-ple allows people to economize on transaction costs, which can broadly be defined as the costs of running a politico-economic system. In particular, a system of private law – consisting of property and contract law – allows people to engage in welfare-improving exchange relations. At the same time, transaction costs may also explain why a unified global order of law and its enforcement does not come into being.

The economic theory of optimal legal areas is based on two functions: the per capita income production function and the per capita enforcement cost function. Both per capita income and per capita enforcement costs of the legal order are functions of

- the degree of specificity of property rights in terms of the content and personal assignment,
- the degree of enforcement of property rights,
- the degree of openness of the economy and
- the size of the club in terms of membership size.

Enforcement costs also depend on whether the club is organized according to the territoriality or the personality principle.[1] Since we are interested in the optimal size of the club we analyse per capita income and enforcement costs as a function of the size of the club (assuming the other variables to take on their optimal values).[2]

11.2.1   The Income Production Function

Paraphrasing Adam Smith's famous statement that the division of labour is limited by the extent of the market one could say that the division of labour is

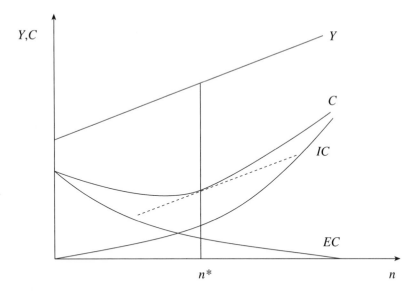

Figure 11.1   Optimal size of the state

limited by the size of the club. Since a deepening of the division of labour leads to higher wealth we can start with the assumption that per capita income increases with the size of the club. Connecting the division of labour with the number of economic transactions, we might alternatively say that the number of transactions increases with the size of the club, thereby increasing the wealth of the members. For the sake of simplicity we further assume that the marginal return of a member is constant, which means that any additional member of the club increases the per capita income by a constant amount. Given these assumptions, the income production function is a linear function with positive slope. This function is depicted in Figure 11.1, in which Y denotes per capita income and n membership size (see the linear curve labelled Y). The slope of this curve depends on the productivity of the human capital of the club members and the outsiders, the quality of the legal orders and the barriers to trade.

11.2.2   The Enforcement Cost Function

The per capita enforcement costs, denoted C, consist of two parts. One part reflects the costs incurred for enforcing the legal order *internally* among the contract parties themselves. This part includes costs of safeguarding domestic contracts and costs of dispute management under the procedural rules of the protective club to which the legal order compatriots belong. The other part of the enforcement costs takes account of the fact that the legal order needs to be defended *externally*, that is, against strangers to the legal order (non-compatriots). This could come about for two reasons: First, a state could attack members of another state in order to opportunistically appropriate their wealth and enslave them. Secondly, if there are transactions between individuals belonging to different states, either tortious acts, contract or criminal conflicts may arise. Thus, private international transactions may result in conflict and ultimately in war unless there is a 'superclub' dealing with such problems on an international scale. Both factors are the source of costs that can be considered as transaction costs of running a multitude of states.

Internal enforcement costs can be interpreted as a function of the number of (voluntary and unvoluntary) transactions performed among the members of the club. We assume that internal enforcement costs increase with membership size as is represented in Figure 11.1 by the curve labelled *IC*. Like internal enforcement costs, the external enforcement costs can be written as a function of the number of transactions between members of the club and foreigners. The number of external transactions decreases with the club size and it also decreases with higher barriers to trade. The external enforcement costs are represented in Figure 11.1 by the downwards sloping curve labelled *EC*.

Overall enforcement costs *C* are the sum of the internal and external enforcement costs. The curve of the overall enforcement costs per capita can be derived by vertical aggregation of the *IC* and *EC* curves. Given the properties of the internal and external enforcement cost functions, as shown in Figure 11.1, the *C* function is *u*-shaped.

We assume that the territoriality principle rather than the personality principal is applied as enforcement technology. As has been shown elsewhere (see Schmidtchen and Schmidt-Trenz, 1990), the territoriality principle is the efficient one. With the personality principle in place the *C* function would have to be shifted upwards in Figure 11.1.

11.2.3 The Optimal Size of a Protective State

State size is optimal if the net gain from membership is at a maximum. The net gain, denoted *G*, is defined as the difference between per capita income and per capita enforcement costs: $G = Y - C$. The net gain is at a maximum where the slope of the income curve *Y* equals the slope of the enforcement cost curve *C*. That is the case with $n = n^*$ (see Figure 11.1); n^* represents the optimal size of the protective state.

The curves in Figure 11.1 labelled *Y*, *C*, *IC* and *EC* represent, respectively, the income function and the total, internal and external enforcement costs functions. As can easily be seen, it is the *u*-shape of the enforcement cost function that is responsible for a finite optimal size of states.[3] The optimal size n^*

can be algebraically calculated by setting equal the partial derivatives of the Y function and the C function with respect to n, which yields the first order condition for a maximum. Solving for n leads to a formula determining optimal size.[4] This formula shows how optimal membership size depends on the parameters of the model. It allows for the following interpretation:

- State size of zero can never be an optimum.
- With a very flat internal enforcement cost function a state of optimal size comprises the world population.
- An increase (decrease) of the internal enforcement costs implies a smaller (bigger) optimal size. The reason is that a change of the internal enforcement costs leads to a substitution of membership for non-membership: with lower internal enforcement costs membership becomes more attractive relative to non-membership, and vice versa with rising internal enforcement costs.
- Analogously, an increase (decrease) of the external enforcement costs implies a bigger (smaller) optimal size n^*.
- A higher productivity of human capital implies higher optimal size of the state because the marginal product of internal human capital rises relative to the external one (the income production function becomes steeper).
- Free trade does not imply world population being the optimal state size.[5]

11.3   ENLARGEMENT

11.3.1   The Modified Model

We now turn to an application of the theory of optimal legal areas. If there were no transaction costs, and if the world population were homogeneous, then the number and size of the nations could be structured in an efficient manner. All you need is to divide world population by n^*. However, this is not the world as we know it. Transaction costs are positive, world population is not homogeneous and history matters. As for the latter, think of the cold war and the iron curtain, two factors that have been operating as constraints to a purely economic determination of the number and size of nations. The political challenge nowadays is not how to implement the grand design, but how to manage the enlargement of the Union. This does not make the model of the preceding section useless, but it has to be modified in the following way. Before enlargement world population is assigned to three groups of states: the European Union (E countries), the Middle and Eastern European countries (M

countries) and the rest of the world (R countries), which have size n_E, n_M and n_R, respectively. We then take the fall of the iron curtain as a factor allowing for a restructuring of the initial assignment of the world population. Enlargement leads to splitting up the former M group into two subgroups, namely new members, denoted Q with group size n_Q, and outsiders, denoted D with group size n_D. Figure 11.2 shows the pattern of this restructuring and the respective group sizes. The upper part of Figure 11.2 shows the initial assignment of the world population, the lower part the assignment after enlargement has taken place. The respective group sizes are indicated in between.

We also take explicit account eof differences in the legal orders by intro-ducing a parameter α which represents the effects of the regulation of economic activities as well as of private law on the productivity of human capital. The higher α, the higher the productivity of the human capital. Productivity serves as a measure for the quality of a legal order. This conven-tion opens up the possibility of a very simple representation of legal order differences.[6]

We assume that in the case of different αs the minimum value is binding. That means, the worse legal order determines the productivity of international transactions. As for the traditional barriers to trade, denoted j, we assume that in the case of two countries having different levels of traditional trade barriers the higher trade barriers are binding for both countries. Whereas both the differences in the quality of legal orders and traditional trade barriers affect national income negatively, the causal chain is different: trade barriers reduce

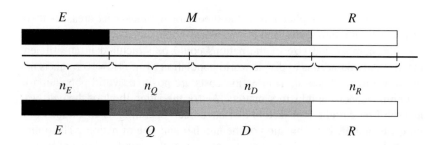

Figure 11.2   Assignment of world's population before and after enlargement

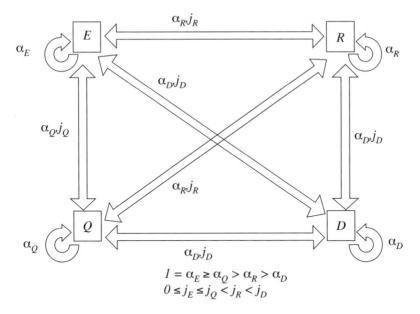

$$1 = \alpha_E \geq \alpha_Q > \alpha_R > \alpha_D$$
$$0 \leq j_E \leq j_Q < j_R < j_D$$

Figure 11.3   Network of transactions

the volume of transactions; legal order differences reduce the 'quality' of an international transaction in terms of its surplus.[7]

Figure 11.3 shows the network of transactions within and among the four groups of countries E, Q, R and D. Double-headed arrows represent the international transactions between two countries connected by each arrow. The curved arrows stand for internal transactions.

Group E's legal order is assumed being better than that of the R and D groups (and it might be better than that of the Q group); see the α ranking below Figure 11.3. Traditional trade barriers are ranked in a reverse order; see the j ranking below Figure 11.3. All internal markets are assumed as operating without any trade barriers.[8] The parameters attached to 'international' arrows reflect our assumption that the lower values of α and the higher value of j are binding.

The abovementioned modifications lead to a slightly modified income production and enforcement cost function. However the pattern of these functions remains unchanged.

11.3.2   Enlargement Scenarios

A full-fledged model consists of two steps. In the first step current Union size, denoted n_E^*, must be determined under the constraint that the size of the M

countries is constant. This restriction reflects the fact that, given the iron curtain, it was impossible for the M countries to join the Union. Enlargement of the Union in the past occurred by taking over members of the R countries.

The second step addresses the enlargement issue. The fall of the iron curtain changed the abovementioned constraint and opened up a new possibility for enlargement. We ask whether from the point of view of the Union it makes sense to allow Middle and Eastern European countries to enter the Union. We leave out the presentation of the first step and assume that the current Union size is optimal. This assumption seems reasonable because the Union got larger in the past but stopped growing.

In order to calculate the optimal degree of enlargement, we start with Union size n_E^* and ask two questions:

> Does enlargement improve the net welfare of the old members of the Union?
> If the answer is yes: what is the optimal degree of enlargement?

Does enlargement improve the welfare of the European Union?
We proceed with the help of a new figure. Figure 11.4 is a modified version of Figure 11.1. The vertical axis measures per capita income and per capita enforcement costs in the Union. We have two horizontal axes. The upper one measures the size of an enlarged Union as the sum of $n_E + n_Q$. Note that n_E

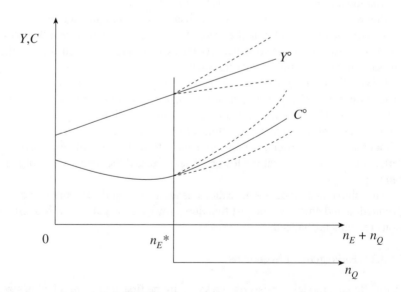

Figure 11.4 Optimal Union size

stands for Union size before enlargement occurs and n_Q measures the degree of enlargement. The higher the n_Q, the more countries are joining the Union. Current Union size is at n_E^*. Since we are interested only in the enlargement issue we take n_E^* at the starting point of a new horizontal axis drawn below the other one. This new additional horizontal axis only measures the degree of enlargement, denoted n_Q.

We started with the assumption that the Union reached its optimal size n_E^*, given the constraint created by the iron curtain. Let Y^0 and C^0 denote the income and enforcement costs functions of the Union, respectively, under this constraint. The optimal size of the Union is given by the value n_E^*, for which the slopes of Y^0 and C^0 are identical (see Figure 11.4). Thus, the values of Y^0 and C^0 at n_E^* reflect the per capita income and enforcement costs for $n_Q = 0$.

Whether enlargement makes sense economically depends on the slopes of the functions Y and C at n_E^*, $n_Q = 0$. If $Y^0 = Y$ and $C^0 = C$ the net gain from enlargement would be zero, since the slopes of the new functions are identical to those of the respective old ones. Therefore, a necessary but not sufficient condition for enlargement is a difference of the slopes of the new curves at n_E^* compared with those of the respective old curves. Graphically, this would show up in a kink at n_E^* for the respective curves. In Figure 11.4 curves having a kink are depicted as dashed curves.

Several scenarios must be distinguished, which are summarized in the following matrix (Table 11.1) and graphically represented in Figure 11.4.

For each scenario one can read off from the matrix whether enlargement is profitable (yes) or not (no). Consider cell 4. The C curve remains the same, meaning that C^0 in Figure 11.4 is the relevant enforcement cost curve; the (dashed) Y curve is steeper than the old Y curve, labelled Y^0. This implies that the net gain from enlargement is positive. To be sure, enlargement would lead to higher enforcement costs but it also adds to per capita income *and* the additional income exceeds the additional costs.

Table 11.1 Enlargement scenarios

		Y curve		
		steeper	same	flatter
	steeper	1 no/yes	2 no	3 no
C curve	same	4 yes	5 no	6 no
	flatter	7 yes	8 yes	9 no/yes

Consider now cell 6. Here the enforcement cost curve still remains the same, but the income curve becomes flatter (lower dashed income curve). This means that enlargement would lead to additional costs exceeding the increase of per capita income. Clearly, this would reduce the welfare of the Union. In a similar way one should interpret the other cells of the matrix.

Scenarios 1 and 9 do not allow for an unique answer. Regarding scenario 1, the answer would be no (yes) if the *C* curve is steeper (flatter) than the *Y* curve; an analogous argument holds for scenario 9.

What is the optimal degree of enlargement?

We have just derived different enlargement scenarios. For all scenarios with a 'no' attached to them in Table 11.1 the optimal degree of enlargement is zero. As for the other scenarios the theory of optimal legal areas provides a rule for the determination of the optimal degree: try to get larger as long as the marginal welfare gain from enlargement is positive. The marginal welfare gain is defined as the difference between the change of the per capita income due to an additional member and the change of the per capita enforcement costs associated with this increase of club size.

The optimal degree of enlargement is reached if this marginal welfare gain is zero. That is the case where the slope of the income curve equals the slope of the enforcement cost curve.

In another paper we derived a formula determining this optimal degree (see Schmidtchen, Neunzig and Schmidt-Trenz, forthcoming). This formula shows that the optimal enlargement depends on the following parameters: the productivity of human capital, the degree of the approximation of law, the quality of the legal orders of the failing applicants and the rest of the world, the traditional barriers to trade among all groups in the world, the internal and external enforcement costs, and the relative group sizes. In Schmidtchen, Neunzig and Schmidt-Trenz (forthcoming) comparative static results are derived showing how the optimal degree of enlargement depends on each of the parameters just mentioned. Of course, the question where exactly the optimum lies can only be answered with the help of empirical data. We would like to stress that all parameters mentioned above can be statistically measured. Thus, the optimal degree of enlargement can be computed.

As already mentioned in the introduction, so called political as well as military considerations are neglected in the model. However, that does not make this model useless. On the contrary, the model can be used to calculate the costs in economic terms of a deviation from the optimum because of political or military considerations. An enlargement policy which claims to be rational must take these costs of political and military considerations into account. Politicians might argue that political and military effects associated with enlargement have to be interpreted as benefits rather than costs. If so, a generalized version of the model used here could be set up in order to provide a more comprehensive analysis. There might be still some readers who are not convinced that a reasoning in optimality terms does justice to the enlargement issues. But they should be ready to answer the question why stopping?

11.4   THE APPROXIMATION OF LAW

As a precondition for access to the Union new members must adopt the acquis. The channel through which approximation affects the Union is in our model parameter α_Q in the income production function. Since for both the law in the books as well as the law in practice, approximation will be a matter of degree α_Q can take on values in the range from α_D (= no approximation) to $\alpha_E = 1$ (= perfect approximation).[9] The higher α_Q the higher the increase in Union per capita income and the higher the optimal amount of enlargement n_Q^* (given enlargement is profitable at all, see the respective scenarios). Since the marginal productivity of new members reaches a maximum at $\alpha_Q = 1$ perfect approximation seems to be the best from the point of view of the Union. However, there are costs to be taken account of. Although the costs of the approximation of law must be mainly borne by the applicant countries, the Union has to consider opportunity costs. The reason is that a realization of a higher degree of approximation of law takes more time. Though the Union would also reap benefits from an approximation of law without immediate enlargement, these benefits might be smaller than those from allowing countries to become new members even if they have not perfectly adopted the acquis. The reason is that with enlargement the negative welfare effects of traditional trade barriers disappear. Thus, there is a trade off that might make enlargement even with $\alpha_Q < 1$ a preferable option. At first glance, a dynamic factor seems to support this conclusion. Being a member of the Union might speed up the process of approximation of law. However, an opposite effect might also be possible. Being a member of the Union means having decision-making rights which could be used by the new members to slow down this process in order to save set up and running costs of a legal order 'forced' upon them.

Is an approximation of law necessary for making enlargement profitable for the Union? Without approximation of law the income production function would be flatter. The worst case scenarios can be read off from the third column in Table 11.1. As it turns out, there is a case in which enlargement would be profitable even without an approximation of law, namely scenario 9. If the slope of the income production function at n_E^* were to exceed the slope of the enforcement cost function at n_E^* the marginal gain of enlargement would be positive. Thus, approximation is not a necessary condition for a profitable enlargement.

Is approximation of law a sufficient condition for making enlargement profitable? Again, the answer is no (see scenario 1 in Table 11.1). In this case the slope of the (steeper) income function at n_E^* is smaller than the slope of the (steeper) enforcement cost function at n_E^*.

One factor closely related to the approximation issue the treatment of which, however, would require a separate model, should be mentioned, namely asymmetric information. We can look at the enlargement issue from the point of view of the principal–agent theory. It then makes sense to assign the role of the principal to the Union and consider the applicant countries as being the agents. Principal–agent theory tells us that a rational player with superior information will take advantage of the other player. Two kinds of asymmetric information are of relevance in our context. The applicant countries have better information than the Union regarding their type. Types can be defined according to the actual degree of approximation of law. Thus, the Union is confronted with a kind of adverse selection problem. The literature about mechanism design, signalling games and screening games provides the analytical tools for addressing this problem (see Dutta, 1999).

Beside *ex ante* asymmetric information, which adverse selection refers to, there is *ex post* asymmetric information leading to a moral hazard problem. In our context this would mean that if the Union would have allowed access without a sufficient degree of approximation of law the Union would be unable to force the new members to act according to its interests, that is, to make progress in adopting the acquis.

However, matters might be much more complicated than discussed, given the fact that nobody knows what exactly the content of the acquis is all about. Of course, in the process of negotiating accession the Union has the power to define the content and to decide whether applicant countries have met the requirements. It should be obvious that this position opens up the possibility for opportunistic behaviour on the side of the Union.

11.5   CONCLUSION

This chapter is a first step toward the development of a theory of optimal legal areas and its application to the study of enlargement of the European Union.

The model presented in this chapter has high explanatory power, since it can identify parameter constellations determining the optimal degree of enlargement. Note that there are no other scenarios beyond the nine listed in Table 11.1. Thus, Table 11.1 is exhaustive. Furthermore, with the income and the enforcement costs the most important variables are included in the model. Of course, the model can be enriched by including 'non-economic' benefits from enlargement such as sustaining peace or other effects discussed by politicians and political scientists.

As already mentioned, the costs of approximation of law have to be borne by the applicant countries (although advice and money is provided by the EU). These costs might be of a considerable magnitude: new laws have to be enacted, new bureaucracies must be set up; a court system has to be installed, lawyers and judges must be trained; the whole legal and institutional structure must be fine-tuned to that of the Union. As we all know, what is enacted by Brussels, Strasbourg and Luxembourg cannot be considered being efficient all the time. Of course, the costs mentioned above might be outweighed by the benefits from membership. But this issue was not raised in the model presented above.

Moreover, the optimal degree of enlargement was calculated from the point of view of the old members of Union. But, what might be optimal for them must not be optimal from the point of view of all parties affected by the enlargement decision.[10]

NOTES

1. Both principles represent techniques of enforcing the law. The territoriality principle means that enforcement is linked to a certain territory. It is 'a strategy to control people and things by controlling area' (Sack, 1986, p. 5). But the protection by a nation's law can also be linked to the person as such (manifest in the form of 'national citizenship') and determined independently of that person's present place of residence (see Schmidtchen and Schmidt-Trenz, 1990).
2. A comprehensive treatment of the theory of optimal legal areas can be found in Schmidt-Trenz and Schmidtchen (forthcoming).
3. For a more thorough discussion of this points see Bean (1973, p. 204), Auster and Silver (1979, p. 29), and Moss (1980, p.25). As an analogy to the theory of the firm, Bean (1973, p. 204) assumes such a shape. Auster and Silver (1979, p. 28f.) point out that opportunism becomes more important with growing membership. In this context, compare Williamson (1967). He confirms that 'the management factor is responsible for a limitation to firm size' (ibid., p. 123). Moss (ibid., p. 25), however, argues that: '[u]nless something is said about tastes or technology of providing public services, it would seem that the optimal size of the "protective state" is the world population'. Nozick (1974, p. 30), also seems to focus on increasing returns to scale.
4. See, for a computation of the formula, Schmidt-Trenz and Schmidtchen (forthcoming).
5. This result contradicts the Alesina and Spolaore (1997) proposition that with free trade country size does not matter since it does not determine the size of the market.
6. Alternatively, one could treat the quality of a legal order as a factor influencing the enforcement costs (or both income and enforcement costs).
7. Note that the variety of legal orders can also be viewed as barriers to international transactions. Whereas for domestic, internal, transactions one monopolist, the protective state, fulfils the task of law enforcement, international, external, transactions make contact with a multitude of legal systems and with the monopoly of power claimed by each state within its boundaries. Furthermore, whereas the legal rules of each protective state can be judged – at least, in principle – as unequivocal, in the international arena we do find a serious 'incompossibility of rights'. Collisions of norms and gaps between different norm systems appear, an accord in court decisions is often coincidental, and the assistance of the judicial and penal institutions in foreign countries is not at all a matter of course. Thus, the nationalization of law and law enforcement results in a specific kind of attenuation of property rights and the

8.   emergence of a special kind of risk, that has been called constitutional uncertainty in international transactions. This kind of uncertainty gives rise to coordination problems of a special kind reflected in corresponding transaction costs. Harmonization of the law and enlargement can be considered as means for the reduction of these transaction costs.
8. The model can be generalized in order to allow for trade barriers also to hinder internal transactions.
9. Note that independent from accession negotiations the fall of the iron curtain already triggered two effects in the subgroup of the *M* countries, which are now applicant countries: first, the degree of openness of these economies went up and, secondly, the basic legal system moved towards one facilitating a market economy, thereby bringing it partly into line with that of the European Union.
10. A comprehensive welfare analysis drawing on the economic theory of optimal legal areas is presented in Schmidt-Trenz and Schmidtchen (forthcoming); see also Schmidtchen, Neunzig and Schmidt-Trenz (forthcoming).

REFERENCES

Alesina, A and E. Spolaore (1997), 'On the number and size of nations', *Quarterly Journal of Economics*, 1027–56.

Allen, L., R.C. Amacher and R.D. Tollison (1974), 'The economic theory of clubs: a geometric exposition', *Public Finance*, **19**, 386–91.

Auster, R.D. and M. Silver (1979), *The State as a Firm. Economic Forces in Political Development*, Boston: Nighoff.

Baldwin, R.E., J.F. Francois and R. Portes (1997), 'The costs and benefits of Eastern enlargement: the impact on the EU and Central Europe', *Economic Policy*, 127–76.

Bean, R. (1973), 'War and the birth of the nation state', *Journal of Economic History*, **33**, 203–21.

Buchanan, J.M. (1965), 'An economic theory of clubs', *Economica*, **32**, 1–14.

Buchanan, J.M. (1975), *The Limits of Liberty. Between Anarchy and Leviathan*, Chicago/London: The University of Chicago Press.

Bulletin of the European Union 'Agenda 2000. For a stronger and wider union', Supplement 5/97.

Dutta, P.K. (1999), *Strategies and Games: Theory and Practice*, Cambridge MA: MIT Press.

Gros, D. and A. Steinherr (1995), *Winds of Change: Economic Transition in Central and Eastern Europe*, London and New York: Longman.

Kronman, A. (1985), 'Contract law and the state of nature', *Journal of Law, Economics and Organization*, **1**, 4–32.

Moss, L.S. (1980), 'Optimal jurisdiction and the economic theory of the state: or, anarchy and one-world government are only corner solutions', *Public Choice*, **35**, 17–26.

Nozick, R. (1974), *Anarchy, State, and Utopia*, New York: Basic Books.

Sack, R. (1986), *Human Territoriality. Its Theory and History*, Cambridge: Cambridge University Press.

Sandler, T. and J.T. Tschirhart (1980), 'The economic theory of clubs: an evaluative survey', *Journal of Economic Literature*, **18**, 1481–521.

Schmidt-Trenz, H.-J. and D. Schmidtchen (forthcoming), 'Enlargement of the European Union and the Economic Theory of Optimal Legal Areas, in B. Steunenberg (ed.) *Widening the European Union: the Politics of Institutional Change and Reform*, Routledge.

Schmidtchen, D. and H.-J. Schmidt-Trenz (1990), 'The division of labor is limited by the extent of the law. A constitutional approach to international private law', *Constitutional Political Economy*, **1**(3), 49–71.

Schmidtchen, D., A. Neunzig and H.-J. Schmidt-Trenz (forthcoming), One Market, One Law: EU Enlargement in Light of the Economic theory of Optimal Legal Areas, Discussion Paper 2001–03: Center for the Study of Law and Economics, Universität des Saarlandes.

Williamson, O.E. (1967), 'Hierarchical control and optimum firm size', *Journal of Political Economy*, **75**, 123–38.

12. Legal and economic principles for the common administrative law in Europe

Jürgen G. Backhaus

INTRODUCTION

The law and economics of administration is still an emerging and somewhat disparate field. The grouping together with regulation in the *Journal of Economic Literature* classification system reflects a very specific view of the field which is not shared on the European continent. Regulation is, by necessity, the imposition of rules on some economic agent, hence an attempt to override market forces through political discretion. The traditional view, on the other hand, as it developed in France and Germany more than two centuries before the modern instruments of regulation were introduced, emphasizes the enabling character of administrative structures so as to allow market forces to develop and economically meaningful decisions to be taken in the interest of economic growth and prosperity.

The structure of this chapter follows from this basic proposition. Section 12.1 offers a succinct characterization of the entire field of the economics of law and administration emphasizing the two different approaches on the European continent on the one hand and the American regulatory system on the other. In order to understand the latter, the basic category is rent-seeking, a concept that is briefly being illustrated. Section 12.2 offers a short survey of the relevant material for further reference. Section 12.3, however, offers an integrative approach. There are economically meaningful principles embedded in administrative legal doctrine which surface to different degrees in both types of legal approaches. These principles offer the best hope to arrive at a coherent analytical approach to the diverse area of administration through the application of law and economic techniques; hence, Section 12.3 offers an albeit brief discussion of these seventeen traditional principles. Section 12.4 discusses problems of European integration in the field of administrative law.

12.1 THE BASIC ISSUES

The classical teaching in state sciences (before the constitutional era) consisted of three parts: cameral sciences, administrative sciences and public finance, with cameral sciences being the craft and knowledge the public manager (*Staatswirt*) needed in order to run public estates and enterprises profitably, administrative sciences providing the civil servant with the requisite knowledge, and public finance being the doctrine of how to raise revenue through taxation with a minimum of harm and how to organize the public budget. Next to this, for judicial functions future judges and civil servants were trained in law. After the French revolution, a clear distinction between the judiciary and the administrative civil service was written into the law (by act of 24 August, 1790) establishing clear rules which administrative procedure had to follow. These procedural rules substantially circumscribed administrative discretion. A separate judicial system was also set up. After the German revolutions of 1848, with considerable delay similar acts were adopted in the German states in the 1860s. Interestingly, the southern states were trying to follow the French example, and this culminated in the systematic adoption and perfection of French administrative law into a complete dogmatic system of administrative principles and law worked out by Otto Mayer.[1] In the northern German states, notably in Prussia, a different approach was taken. Here, Rudolph von Gneist (1888) became important and tried to base his German law of public administration on constitutional and administrative principles he had found by studying British legal history.[2] Basically, and by way of simplification, we can say that the French approach emphasizes rules, procedures, and clearly circumscribed acts (with the administrative act (*Verwaltungsakt*) as the centrepiece) while the British inspired approach tries to structure the discretion of the civil servant by means of general principles that should guide his behaviour. Both approaches have the primary purpose of generating certainty of the law, in particular as far as protecting the citizen against state abuse of power is concerned.

Administrative law in the United States has quite different roots. While the protection of the citizen is mainly contained in the Bill of Rights, administration as a much more recent phenomenon has primarily taken on the form of regulation. While the entry does not even exist in the *Encyclopedia of Social Sciences* of 1931, in the next edition, the *International Encyclopedia of the Social Sciences* (1968) an article written by Clair Wilcox clearly states:

> In its broadest sense the term 'regulation' may be taken to comprehend all of the controls the government imposes on business of all kinds. In the narrower sense in which the term is used here, it is limited to the control of the services provided and

> rates charged by private enterprises engaged in the provision of transport, commu-
> nication, electricity, gas, and other utility services. (Volume 13; p. 390 II)

By now, regulation covers any conceivable activity of private citizens, not just industries (also including banking, insurance, all manner of education, health care, other types of care, publishing, even how religious organizations need to be run (regulation through the tax code) and covering even to the use of the English language. Often, regulation is effected through amendments (riders) to the federal or state budgets, when to the budgets of particular agencies specific charges, tasks, procedural prerequisites or other instructions are being added. Any conceivable political purpose can be achieved through this mechanism.

Most recently, the classical statement of this approach is given by the leading scholar in American law and economics of administration, Susan Rose-Ackerman (1992). There is substantial opposition to this approach as well, but it has certainly not reigned in the exuberant growth of regulation in American society and where the American example has been followed (notably also on the European continent). Perhaps the foremost example of this opposition is Robert H. Bork (1990). Bork's position can be readily stated. His point of departure he makes abundantly clear:

> In the past few decades, American institutions have struggled with the temptations
> of politics. Professions and academic disciplines that once possessed a life and
> structure of their own have steadily succumbed, in some cases almost entirely, to the
> belief that nothing matters beyond politically desirable results, however achieved.
> In this quest, politics invariably tries to dominate another discipline, to capture and
> use it for politics' own purposes, while the second subject – law, religion, literature,
> economics, science, journalism or whatever – struggles to maintain its indepen-
> dence. But retaining a separate identity and integrity becomes increasingly difficult
> as more and more areas of our culture, including the life of the intellect, perhaps
> especially the life of the intellect, become politicized. It is going to be denied, but
> anything counts, not logic, not objectivity, not even intellectual honesty, that stands
> in the way of the 'correct political outcome'. (Bork, 1990, p. 1).

In the case of the two architects of administrative law so far mentioned, Otto Mayer and Rudolph von Gneist, it is clear that their principles have flowed from sources separate from politics, as the purpose was to protect the citizen from political abuse of power. Bork now criticizes modern American law practice and notably regulation for turning this original purpose on its head. At the heart of traditional American public legal doctrine lies the notion of due process, with many separate manifestations of this basic principle. One of them is economic due process, the respect of private property rights and unimpeded market forces. Bork takes up a typical example of judicial excesses for his criticism:

The notion of substanties due process had been used by prior Courts to protect both economic and non-economic liberties, but there had been some indication prior to the New Deal Court that the protection of economic freedom was likely to decline. In 1935, a five to four decision in Nebbia vs. New York, upheld a New York statute empowering a Milk Control Board to fix maximum and minimum retail prices for milk. Nebbia was convicted of selling milk too cheaply in his grocery store. The effect of the statute, and its obvious purpose, was to transfer money from consumers to milk producers. (Bork, 1990, p. 57)

The issue that becomes pressing is: what can economic analyses accomplish in the face of these disparate approaches in administrative law?

Basically, we can distinguish three lines of development. Originally, the concern centred on protecting weak market participants, hence giving material or substantive as opposed to formal or procedural meaning to the term 'due process'. To this realm belong attempts at using economic analyses in order to contain market power. This is the origin of anti-trust legislation and adjudication, and it is also the origin of supervising the pricing behaviour of monopolies when the formation of monopoly power cannot be prevented in the public interest. This is the origin of public utility regulation, and this is the reason why regulation started out in the network industries. Clearly, legislation was guided by the then prevailing economic theory.

However, it did not take long before captains of industry realized that economists may disagree, and that using their theories in court can help imposing burdens on competitors. The case cited by Bork may be a case in point. This theory of regulation has been explored in great detail with many theoretical (George Stigler stands foremost, who received the Nobel Prize in Economics for his work) and empirical studies, notably in the *Journal of Law and Economics*. By way of illustration, the recent merger of Daimler and Chrysler immediately led to the demise of the lobbying institution of the big three Detroit automobile manufacturers, the American Automobile Manufacturers' Association, as lobbying in the interest of domestic industries against foreign competition no longer made sense for one of the three (*Wall Street Journal*, 1998). In this context, the theory of rent seeking has become one of the most important tools. It identifies the gains from limiting competitors' access to markets and thereby not only provides quantitative measures for the welfare cost of such regulation, but also quantitative measures for the extent to which resources will be made available to gain such regulatory rule-making.

Thirdly, in the spirit of the new law and economics, the law and economics of administration will try to understand the workings of particular administrative principles, procedures and structures and try to identify the most appropriate one for any particular set of circumstances.

12.2   THE LITERATURE

The literature on the law and economics of administration is extremely diverse, stemming from the different traditions and stemming from the very recent interest in the application of economic analysis to this field. To be sure, this recent interest is a revival of interest; there used to be a strong interconnection between economics and public administration, as witnessed by the title of what once was Germany's leading journal in economics. *The Annals of Economics, Administration and Legislation.*[3] For these reasons, the review of the literature has to be somewhat eclectic.

One aspect that is notable in the *New Palgrave Dictionary of Economics and the Law*, although to a much lesser extent than was the case in its predecessor, the *New Palgrave Dictionary of Economics*, is a certain Anglo-American bias, in particular with respect to the institutional assumptions underlying theory and underlying the system of classification. Newman certainly has tried to compensate for this bias by including explicit treatments of European issues and intellectual figures. In this respect, however, the *Elgar Companion to Law and Economics* goes several steps further.[4]

Next to reference works in the law and economics area broadly conceived, we also witness almost simultaneously the publication of several anthologies reproducing classical and standard articles in the field and some selected book chapters as well. Three such analogies have appeared in recent months.

Kenneth G. Dau-Schmidt and Thomas Ulen have collected slightly more than 50 classical articles in their *Law and Economics Anthology*. It is clear that this anthology is supposed to support an upper-level law and economics course which probably also features an introductory textbook, which the anthology is supposed to complement. This can be useful for a seminar-style teaching approach, and even if library facilities are limited such as might be the case in a business school. The anthology is well balanced with an obvious focus on the American literature. The anthology has seven roughly equally long chapters, with chapter 1 providing introductory material by Richard Posner, Cento Weljanowski, Arthur Leff, Robert Ellickson and the problem of social cost by Ronald H. Coase.

This last entry is at the same time the springboard for the entire chapter 2, which is exclusively devoted to the debate over the co-sterum. Chapter 3 covers the economics of property with an introductory part (contributions by Harden and Ellickson), a section on the efficiency enforcement of property rights, and the economics of intellectual property and the economics of taking and regulatory taking. Clearly missing from a European point of view are the transitional issues that the devolution of formerly state socialist industries present to the law and economics researcher in the area of property.

Chapter 4 is devoted to the economics of contract law with articles on the foundations, on formation defence and performance excuses and the economics of remedies for breach of contract. This literature is clearly steeped in the common law tradition; the European civil law tradition would require different contributions. Chapter 5 is devoted to the economies of tort liability with a large section on liability and a somewhat smaller one on damages; chapter 6 deals with the economics of criminal law emphasizing the traditional models and critiques of the traditional economic model of criminal law to which the first editor of the anthology has also contributed. Finally, chapter 7 features the efficiency of the common law debate with all the relevant articles. The issue of whether the civil law is also developing towards efficiency, albeit through different processes including codification, is obviously not addressed.[5]

The roughly 50 articles collected in Wiener Katz (1998) are more likely to be used as a background source for a course in law and economics in a law school. The editors were concerned that many law students or practitioners of law and economics when they have a background in law are not sufficiently aware of the economic methods they are supposed to use, or at least the use to which they need to put them to assess their analytical work or work on cases. Hence, the articles emphasize these foundations. The collection consists of nine chapters. Chapter 1 is devoted to the methodology of an economic approach and features classical articles by, among others, Gary Becker, Thomas Schelling, Mark Blaug and also Friedman's important article on the methodology of positive economics. Chapter 2 stresses two competing economic models of law essentially emphasizing the difference between what has above been distinguished as the Chicago and the Yale approach. Chapter 3 offers a survey of basic applications with entries on property, tort, contract, criminal law and procedure. Chapter 4 is devoted to refining the model with an emphasis on strategic behaviour and chapter 5 gives further refinements, here with an emphasis on risk and insurance. Chapter 6 does the same with respect to information, and chapter 7 offers the fourth set of refinements emphasizing bounded rationality. Critiques of the economic approach form the content of chapter 8, with side by side a liberal critique, a paternalist critique, a radical critique, a sociological critique, a communitarian critique, and the specifically American legal realism (Leff) criticism. Family law is considered a frontier of law and economics analysis, and this is the subject of chapter 9 with three well-chosen contributions. Each chapter closes with a section called 'Notes and Questions', giving essentially motivated exam questions and additional references to the literature. By far the most astonishing of the recently published anthologies is a two-volume work by Warren Samuels (1998). The two volumes contain almost 50 reprints and a very extensive introduction by the editor, a practical joke Warren Samuels' style entitled 'Introduction: some early journal contributions to law and economics', an in-depth essay spanning over more than 80 printed pages. The articles have been reprinted from the original journals, and there are short biographical and bibliographical entries. In addition to the highly useful introductory essay, there is a combined name and subject index, essentially making the entire work highly accessible in particular in combination with textbooks and encyclopedias. The selection necessarily has to focus on English language articles. There is a very strong emphasis on American authors, but the British contribution is present (Pigou, Robinson, Duncan W. Black). The contribution by the American institutionalists has been heavily emphasized, there are for instance six articles by Robert Lee Hale, yet care has also been taken to look at other traditions when that was feasible. For instance, the editor unearthed two English contributions on law and economics by Georgio del Vecchio from the *Journal of Social Philosophy* and the *Villanova Law Review* respectively. Since few libraries today can give their students access to such a large number of journals as used by the editor, and to the old stacks in particular, one is compelled to feel grateful to professor Samuels for having put this collection together.

Given the fact that the contributions surveyed in this review chapter have all appeared over a very short span of just a few months, and all of them have as their aim a consolidation of disparate research in overview articles or a collection of classical articles so as to make them available to the ongoing research, law and economics as a subdiscipline in economics must be said currently to be undergoing a phase of substantial consolidation and growth, securing its intellectual foundations, systematizing its canon of teachings and spreading its purview into neighbouring disciplines.

12.3   LEGAL PRINCIPLES IN ADMINISTRATION

In principle, any act of administration requires a legal base. This will particularly be an act, a statute, a decree, a budgetary allocation or even an international treaty; yet next to those general and specific, positive and procedural norms, there is a different set of sources of law, the so-called principles. The principles tend to have their origin in the academic literature, where they have been derived (found) through the analysis of different bodies of the law; they tend to become proper sources of the law by being upheld in decisions of higher courts. The principles can be differently worded and differently grouped. In American law, fewer principles are accepted but they are given a broader meaning still subject to substantial interpretation. In European administrative law, the number of principles tends to be larger, and they tend to be more specific. Important, however, is the underlying insight that the principles are in full agreement with economic reasoning, hence they can serve to facilitate the economic analysis of an issue in administrative law.[6]

In the continental tradition, we can distinguish twelve general principles and another five specific principles, giving us a total of seventeen. The general principles are:

1. The principle of human dignity. Administrative procedures or acts cannot mechanistically be designed, they have to take into account the entire human being in its fullest capacities. This is important from an economic point of view, since otherwise acts of communication which are necessary to produce the requisite knowledge cannot be initiated (Hayek, 1945). This disallows rubberstamping as practiced by UN agencies.[7]

2. Prohibition of arbitrary measures. Any administrative decision must be based on a reasoning that can be rationally reconstructed. This is, of course, a requisite for economic analysis to be applicable. Arbitrary decisions that cannot be based on a rational motivation according to this principle are void.[8]

3. Principle of equality. Under the law, all citizens must be treated equally. Otherwise, markets could not readily operate, and administrative decisions and structures form the institutional framework in which market exchange takes place.

4. Principle of good faith. All administrative decisions must be made in good faith. If this were not the case, the requisite information would, again, not be forthcoming and the decision could not form a basis for an environment in which economic agents can take decisions on the basis of facts.

5. Principle of legal certainty. The purpose of administrative activities is to create legal certainty. This, again, is important in order to create the framework in which market-based decisions can take place.

6. Principle of justice in each individual case. The general principles of justice must apply in each individual case. It is not sufficient for justice to prevail in a general sense, as in the case of the Kaldor-Hicks compensation possibility criterion. The compensation, in this instance, would actually have to take place.

7. Taking in the public interest and with compensation. Executive exclusive power can only be exercised to the disadvantage of a citizen if this exercise is required by the public interest and if the citizen is being fully compensated. Here we note that the administrative transaction is required to get as close to a market transaction as possible.

8. Prohibition of chicanery. An administrative measure can only be used for the purposes for which the administration had been set up and for which it had received executive power to use the measure. This is closely linked to:

9. Misuse of legal forms. A legal form of administration can only be used for the purpose for which it had been designed. Both of these principles, again, try to ensure that the state through its executive power could undermine the results of market exchange. For instance, an administrative agency cannot be set up in the form of a limited liability company so as to avoid the compensation requirement of principle 7.[9]
10. Principle of upholding legal customs. An administration has to take into account the customs prevailing in a particular community, as does every merchant. This is in order to ensure that even those parts of the law that have not been codified (typically due to massive problems in gathering the proper information) have to be respected by the state.[10]
11. Principle of subsidiarity. This principle ensures that the smallest viable agency needs to assume any specific public function. The underlying purpose is efficiency and expediency (Backhaus, 1995, 1997a, 1997b, 1997c, 1998).
12. Prohibition of an excessive use of executive power. This principle requires that only so much executive power be applied as is necessary to achieve a specific legitimate purpose. Executive powers are hence looked upon as if they were under a budget constraint. The administration must make as parsimonious a use of its power as it can.

More specifically, there are five additional principles referring to peculiarities of administrative procedure:

13. Principle of guarding the public interest. In all its administrative decisions and acts, the agency needs to uphold and guard the public interest, that is, there must be coherence between the activities of the different agencies.[11]
14. Right and duty to minimize a danger for the public. Here, again, an agency cannot claim immunity for not preventing some public danger due to lack of a specific charge to do so.
15. Prohibition to decide in one's own affairs. If an agency becomes a party to a dispute, it cannot decide in its own affair. The matter has to be referred to an impartial judge, as would be the case in market transactions.
16. Prohibition to levy charges for administrative acts. Acts of general administration need to be financed through the general budget. Since they have to be taken in the public interest, there cannot be a *quid pro quo*, and the agency cannot sell, for instance, building permits.
17. Principle of due process. This principle requires that an administrative agency engage in as extensive a search for information as possible, giving those affected by its decisions a chance to come forth with relevant information.

Interestingly, the principles of *ultra vires* and precedent are not generally acknowledged in continental administrative law, although they form the cornerstone of British and American legal doctrine.

12.4 PROBLEMS OF EUROPEAN INTEGRATION IN ADMINISTRATIVE LAW

The 17 principles worked out in Section 12.3 have received new relevance due to a situation that has come about as a consequence of the peculiar history of administrative law as an academic discipline. Since this subdiscipline of administrative law is very much a Franco-German product, and has not been similarly advanced in the Anglo-Saxon world, there are member states in the European Union which have a strong tradition in administrative law, and there are others which have hardly any tradition in this field. It so happens that the European Commission is composed of commissioners who have to be drawn from the different member states according to a more or less agreed upon formula. It therefore also happens that in crucial areas of European legislative action, a commissioner may be active who has no background whatsoever in the administrative traditions that have prevailed on the continent, although the European Community as a whole works according to French administrative rules which are, as has been explained above, very similar to the German ones. In several areas, such as competition policy, this has led to substantial friction. The staff of the commissioner for competition, for instance, in persuasion and style is very much steeped in the British model, which leads to a straightforward application of economic models without taking steps to translate these models into institutional reality, a procedure which Schumpeter has called 'the Ricardian vice'. If such an approach is combined with a lack of regard to the traditional principles of administrative law, serious friction can arise (Backhaus and Hansen, 2000).

Most of the principles mentioned above are relevant in these cases. First, policies should never *mechanically* be designed or applied, but should be tailored to the situation in question. Secondly, measures should not be arbitrary, but well reasoned after (thirdly) a careful consideration of the facts in question. In the case of the German booksellers, the facts on which the decision of the Commission rested were in dispute, and there was no public hearing in order to resolve such disputes. Although similar systems of organizing the book trade prevail in the German language area, France and the Netherlands, Germany had been singled out in violation of the principle of equality. The Commission's decisions were fourthly not made in good faith, as the Commission withheld crucial information and even proceeded to raid the offices of one of its partners in discussion, the German Booksellers'

Association, which had and could not have any part in the alleged (but not proven) allegations of creating a booksellers' cartel. Through such actions, fifthly, the Commission created substantial legal uncertainty. By attacking the entire publishing industry of an entire language area, the Commission hardly did justice to each individual case. Since, according to the views of many German economists, the German Booksellers' Association and most individual booksellers, the measures taken by the Commission are unlikely to further the interests of the consumers, the purported purpose, the measures taken by the commissioner for competition smack of chicanery (principle 8). The initiatives by the commissioner have the objective to overturn centuries old customs (principle 10). They amount to a heavy-handed approach to deal with a cultural entity (the German language area) from the centre and not the periphery, in clear violation of the principle of subsidiarity. It can hardly be claimed that there is competition between German, French, English, Spanish or Italian books. Hence, the appropriate level of dealing with the problem must certainly be found in the German language area (principle 11). Raiding the offices of one of the partners in discussion must certainly be seen as excessive use of executive power (principle 12). And finally, withholding the relevant legal documentation on which administrative decisions are taken is in violation of the principle of due process (principle 17). This short run-down, given a very specific case, has served to illustrate the point that the principles of administrative law, as they embody economic reasoning, can usefully be introduced in arguments about the performance of the European Commission in particular and in processes of European harmonization more generally.

CONCLUSION

The law and economics of administration is an extremely broad and disparate field which is currently undergoing precipitous change. It can be shown that the classical principles of administrative law are closely tied to the relevant economic doctrines and can hence serve to facilitate the economic analysis in the area of administrative legal problems.

NOTES

1. Otto Mayer (1846–1924) became a professor in Strasbourg in 1883 and in Leipzig in 1903. He published his *French Administrative Law* (französisches Verwaltungsrecht) in Strasbourg in 1886 and his *German Administrative Law* (deutsches Verwaltungsrecht) in two volumes (1895–96).
2. Rudolph von Gneist (1816–1895) (1888), professor in Berlin in 1844. He published his *Contemporary British Constitutional and Administrative Law* (das heutige englische

Verfassungs-und Verwaltungsrecht) 1–3, 1857–63, the *Rule of Law* (der Rechtstaat) Berlin 1879 (2) and became important through the Minister Count Eulenburg under the Chancellorship of Prince Bismarck and the reign of Emperor William I.

3. It has now been superseded by *The German Economic Review*, but the publisher who owned the rights to the journal has continued it under the traditional name of *Schmollers Jahrbuch*.

4. Jürgen Backhaus (1999). The purpose of this companion is to provide a reference work for the active researcher in law and economics. In composing this companion, care has been taken to avoid a possible overlap with other works in the field. In particular, this work does not aim at duplicating the ambitious *New Palgrave in Law and Economics* which aims at balancing the pointedly formal focus of the *New Palgrave* by emphasizing institutional economics. A comprehensive set of articles mainly in the Chicago tradition of law and economics allows us to focus on other mainly European aspects of law and economics and the historical sources of law and economics' research. This explains the structure of the *Companion*.

   The *Companion* appears in two parts. Part one covers main areas of law and economics, including basic issues as well as different sources of the law, whereas part two offers twenty-two scholarly biographies of main figures in law and economics. These biographies have been written with a view to allow further research into neglected areas in the field which have been taken up at some point but are not part of the current scholarly discussion in law and economics.

5. See the special issue of the *European Journal of Law and Economics*, volume 7, devoted to this matter.

6. In Germany, these rules are contained in Basic Act articles 1, 2, 3, 4, 5, 6, and 7.

7. In Germany: Basic Act, article 1.

8. In Germany, this is called *Willkürverbot*. Under some circumstances it is doubtful that the legal consequence is outright voidness; there may be other but similar legal consequences (Act of Legal Procedure, articles 44, 45 I N. 2). Even the lack of any reasoning doesn't make the decision void; even with an illegal reasoning an administrative act can be valid (if the result is legal).

9. In Germany, it can be, but the compensation cannot be avoided by that construction.

10. For Germany, this may be doubtful. (*Gewohnheitsrecht* in German).

11. However, in Germany each agency may have the competence to define for itself what the public interest is.

REFERENCES

Backhaus, Jürgen G. (1995), 'Subsidiarity and Ecologically Based Taxation: Aspirations and Opinions', in Sabine Urban (ed.), *Europe in Progress*, Wiesbaden: Gabler, pp. 223–63.

Backhaus, Jürgen G. (1997a), 'Christian Wolff on subsidiarity, the division of labor, and social welfare', *European Journal of Law and Economics*, **4**(2–3), Boston: Kluwer Academic Publishers, 1997, pp. 129–46.

Backhaus, Jürgen G. (1997b), 'Subsidiarity and Ecologically Based Taxation: A European Constitutional Perspective', in C.K. Rowley (ed.), *Constitutional Political Economy in a Public Choice Perspective*, Boston: Kluwer Academic Publishers, pp. 281–310.

Backhaus, Jürgen G. (1997c), 'Subsidiarity and ecologically based taxation: a European constitutional perspective', *Public Choice*, **90**, 281–310.

Backhaus, Jürgen, G. (1998), 'Christian Wolff on subsidiarity; the division of labor and social welfare', in Jürgen Backhaus (ed.), *Christian Wolff and Law & Economics*, Hildesheim, Zürich, New York: Georg Olms Verlag, pp. 19–36.

Backhaus, Jürgen G. (ed.) (1999), *The Elgar Companion to Law and Economics*, Cheltenham, Northampton: Edward Elgar Publishing Ltd.

Backhaus, Jürgen G. and Reginald Hansen (2000), Resale price maintenance for books in Germany and the European Union: a legal and economic analysis, Memograph, University of Frankfurt.

Bork, Robert H. (1990), *The Tempting of America: the Political Seduction of the Law*, New York: Freepress.

Dau-Schmidt, Kenneth G. and Thomas Ulen (eds) (1998), *Law and Economics Anthology*, Cincinnati, OH: Andersen Publishing Company.

Hayek, Friedrich August von (1945), 'The use of knowledge in society', *American Economic Review*, **35**.

New Palgrave Dictionary of Economics, London: Macmillan.

New Palgrave Dictionary of Economics and the Law, London: Macmillan.

Rose-Ackerman, Susan (1992), *Rethinking the Progressive Agenda: the Reform of the American Regulatory State*, New York: Freepress.

Samuels, Warren (ed.) (1998), *Law and Economics: the Early Journal Literature*, London: Pickering & Chatto.

Wall Street Journal (1998), 'The big two shift gears on the best way to reach Washington', Friday November 27, 1998, pp. A1 and A12.

Wiener Katz, Avery (1998), *Foundations of the Economic Approach to Law*, New York, Oxford: Oxford University Press.

Wilcox, Clair (1968), 'Regulation of Industry', in David L. Sills (ed.), *International Encyclopedia of the Social Sciences*, vol. 13, New York: Macmillan, p. 390 II.

Index